Joyce Storey won the Raymond Williams Memorial Award for *Our Joyce* and *Joyce's War* when they were first published by Virago Press, who also published *Joyce's Dream*, the final volume of her autobiography. *The House in South Road* is the collected and abridged edition of the three volumes.

The House in South Road

An Autobiography

JOYCE STOREY

Edited by PAT THORNE

virago

VIRAGO

Published in Great Britain by Virago Press 2004
Reprinted 2004 (twice), 2005, 2006 (three times), 2007 (twice),
2008, 2012

Originally published as three individual editions as
Our Joyce, *Joyce's War* and *Joyce's Dreams*

Original stories Copyright © Joyce Storey 1987, 1990, 1995

This edited and abridged edition Copyright © Pat Thorne 2004

The moral right of the author has been asserted.

A CIP catalogue record for this book
is available from the British Library.

ISBN 978-1-84408-046 -5

Typeset in Sabon by M Rules
Printed and bound in Great Britain by
Clays Ltd, St Ives plc

Papers used by Virago are from well-managed forests
and other responsible sources.

 MIX
Paper from
responsible sources
FSC® C104740
www.fsc.org

Virago Press
An imprint of
Little, Brown Book Group
100 Victoria Embankment
London EC4Y 0DY

An Hachette UK Company
www.hachette.co.uk

www.virago.co.uk

Joyce dedicated her books to her four children, and this edited version is likewise lovingly dedicated to my sisters Jackie and Julie, and my brother Darrell.

PAT THORNE
Boscastle, Cornwall
February 2003

Early Days

My mother had carried me with bitterness and resentment. Just fifteen months earlier, she had given birth to my brother Dennis, and six short months before that she had been marched up the aisle by a tight-lipped father determined to make an honest woman of her. She recalled that it had been Harvest Festival time, and the Bourne Chapel was decorated with sheaves of golden corn. In the windows stood tall pots of bronze and yellow pom-pom chrysanths. Although the sun shining through the stained-glass windows was warm and touched the altar rail where she stood, she felt sick and cold. As she walked slowly past the shiny black pews with their red covers, her hand hardly touched her father's out-stretched arm.

My grandfather, Philip Cockram, was a big man with a big booming voice to match. That voice, plus the buckle-end of a strap, was all he needed to exact obedience from his

1

brood of six children. My mother often felt the strap on her unprotected legs. Even Philip's wife ran from him like a scared hare, and each night, with the sound of his key in the lock, in her fresh-laundered pinny, she would be ready with her hand on the big black kettle, which had been singing on the range, waiting instantly to pour the water into the china teapot. 'The master's coming,' she'd say.

As she neared the altar rail, Gilbert Charles Dark, the son of Nathaniel Dark, the local coalman, stepped forward to greet his bride, and her legs felt strangely heavy, as though they were protesting at this enforced union. He had pursued her with some considerable persistence after first meeting her in the park where she was walking with her sister Amy, and he raised his white boater to them both. Amy had giggled, and then gone home to whisper to her father that the Dark boy had paid attention to 'our Nell'. After that, he actually came calling, and always produced a red carnation from under his hat. Philip invited him to tea and asked a lot of questions. Gilbert was apprenticed as a brass moulder and his job so far had protected him from being conscripted for the army, but now that he was twenty-one he would shortly be sent to Coventry, to a munitions factory.

That was that, and as far as Philip was concerned they were officially engaged. No more messing about: he wasn't having his daughter flitting from one bloke to another, giving him a bad name. Nell could be a handful, a bit headstrong and high-spirited. She had an uncanny knack of looking a chap straight in the eye as though she was mocking him. A couple of babbies would soon get the fancy notions out of her head; a chap knew where his wife was when she had a babby in her arms . . .

'Who giveth this woman?' the vicar's voice was saying; and Philip's booming answer must have sounded like a death knell. 'We give our lives so glibly into another's keeping,' she once said to me.

It had been a quick, furtive fumbling that hot July night in St George's Park. Once again, it was her sister who silently and slyly whispered to their father that Nell had been sick one morning when she had run all the way up Castle Street and across Castle Ditch to the Pithay to arrive at Fry's Chocolate Factory. Amy was a foremistress in the packing department and saw her sister, white and trembling, fighting uncontrollable waves of sickness. Nell arrived home one night shortly after this to find Chas, as she called him, sitting on the horsehair sofa and her father standing by the fire.

'Well, my girl,' he said, 'it looks as though we shall have to get thee wed. Thy lad'll do the right thing by 'ee, and you've a house to move into – his two sisters'll let 'ee half their house up Kingswood way.'

And so it was that Chas brought his unwilling bride back to the house at South Road in a terrace of stone-built Victorian houses. His two spinster sisters agreed on a rent of six shillings a week. The following April, my brother Dennis was born and the two of them, Ada and Flo, twittered with excitement and hurried from work to coo over him and carry him into the front parlour which was their domain. Chas was now in Coventry on war work and making spasmodic visits home. Three months later my mother, pregnant again, hardly noticed how frequently the baby disappeared into the other room, or even heard the bolt being drawn across the door. In July of the following year I was born and my father made a flying visit to Bristol to see us.

He hoped for a reconciliation when a little girl was born. He loved my mother passionately, but he couldn't express what he felt; a lack of education dammed him up, and he could find no expression in words. There was no aggression in my father and he would cry with vexation or just bite his lip and turn away. He would have done anything to please her, but she never forgave him for robbing her of her youth. In the years that followed, she played her part as wife and mother. She cooked, she bottled and she sewed. When money was scarce, she could produce a meal from a few scraps, and her nimble fingers were never still. She invented things from cardboard for us kids to play with and she could paint and make paper flowers and big fat Christmas crackers. But when she met my father's gaze, a hard look would come into those dark brown eyes of hers, as though the warmth was suddenly withdrawn, and my dad would bite his lip and walk away.

I was sixteen months old when the war came to a close and an uneasy armistice was signed. Trainloads of war-scarred and battle-weary soldiers returned from France. They were to suffer one last humiliation. Not from gun-shot or blast, but from a killer flu virus that struck when body resistance was at its lowest and took off as many casualties as did the war. My father returned from Coventry with streaming eyes and a high temperature, and by Christmas 1918 everybody at 18 South Road was confined to bed, including me.

Spring brought promise of better things, and Dad found work at a local foundry called Jackson's that had started up at the top of the lane. Two minutes and he could be in the yard. Sights, sounds and sensations filled my life now, and one of my earliest memories is that of Jackson's furnace when it started up at six in the morning and hissed to a final gasp and splutter at six at night. It thumped its way through the day and shot fiery red sparks into the sky, and on wash-days my mother shook her fist at the black monster because it shed dirty smuts all over her clean washing. My father brought me red sand from the foundry to play with, and made me a sandpit, and he brought my mother's big wooden sewing-machine top for me to use as a boat. But it was out-side the battered old gate, with its peeling paint and loose, rusty lock with the spindle on the brass handle that came away in your hand, that life began.

We had a white collie dog called Lady and together she and I made for the back gate and freedom. Lady had long since mastered the art of removing that handle, and she barked and wagged her tail when she saw the children. Outside the back door was a square of bare earth called The Patch, which faced the backs of the last ten houses. A lane skirted The Patch and led up and around Fry's Farm, with the corrugated fence of Jackson's taking up the other side of the lane. Facing the other ten houses in the terrace was a shoe factory, so we were the lucky ones. We had this half-acre of dirt to play on. The boys played football, rounders, kick-tin and marbles; and the girls ran wooden hoops, played with dolls or prams, or did skipping or hopscotch.

But it was The Mountain that Lady and I always made for. The Mountain was a mound of earth at the far end of The Patch piled high up against the doctor's house. It had started off as rubble, where everybody threw the stones and rubbish when the men had cleared The Patch for the kids to play on, but now it was a mountain and an exciting adventure playground. I slipped and heaved and fell. I scraped my knees and hands and finally made it to the top. Several of the older boys tried to be protective and carry me but I resisted all efforts to help and squirmed and wriggled away from them. My mother came out sometimes to drag me away, and I'd scream until a fit of coughing stopped me from making any other sound at all. The flu had left me with a cough and my mother sometimes looked at me with alarm.

I was three before I finally manoeuvred The Mountain. Lady bounded ahead of me and barked her encouragement from the top, whilst I puffed and panted and grew red in the face, completely oblivious to the stings from nettles or the stones that grazed my knees. Red clay stained my knickers when a sudden slip forced me to fall on my rear and have to start all over again, but with Lady still barking tantalizingly from the top I would pick myself up, rub my grubby hands on my clean dress and the long haul up would start again until, lobster-faced but triumphant, I joined Lady at the top. I'd jump up and down with fiendish glee, with Lady barking madly. We made such a racket that my mother would look up from her sewing machine, notice the gate was open, and come tearing round the corner to snatch me up and haul me inside the gate again. Then my frustration was so great that I jumped up and down with rage and shrieked with temper and again a fit of coughing would leave me pale and shaken.

Sometimes it was one of the roughnecks who would take a turn at retrieving me from the top of 'that muckheap', as my mother called it, but I'd wriggle so furiously from his grasp that sometimes it was the both of us that took a tumble, and the lad would look apologetic and mutter, 'She ain't half got a paddy, your little un, missus.' Looking back, it must have been fairly obvious, even then, that many would try but few would succeed in subduing me.

Despite all the efforts to bar The Mountain from me, it remained a challenge and a desperate goal to win, for there was no way to explain what the view from the top revealed for me. Over the wall was the doctor's house, and along the wall that divided the house from Fry's Farm was a row of tall proud cypress trees, looking like sentinels in dark green uniform. Blue delphiniums, red and pink larkspur and lupins graced the far wall. There were green lawns and gravel paths, and then suddenly from behind the big glass conservatory two young boys would come tearing on their three-wheeler bikes. They would look up when they neared the wall and wave to us. And every time they came round this would be the signal for Lady's barking and my ritual dance to start all over again.

The women from our row of houses would sieve the ashes

from their ranges all along the lane. The rain always left great pools of muddy water and attempts to fill them in or break up the clay of this unlovely earth only made it worse. Ma Saunders came out first, wearing a green cardigan always full of holes and her long black skirt covered with a piece of coarse brown sacking tied round her waist several times with black tape. Most women had their hair tied severely back, either in a bun or covered with a dust cap. Ma Saunders always wore her husband's cap. My mother broke the rule; she wore a band of black velvet and her soft dark hair framed the whole of her forehead and gave her a soft, feminine look. Ma Saunders was always retrieving hairpins, and tiny wisps of hair escaped from beneath the brown cap she wore. She would stare disapprovingly at Lady and me perched on top of the mound of earth and wag her finger at me: 'Stop that noise, you baggage, and come down from there – I'd tan yer backside if you were a lass of mine.'

Lady and I looked at each other. We both knew she was the enemy and we both knew exactly how to deal with her. As soon as she made a few steps up The Mountain and stretched out bony hands to grab me, we would both set up such a din. I screamed right in her ear, and Lady growled and showed her teeth so that Ma Saunders would stumble, fall on one knee and then beat a hasty retreat, muttering, 'Temper like a racehorse, that kid.'

Meanwhile, the doctor's two boys were very interested in the rumpus that Lady and I caused, and I'm sure they would have loved to be allowed outside. I learned much later that their names were Aubrey and Philip, but I settled for 'Bree'

8

and 'Lilip'. Come hell or high water, I contrived, with the help of Lady and all the cunning I could muster, to be there every day to gaze in awe and wonder at the garden, and to wait for that moment when the boys came tearing out of the bushes by the conservatory. They would yell and wave, and Lady and I went wild with excitement.

Shadow of Illness

The roughnecks were playing football right by the doctor's surgery. We were in our usual vantage place on the top of The Mountain, with Lady barking and me jumping up and down. Several people going into the surgery had glanced up in alarm as the ball screed towards them, and Mrs Wilson from the end house, who had been practising her scales (she was a singer), suddenly broke off in the middle of a high note to shout through the open window to them to 'Pack it in!' Her husband kept pigeons and was whistling softly by the loft, trying to get them in. When the ball hit the top of the wall and skimmed over into his yard, he suddenly made a quick movement through the back gate and without any more ado lambasted the first lad that he saw across the head and shoulders. The assault lasted for several minutes whilst everyone looked on in stunned silence – even Lady didn't bark. Mr Wilson must have exhausted himself and grown tired of meting out punishment, because he suddenly stopped the bashing and stalked back as quickly as he had shot out, and resumed whistling for his pigeons as if nothing had happened.

The shocked silence was broken by one of the bigger lads giving the ball a hefty kick, which came straight in my direction and caught me full in the midriff, winding me so that I fell and rolled down the hill and lay on the ground gasping for breath. Fortunately, an elderly man going into the surgery witnessed the whole thing and rushed forward to pick me up and carry me to the doctor's. Doctor Britton was young and efficient. He first enquired from the knot of small boys crowding round the door with anxious faces who I was and where I lived. He learned from a babble of voices all speaking at once that I was Chas Dark's babby, and a dozen grubby fingers pointed to the open yard of our house just three doors away. He told them they must take their ball and play in the field at the top of the lane and very sheepishly they quietly dispersed. My mother and father were informed and were now ushered into the surgery, white-faced with anxiety, and Dr Britton spoke to them for a long time. Then my father picked me up and carried me over his shoulder back to the house and laid me on the hard sofa where I cried again because the horsehair stuck into my legs. My mother made a soft kapok mattress to put under me and only then did I drift off to sleep.

I did not know that I was ill. The bouts of coughing did not convey a message that I was in any danger; or the sudden interest in me, or the talks with my mother that left her looking worried. I doubt if the expression 'fifty-fifty chance' that I overheard would have meant much anyway.

Then came the morning when Lady and I once more made for the gate that was already half open. She bounded through, stopping only to bark at a wolf spider busy spinning a web across the top of the half-open gate. As the sun shone through the web it glistened like silver. I stopped to watch the spider weaving busily away, and I suddenly thought of my mother and how her fingers wove the fine crochetwork into a pattern as intricate as any spider's web.

Lady bounded towards The Mountain and Ma Saunders was deep in conversation with Mr Fry from the farm halfway up the lane. A big cart drawn by two horses was immediately behind them – a man had just thrown his shovel into the cart and was heading towards the road. When my line of vision was finally cleared, what I saw made me stop dead in my tracks. I was facing an unscalable eight-foot wall of stark grey stone – The Mountain had gone. Ma Saunders' black skirt swept against me just as I was about to howl my protest to the four winds.

'That's stopped your little gallop,' she said maliciously, and disappeared into her back yard.

Despondently we gazed at the tall, bare wall. Never again would I climb to the top to gaze into that garden paradise, or see the familiar faces of the two boys. Large tears rolled down my face whilst Lady sighed too and nuzzled her nose into my hand. We walked slowly down to the surgery door. The black wrought-iron gates were closed and locked. As I peered through the bars of the gate and even into the conservatory, there was no sound or sign of the two boys. Another wall completely obstructing the side and front of the house carried on right into South Road until you came to the big, blue-painted, wide wooden gate which swung open to reveal another lawn with waving pampas grass and a big expanse of gravel path that swept in a wide arch right up to the front door. In the corner of the garden you had to pass under a beautiful red hawthorn tree. The scent of the blossom when it flowered in the spring was sweet and heady. My mother said it was sickly, but I loved it. As we rounded the corner I found to my unutterable joy that the gate was open to its fullest extent.

The gardener was collecting up some rose limbs that he had been pruning, the wheelbarrow and his spade were well in evidence and I could see his little bobble cap and his thick white socks turned over his wellington boots. Without realising it, Lady and I advanced into the drive, and at that moment the two boys came tearing round the corner on their trikes, the wheels making a crunchy sound on the gravel. They pulled up slowly as they caught sight of Lady and me standing there so audaciously in the middle of their drive, and shyly offered a greeting. Lady offered a paw and wagged her tail. The two boys were curious about me and captivated by Lady, who barked to let them know that she too would love to play. I jumped up and down to express the joy I felt.

Hearing the rumpus, the gardener sauntered over to us and, when he recognised me from the previous week, bent down to enquire if I was all right now. I nodded my head up and down vigorously, and he patted my head and touched my curls. At that moment, Dr Britton strode through the gates and eyed this domestic scene with some amusement.

Then he too bent down to enquire as he touched my midriff, 'Does it still hurt here?'

I shook my head from side to side, then pointed to the two boys still amused with Lady lifting her paw in a gesture to be friends. 'Lilip,' I said, pointing. 'And Bree.'

'I see you have made the acquaintance of my two sons,' he said, laughing. 'Now we must go and find your mother. I have some news for her.'

He took my hand and I waved goodbye to the two boys. Little did I know, but it was to be some time before I saw them again. Events were moving swiftly now and I was to face the first upheaval of my life. At the moment though, with one hand in Dr Britton's, I felt elated. Even the loss of The Mountain faded into insignificance at the discovery that morning of the open gates and a first-hand glimpse of that wonderful garden and the two boys excitedly riding towards me on their trikes. As we came into the yard, my mother was hanging out some washing but she glanced up sharply when she saw me with the doctor. They stood for several minutes talking in low tones and my mother looked serious and was very silent. When he had gone, she leaned against the side of the water barrel for a long time, then she sighed very deeply and once more began to hang the washing on the line.

With the November fog and the fast approaching winter, my cough grew steadily worse and there were days when I never moved from the hard, uncomfortable horsehair sofa that became my bed. Too exhausted even to cry after one of those bouts of harsh brittle spasms of coughing, I would lie for hours just staring at the faded wallpaper with its pattern of mauve and pink flowers, and sometimes imagine I saw fairy faces and animals in the contour of the pattern. Above the sofa was a picture of Frenchay Glen in a large Dutch gilt frame, and on the far wall was a picture, also in a gilt frame, of a stag with huge antlers standing proud and erect and called 'The Monarch of the Glen'. My mother said that both paintings had been the work of a man who would offer his talents liberally to anyone who would buy him a pint. The quiet restfulness of the trees in the picture would soothe me and I could almost hear them rustle softly. I could feel the sun shining through the branches and I longed to be able to get up and go with Lady outside the battered old gate. Lady was my constant companion and would sit for hours with her head resting on the bottom of the sofa and occasionally giving a big sigh as if to say, 'When are you going to come and play?'

When Dr Britton came he looked very grave, and once I heard him tell my mother that it was now very serious indeed and that both my lungs were affected. She must make up her mind about something very quickly so that he could make the necessary arrangements. Towards evening, when Dad came home from work, he would come straight over to look at me and enquire of my mother what the doctor had said. I would hold out my arms to him, but he would say coaxingly, 'Just wait for Dad to have a wash first.'

I would hear him splash about in the sink by the back door and when he came back in he always smelled of carbolic soap and his clean shirt would be a collarless striped one. Then he'd pick me up and walk up and down the room with me, patting my back in a rough, kindly way that eased the pain of where I'd lain so long on that hard sofa. At the same time, he hummed a tune in a strange kind of trembling with his lips. He kept up this pacing up and down until he successfully eased me off to sleep. He was very gentle and I never knew the exact moment when I came into contact with the hardness of the sofa once more.

That winter I almost died. Of this of course I have no knowledge, but only a hazy memory of floating without effort and without pain towards the window where, although it was night-time, I thought I saw the doctor's garden with the mauve and pink delphiniums and the lupins and the larkspur and the bees buzzing from flower to flower. I was just about to drift down from the windowsill into the sunlit garden when I heard my mother urgently calling me back.

'Come back,' she said. 'I won't let you die. Come back – oh, come back!'

I returned rather violently, or so I dreamed, for it seemed I had fallen off the sill and down onto the floor with a bump. Many years afterwards, when my mother related this incident about the night I almost died, these were the very words she said she had called out to me when I'd gone into a convulsion and she called me back from the edge of death.

Painswick

*T*he long winter had gone, and the birds were singing out-side the bedroom window that spring morning when I heard a sound of bustling activity from the kitchen below, and then Dad called to my mother to hurry or we would miss the train. During the last few weeks, my cough had eased a little and my chest was not so painful, so I was almost excited about the prospect of a train ride, for I had never been on one, or even on a station. My mother carried me downstairs, where the pile of new knitted garments lay ready and waiting. When the new vest was put on I cried for it was itchy and irritated me, and for fear of bringing on a fresh spasm of coughing my mother conceded and brought out a soft cotton one with half-sleeves. This satisfied me, and I was finally dressed in the green cape and hood with tiny mittens to match, and strapped into the pushchair that my mother had borrowed for the occasion. Dad packed a flask and sandwiches and, when he had checked that he hadn't forgotten anything, we made our way down the path to the back gate and out into the lane. Lady barked at us from the sitting-room window. I never saw Lady again, and my very last memory of her is those sad eyes looking at me from the window.

Of the actual journey to Painswick in the train from Warmley Station I have no recollection, or of the seriousness of the occasion. It was not uncommon for children or adults to die of tuberculosis, a disease that affected the chest and lungs, and which I had contracted with both lungs affected. Fortunately for me, Dr Britton, an up-and-coming bright young doctor, was very much in favour of the open-air clinics that were just beginning to appear in England for the treatment of the complaint. Hitherto, only people who could afford to go to Switzerland stood any chance of returning home in good health. Careful diet, exercise and rest and plenty of good clean fresh air was the recipe, and now a few of these places had opened up in England – still at the experimental stage, they said.

I had been chosen as a small guinea pig, along with twelve other children whose ages ranged from six months to twelve years, to go to an open-air hospital at Painswick near Stroud. That was why my mother had made all those knitted woollen garments and that was why I was on my way dressed in that green cape and watching all the fields rush past. But I knew nothing of that. I thought I was just going for a ride. Hinton, Dinton, Durham, Doynton, Absom, Wick, Pucklechurch and Syston. These were all the little halts where a slow train would stop and my father could rattle them all off like a children's rhyme. Much later I would get to know and love them, for they were to be the source of endless pleasure when Dad and I would explore them on our bikes.

Right then, only a few vivid memories etched themselves indelibly on my mind. The starkest of all was the wide white gate we opened, leading up to a long white wooden bungalow with a verandah all round it. At the bottom was a gate that led into a field that extended right up the other side of the bungalow. As we walked up the path, I have a vivid memory of the big oak tree standing there like some great kindly giant. It must have been a very old tree, for several of its great branches thrust out peculiar, gnarled, deformed shapes. I grew to love this great giant of a tree. The deformed limbs made easy steps on which to climb, and when I grew well again I spent hours curled up amongst the leaves and not even daring to breathe when they came calling or looking for me lest they discover my precious hiding place. I told it all my secrets and in the summer I would retire to this part of the garden to lie beneath its branches and be lulled to sleep.

A lot of parents and children were seated or standing in small knots, waiting to be called into the bungalow. Matron would call a boy or girl by their Christian name first and come and take them by the hand. She had a white collar and cuffs to match. At the time I did not think it at all strange that I should be in a place like this. I thought it was all part of the lovely treat that I had been taken for a ride and now into this nice garden. It had been a long day, and I was beginning to feel very tired and ill. I wanted to go home now and go to sleep. At last my name was called and the lady with the white collar and cuffs came out and took me by the hand and into the house.

At the end of the verandah was a tiny little room which contained twelve little pegs from one of which hung a towel with my name on it; also on the peg was a bag with a big 'JD' embroidered on it and in which I recognised the brown whalebone bristle brush which my mother used to brush my hair every morning. I was told to take off my clothes and when I had done so I was given a cotton vest, and then a brown cotton tunic and a pair of brown shorts. No socks, but a pair of plimsolls took the place of the brown leather shoes I had been wearing. All the clothes that my mother had so painstakingly knitted were taken away. Years later, my mother would relate how she had received the parcel and wept bitter tears. 'They have taken her up there to die,' she wailed in despair.

I was given a brown wicker basket with a white disc on the front with the number fourteen on it, and was told I must put my clothes in it every night and be responsible for it. Tea would be very soon, she said. Once again, I thought that as long as my mum and dad were there in this house it would be all right and we would be going back home tomorrow. I went in search of them and, as the twilight came and the shadows lengthened, a kind of panic took hold of me. In desperation I raced towards the entrance gate. I saw a woman crying at the gate and giving one last anguished look back towards the bungalow. The sound of several children sobbing from the interior of the place made the terror rise in my throat, almost stifling me. A nurse ran up to me and, taking my hand, turned me back towards the house.

'Your mummy wants you to be a good girl. You are going to stay in this nice house with us. You will like that, won't you? And you will have all these children to play with.'

I remember the room alongside the paddock and the bread and butter and jam laid on for tea. And I remember those three great shudders that went through my body and the anguished, stifled sob that never came out. I had been a bad, bad girl. Those temper tantrums that everybody predicted would get me into trouble finally had. 'They' had come for me at last, and now I would never see my mother or father again. My mother no longer loved me and had rejected me. I would have to be good from now on.

The nurse stopped for a while when she saw I wanted to say something, but no sound came. At any other time I could scream my frustration to the wind, but now it seemed I could hardly breathe. I tried to get out the word 'Mummy', but all the fear and terror of being left alone in this place was trapped deep down inside me. I gave three great shudders that almost convulsed me as the nurse picked me up in alarm and carried me into that strange place, and fussed over me until at last I must have slept.

I never forgave my mother.

I came to love that house at Painswick. The nurses took us for walks in the countryside, and we took off our plimsolls, tied the laces together, hung them round our necks and walked barefoot along the streams that babbled through the quiet country lanes. We slept on the open verandah in rough army blankets tucked up snug and tight. Our beds were made up in a special way so that no matter how you wriggled the blankets stayed tight around you. Only if the rain beat in or the weather was really bad were the shutters pulled across. I grew to know and love the sounds of the night, to hear the cry of the owls, the bark of a vixen, and to wake in the morning to the sounds of woodpigeon and the dawn chorus of blackbirds. And I loved to hear the rustle of the wind through the trees, and to see the sunrise or the clouds scudding across the sky. Sometimes a young man would take us for long walks. He would make us run for a while, and then fall flat on our faces and pant hard for several minutes. This was to expand our lungs and to expel all the bad air. He would make us roll down a hill, over and over, in a grassy field. And sometimes we would collect twigs and sticks and light a fire and dance around it like mad dervishes.

My mother and father came to see me at Christmas. They sat along the side of the room in high-backed chairs and watched us from a distance whilst we tucked into jellies and cakes that the staff made for us, all the while swinging our bare feet under the table. I kept watching them and hoping they would come to tell me I was going home. But more than anything I wanted them to come and cuddle me and tell me I hadn't been a bad girl, that they loved me and wanted me back. For some reason, I honestly thought I'd been sent away to be punished for my bad temper. Maybe my mother thought it best not to come to talk to me. Maybe she'd been told that to be upset again would undo all the good progress I was making. Maybe, as I was settling down well, she had been told to watch but not communicate. I had no way of reasoning any of this, and it was only later that I came to understand that she must have suffered as much as I did. The feeling of suffocation arose once more when I thought of being comforted and held close and she didn't come to me. When I looked up for the third time, I saw only the empty, hard, upright chairs where they had been sitting.

They had gone.

It seemed my life would go on for ever in these serene and idyllic surroundings. Kingswood, The Patch, and that cold Victorian house in South Road faded from my mind, and only the guilt that I had done something bad stayed like a dark and silent shadow somewhere deep down inside me. From the first day when I had shuddered so violently at the disappearance of my parents I had sworn always to be good and never again show any burst of temper so that I could go home and live with them again.

We were escorted every morning to the schoolroom in the village and I set to with a will to learn the tasks set before me. I learned to tie bows in record time. The cardboard clock face was harder and I sometimes made myself sick with anxiety when just a hint of impatience showed on a teacher's face. I learned to be as quiet as a mouse as soon as I saw a finger raised to lips, and to stand to one side to let the next girl pass through the door at tea-time, and to close the door noiselessly behind me.

But words were the best magic, and soon I was reading simple picture books that led me into a world where adults couldn't reach me, touch me or hurt me. And this, together with the walks and the countryside, filled my soul with a joy and peace I could not describe. So whilst my body filled out and rounded and my face took on a healthy hue, I also became a silent, solitary child who found more pleasure playing alone than with others, except that I was never alone. I heard voices in the wind, felt the sun warm on my back, and when I ran through the tall grasses I would shout aloud in joy.

The days and months passed, each one very much like another, and I found a kind of stability in their sameness; I began to feel secure in the constancy. In the playroom I found a battered celluloid doll with a bashed nose and cracked face. I adopted it and carried it everywhere. It resembled a boy doll and, because it was warm to the touch and not cold like a china doll, I cuddled it and kissed it and held it close to me. I talked to it for hours and together we would hide away in my secret place in the tree.

There came a day when something different did happen. I had just reached the classroom when one of the teachers told me that I had been a good girl and now I was better I would be going home again. My father would be coming to fetch me the next morning. I was five and a half and had been away from home for eighteen months. There were so many things I had to do now. Say goodbye to Maisie the horse who had so often ambled up to the window of the dining room where I would feed her all the crusts I so hated eating, and take off my shoes for one last time and wade in the stream that ran along the bottom of the paddock. Most of all I wanted to wrap up my boy doll. Someone had told me that we couldn't take any of our toys out of the home because it was a fever hospital and wasn't allowed, but I sneaked a large piece of brown paper and I thought that if I wrapped up my doll in a parcel and took it out hidden in my clothes nobody would be any the wiser, so I remember sitting on the verandah and trying to wrap up this boy doll.

Then a shadow fell across the step and I saw my father with his blue eyes smiling down at me but looking slightly embarrassed at the obvious change in me, as though I was a strange new person he hadn't seen before. Then I stood up and said I hoped he wasn't too tired from his journey and that I was all ready if he wished to go. The only memory of the journey is the indescribable discovery of the loss of my boy doll and the knowledge that they must have snatched it at a time when I was preoccupied. The treachery was too much to bear but I dared not cry because I had promised to be good and tears would complicate things. As we approached Warmley Station my father suddenly repeated the names of the local stations we were passing through: Hinton, Dinton, Durham, Doynton, Absom, Wick, Pucklechurch and Syston.

My mother was at the station to meet us. So were Aunt Flo and Aunt Ada and my brother Dennis in a new white sailor suit and hat and white doeskin boots. He immediately turned his back on me and for shyness hid his head in Aunt Ada's skirt.

Aunt Flo said, 'Haven't you grown into a big girl, Joyce?'
Aunt Ada said, 'You'm like a farmer's wench.'

My mother looked at me for a long time but didn't say a word and I remember that my father went towards her but she turned away and then he hustled us all out of the station and we walked slowly home up Warmley Hill past the Tennis Court Hotel and up to the tram terminus. We walked past Kingswood Church and the clock tower and into Regent Street, past the Regent Cinema and the sweet shop and garage next door, then round the corner into South Road with Moons the Ironmongers on the corner, owned and run by two odd little spinster sisters. And so home to that cold Victorian house that, even now like a dark shadow beckons, with its unhappy memories still sharp and crystal clear.

My mother took me upstairs to show me the back bedroom that had been freshly whitewashed for me; the medicated smell that still lingered reminded me of the Infirmary. An iron hospital bed and a chest of drawers were the only furniture, but a corner wardrobe and the curtains at the window made a gay contrast in chintz with a pattern of large roses, and my mother had made a colourful patchwork quilt for the bed. On the bed was a new china doll that had been dressed by my mother, but I hardly looked at it for I remembered the warm celluloid boy doll that I had left behind at the home, and once more I struggled with emotions that were made all the harder by having to repress them.

Our big kitchen had a shiny black range and my father had made up the fire and laid the cloth for tea. Dennis was nowhere to be seen and had disappeared into the front room with the two aunts. I sat at the table with a huge piece of cake in front of me and a breakfast cup full of tea. I waited for grace to be said and my mother smirked when I asked if I should say it.

'You can forget that rubbish,' she said. 'You're home now.'

'Would you please pass the bread and butter?' I said politely.

My mother laughed and said mockingly to my father, 'We have a proper bloody lady here.'

Then I asked about Lady and was told that she had been put down. I felt desolation that was almost unbearable. I felt as though Lady was waiting for me to open the back gate and we would go out and explore the waiting world beyond the gate together. I suddenly wanted the familiar surroundings of the past few years: the wide open verandah where you could lie snug and warm and hear the hoot of an owl or the cry of a vixen and smell the smoke from a wood fire and the wild honeysuckle. See the clouds racing across the sky or the moon riding amongst the bright stars and then wake on a cold and frosty morning and run across the frozen blades of grass and see the lacy spiders' webs in the hedges. That night as I lay in that lonely back room, I looked out onto a bare blank wall and cried to go home. 'I want to go home,' I wept softly into the bedclothes so that they shouldn't hear me. 'I want to go home.'

Schooldays

*I*n the days that followed, I went to school. Two Mile Hill School was an elementary school for working-class children and stood on the top of the hill that loped all the way down to St George. I had been used to a quiet little class of about half a dozen children with at least three teachers, which meant that we sometimes had a whole period of individual attention. Conversation was subdued and a loud giggle was instantly suppressed when a finger was pressed to the lips. Now it was all noisy activity, with little boys showing natural aggression and taking coveted possessions away from other children, and a vast expanse of playground where the children divided. The boys played their boisterous games and the girls found quiet corners to play skipping and pottle, or to bring brightly coloured wool and make uneven lengths of knitting. I hated the noise and the confusion and the bullying. Even the blowing of the teacher's whistle disturbed me, and although it taught me at the first sound to get immediately into line, I have never lost the desire to throttle the person who dares desecrate the peace, and to regiment and condition young minds. I rebelled then as I do now, and my bland expression belied the dark thoughts that lay smouldering and unspoken.

Every morning on our way to school we stopped at the top of the lane to watch Tom Pillinger making the sparks fly off the anvil as he shoed the lovely shire horses at the forge. The chink of hammer on steel and the hiss of steam when the new shoe was plunged into water were fascinating and we stood and watched in rapt silence, unable to move until the faint sound of the bell galvanised us into action.

Every Friday I was excused school because I had to attend the clinic at Warmley. We would have to walk the two miles down and back in order to obtain a free jar of cod-liver oil and malt; I also got a glass of free milk three times a week at school. I loved the cod-liver oil and malt and would often rush in from play to take a spoon and dip it in the jar to savour the treacly stuff. We had a big pantry under the stairs and all kinds of delicious smells emanated from there. Mum made wine and there were always delightful mysterious things happening inside the big stone jar where the wine was fermenting. Sometimes, when it had been bottled and corked, we would suddenly hear a loud bang and the cork would fly out from the bottle and all the wine would dribble down the sides like coloured froth. We often came in from play and took a great swig from a bottle of elderberry or gooseberry or dandelion wine, then cut a huge chunk of crumbly Cheddar cheese. Other favourites of mine were sticky condensed milk or golden syrup on bread, or pork-dripping on toast. We made toast on the big range, holding the bread close to the fire on the prongs of a long toasting fork.

On Sunday I went to Sunday school, and every Sunday afternoon my mother met me and we walked down Two Mile Hill to St George to have tea with her parents, Gran and Granfer. All the family gathered and we'd all sit round a big wooden table and have seedy cake and prunes for tea. My grandfather was a big man of six foot with a moustache and a shock of baby-fine white hair. He used to sit in a big wooden chair by the open fire and recount stories of murders that were published in a paper called *Thompson's Weekly News*. Nobody dared interrupt him, and all us children had to stay as quiet as mice. We were not allowed in the front parlour; that was a room that stayed musty with disuse, and a big aspidistra blotted out the light from the window that looked out onto the street. Gran always sat in her chair on the other side of the fire and often fanned herself with her apron. She suffered from hot blooms – a condition my grandfather said was peculiar to women. But by the way he hollered and shouted at her I would have staked my life that her condition was entirely due to him. He had a way of dominating her completely so that, if and when she spoke at all, it was in a quiet and timid way, and if she didn't move at his first demand he would raise his voice to a shout, and then she would almost run to do his bidding. I hated my grandfather with a passion, and he seemed to view me with the same dislike and contempt he held for my father.

'Chas Dark has no spine,' he announced to all and sundry. 'And our Nell's that headstrong she needs a heavy hand. She's too strong a personality for Chas, and he'll rue the day.'

My father sat there tight-lipped and silent in front of the whole family, none of whom said a word in his defence.

One day Granfer took some watercress from a plate and suddenly flicked the water at everyone sitting round the table, slapping his sides and roaring with laughter at their surprise. I jumped, along with everyone else, but hadn't been at all amused. 'I didn't find that at all funny,' I said.

Granfer's face went a pale shade of purple and he roared loud enough to make everyone tremble and look uncomfortable. He fixed his watery blue eyes on me and exploded with rage, 'And what, young madam, would you find amusing?'

'I would like it, Granfer, if you shouted less at Gran and the rest of us.'

My mother tried to hide her smirk, for she had often felt the buckle-end of his strap across her young legs. She had a champion now, in me. My father had suffered insults enough and he was right there now to defend this innocent if audacious remark. But Philip was already turning to his son-in-law.

'You are not a man at all if you can't control the wilfulness of your daughter nor the wildness of your own wife. The young un is going the right way to end up on the front page of the *News of the World*, and our Nell will lead you such a dance, you'll not know if you're on yer ass or yer elbow.'

31

Gran's face had gone turkey red and she was fanning herself vigorously with her apron. The rest of the family got up to go, but Granfer's booming voice demanded that they stay. So we all glared at one another until Auntie May said in her calm tones that she thought things had gone far enough and that she and Alfie, her husband, wanted to get ready for chapel and as they were in the choir they would have to be excused.

Sometimes, though, the family gatherings could be fun and we would have enjoyable evenings together with Granfer playing the organ. We would all sing those lovely old hymns and songs like 'We shall meet but we shall miss him, there will be a vacant chair,' or 'Have you had a kindness shown? Pass it on.' Alfie and May had good voices and they could sing and make us all join in. Auntie May lived in rooms across the street. Hardly anybody in those days could afford a house. Perce, who was the youngest of my mother's brothers, wanted to be wed and was demanding that Granfer open up the front parlour for him and Gladys. He would have his own way, too, my mother said.

Every Whit Monday there was a trip up the river in a barge. This was the event of the year, when Granfer played his silver-ended squeeze-box and we would all sing, 'We are out on the ocean sailing to our home beyond the sea.' We would sail right up to Bees' Tea Gardens and all the kids had a wonderful time playing hide-and-seek and going down to the river's edge where we could watch the rush of water tumbling over the weir. The sun was always warm and there would be masses of bluebells in the woods. Young lovers walked hand in hand along the riverbank, and we were given pennies by uncles we hadn't seen for ages; parents became reckless with hard-earned cash and we would be given an unexpected ice cream or glass of lemonade.

Whitsuntide was an exciting week, when all the Sunday schools marched with banners flying and bands playing. The traffic was halted and the crowds lined the streets all the way from Kingswood right down Two Mile Hill to St George. You had to be up early in the morning to get right at the front to see all the things that went by. Before I started to go to Zion Chapel, I used to dance in front of the man with the big drum. I loved the wild abandon; it was like the freedom of the fields, giving yourself up to the music and the beat of the drum.

When all the Sunday schools had marched down as far as the Worlds End pub at St George, they turned and came back to Soundwell Road at Kingswood. G. B. Britton was a local shoe manufacturer and owned a big house at Lodge Causeway. Outside the gate on the day of the march was always a man with a big basket of buns, and we all had a bun and some fruit and nuts and then we were allowed into Mr Britton's garden. It was like fairyland, with rose gardens and bowers and unusual trees. I loved being in the garden and spent the entire time in a magical world of my own, lost with the trees and the flowers and my own imagined companions. It was in a quiet corner of the garden that I met Mr Britton. He came upon me as I was deep in conversation with one of my imaginary people, and with considerable politeness (and trying to hide his own amusement) apologised for interrupting us.

At that time I had the most beautiful hair, which fell to my waist in six complete ringlets and was the colour of burnished gold. Every morning my mother brushed it with a whalebone brush until my scalp tingled and my hair covered my shoulders in glorious waves. When everyone else had to put their hair into rags or pipe cleaners to make it curl, mine was a sea of natural waves and colour. By the time I came home at lunchtime, my hair had developed a character all its own and had transformed itself into six fat, perfect curls. Even when you inserted a finger right through the tip of the ringlet you could not disturb its splendour, and my mother used to tie the whole six curls with a ribbon every afternoon. Mr Britton positively glowed and patted my head and waxed enthusiastic about my hair. Then he presented me with a perfect white rose and told me that his wife adored roses and that all the roses in the garden were hers. On the spur of the moment I asked him if I could come and sit in his garden again, and he said quietly that I could come anytime I liked.

The Lilac

The lilac, a deep, deep mauve, hung in glorious profusion over the wall that divided my grandparents' garden from the house next door. The tree belonged to Ma Parsons, and had never been trimmed back. Now, after a sudden May shower, it hung, heavily scented and beautiful, in all its springtime glory. The more I gazed at it, the more convinced I became that Gran would love to have some for her sideboard, or in the centre of the deal table in the kitchen. Back home there were jars of flowers everywhere, even on the windowsills. Bright yellow buttercups, cowslips and bluebells, and soon there would be big white moon daisies that we brought home from the meadows. Here there was nothing except the dark green aspidistra that stood on the small table in the bay window of the front room.

I was already snapping and tearing at the heavy-laden limbs of the lilac when I saw out of the corner of my eye my grandfather bearing down on me, his face livid with rage. I was used to him bellowing and shouting, but unlike my grandmother who ran to do his bidding like a scared rabbit, I merely waited for him to come up to me.

'And who, might I ask, give you permission to pick the lilac?' he said in a voice like thunder. 'That bush belongs to Mrs Parsons next door and is her property.'

'It's over your side of the wall,' I said simply.

Now absolutely purple with rage, he snatched the blooms away from me and marched me through the hallway and into Ma Parsons' next door. She was a tall, skinny woman and now emerged from her back kitchen with a dirty tea-towel in her hand. She was attempting to dry a black saucepan that was so ingrained with grease and grime that it was making the tea-towel even dirtier with each wipe she made. She peered enquiringly at the pair of us as we advanced towards her, and blinked with small, watery blue eyes. She wore a black skirt pulled across her waist and secured with a large safety pin; her blue cardigan was faded and rolled up at the elbow. There was a gaping hole on the shoulder and this had been loosely drawn together with a different shade of wool.

'This THIEF,' and Granfer emphasised the word, 'has taken it upon herself to pick your lilac. If she were a wench of mine, I'd take a strap to her. Just wait till our Nell comes in tonight to fetch her, I shall have a few words to say about the liberties she takes.' Then, turning to me, 'Apologise!' he bellowed, shaking me until my head began to rock from side to side. 'Just say you are sorry, you little THIEF.'

'I am not a thief,' I shouted back at him. 'And don't you dare touch me.'

Shaking myself free, I turned and fled, leaving both of them staring back at me, one in a blind mad rage, and the other with a look of utter surprise in her watery eyes.

I ran out into the street. At the top was Avondale Cemetery. I ran like the wind through the gateway and hid behind a big tombstone until my anger and fright had subsided. When I was quite sure that no one had followed me, I began to play quite happily among the gravestones. I imagined that all the dead people were being held captive under the ground. I would go up to the grave and say dramatically, 'Take my hand and I will set you free.'

Then I saw the gravedigger leaning on his shovel and looking at me, so I ran in the opposite direction so that he couldn't see me. From a grass verge, below the vale was the river snaking its way along the Netham and skirted by woods on either side. I curled up on the bank and went to sleep.

When I opened my eyes, it was cold and I was hungry. I wondered if my mother had arrived to fetch me back, for she had dropped me at Gran's that morning before going to the clinic with our Dennis. I wondered if I should venture back now. I saw the gravedigger glancing my way and I scooted out of a side turning and into the street. As I tiptoed along the passage, I heard Granfer still bellowing and telling my mother the tale. I peeped through the crack in the door and saw Gran fanning herself with the end of her pinny. His loud voice must have brought on one of her hot blooms. Dennis was sitting on a stool in front of the range; he was holding a big piece of cotton wool to his mouth and he looked fed up and miserable.

'I tell 'ee, Nell, you'm goin' to have trouble with that girl if you don't curb the high spirits of ern. I only tell 'ee fer yer own good. Spare the rod an' spoil the child.'

'Knock one devil out and let half a dozen in,' said my mother. 'I can't say the strap ever did a lot fer me.'

Granfer began to spit and splutter. 'No, I didn't spare the rod and I kin hold my head up with all the buggers down the street.'

'You might be able to hold your head up, but I couldn't sit down fer days!' retorted my mother. 'Neither did I forget it, or think it did me much good.'

He was staring at her now, unable to believe that she was standing up to him. I slipped in quietly and stood by her side.

'Besides,' she went on, 'what was so wrong in our Joyce picking a bit of lilac? And over your side of the wall an' all, it's yours to pick if you've a mind to. Old nose-bag will have a field day with the story you've given her. Haven't you any thought for me without filling her mouth with gossip?'

To my utter amazement, my grandfather's face began to crumple and he actually began to whine. 'I never meant no 'arm, Nell,' he snivelled. 'I only wanted to point out to 'ee what a headstrong wench thy Joyce is. If she ain't curbed now, she'll land up on the front page of the *News of the World*.'

'You call her headstrong because she has a bit of spirit and that is what you'd like to thrash out of her, like you tried to thrash out of me and all your other kids. Well,' and she leaned towards him as she spat out the words, 'let me tell you something. She has something of my spirit and I glory in it, and neither me nor her father will raise one finger to beat that out of her like you tried to beat it out of us.'

Looking very grim and triumphant, she stood up to depart. Instinctively both Dennis and I moved to her side, Dennis with the wad of cotton wool still pressed to his mouth and looking very white and sick. When she got to the door she turned again to her father.

'And don't go taking out yer nasty temper on our mother,' she hissed at him. 'Or you'll have me to reckon with.' She pushed her face right into his then and said, 'And no more smart remarks about Chas not being man enough to keep his wife in order, for I've been the butt of your vile jokes for long enough. You threw me at this man, so don't undermine our marriage now.'

Granfer actually looked scared now, and I saw his small beady eyes fill with tears. He looked rather pathetic as he stood in his doorway and saw us go.

The rain that had threatened all day now began to fall in big fat drops. We hardly heard him call to us from the doorway, 'Bide a bit, Nell, till the rain goes off.'

But we had already turned the corner and were heading for the long trek home.

Ada and Flo

I hardly ever saw my brother Dennis. He was locked away somewhere in that silent front room. Sometimes on a Sunday I knocked softly on the door and asked to be allowed in and they would let me.

There were several things in that front parlour that I loved to stand and look at. One was the blood-red epergne that occasionally had carnations or roses in it and looked very grand and regal. It gave the room an air of great splendour, an elegance that belonged to the gentry who lived in mansions just like the ones you saw in magazines. The other was a wondrous thing full of magic that filled me with excitement so that my eyes shone. It would have been worth throwing a tantrum to be allowed in that room just to see it. To the left of the fireplace was a gas jet complete with gas mantle. When the gas was turned on in the evening, the whole room was bathed in a soft yellow light. In order to obtain this light, pennies had to be fed into a red metal box, which was behind the front door in the passage outside. My mother contributed two pennies and the two aunts the other two, carefully placing them on the mantelshelf until they were needed. Four pennies took you up to ten o'clock, when the gas ran out and left you in darkness until you inserted more money in the meter, but nobody ever extended the lighting after ten.

Round Aunt Ada's gas mantle was a glass shade made of long crystal glass drops that caught the light and danced like a thousand tiny stars, and when they were ever so slightly touched they jingled like fairy music from a magic sphere. I could weave a thousand dreams from just one touch until I was brought back to cold reality by Aunt Ada boxing my ears and telling me, 'Leave the bloody thing alone, or is that something else you want to destroy? You don't see our Denny fingering things and always wanting to break them.'

It had been to this room that they had brought 'our Denny' when he had been six months old, when my mother found herself pregnant a second time and was devastated by the discovery. She hadn't minded the aunts twittering over him and caring for him. In the years that followed my birth and the resulting health problems from TB she must have been glad of the help and care Ada and Flo lavished on the boy, and they certainly took care of his every need. They waited on him hand and foot and when they took him for walks or wheeled him out in the pram they told everyone that he was their son, sent by the good Lord to them.

This state of affairs lasted until I returned from Painswick, when a single voyage of discovery led me to the front parlour and the knowledge that there was another child to play with behind the locked door. It seemed now that I was the cause of a general disruption in the normally quiet running of the home. My faint tapping on the door would for the most part be ignored and I would have to walk disconsolately away. Sometimes Aunt Ada's hard, brittle voice shooing me away sent me back to the corner in the kitchen where I sat on the box fender and looked out at the dark blank wall.

Sometimes, though, Aunt Flo, the gentler of the two, allowed me to come and sit round the fire with them, and Dennis let me read his comics. Aunt Ada sometimes read to us in a flat, expressionless voice and then we had a fit of the giggles and fell about, clutching each other, helpless with laughter. It nearly always ended up with me being shoved outside the room and the bolt drawn across the door once more.

When we went to school, I went out the back way and Dennis through the front. If we walked home together, I stopped only long enough to see Ada let him in, and then I ran around to the back and let myself in that way. In the end it led to trouble and I, of course, was the root cause of it. Dennis was a kind boy and I enjoyed being with him. He shared his books and his toys with me and had a sense of humour that made me laugh and giggle. He had expensive toys that the two aunts bought him and kept hidden until I was safely out of the way, but it was a simple John Bull printing outfit that was the cause of all the trouble.

You simply put the little individual characters into a wooden frame with a pair of tweezers, then pressed the completed sentence onto an ink pad and then onto a piece of paper. Hey presto! You could make up your own magazine. We had already experimented with our thumbprints and the whole of our palms, and the tablecloth – all starched and stiff and pristine white – seemed too inviting and appropriate to miss out, so I pressed a perfect imprint onto the table-cloth. Dennis sensed danger before I did, and just as a perfect pair of palmprints appeared on the cloth a shadow fell over us and a long bony hand thumped me on the back.

Dennis whined, 'Our Joyce did it. She made me do it.'

'There's no end to your wickedness. I'm going to get the Black Maria to take you away – they will put you in a strait-jacket.'

All this and more from Aunt Ada, but it was the thought of the Black Maria that filled my soul with such dread that I began to sob uncontrollably and to kick and scream at the thought of being taken away forcibly and put in a strait-jacket where I might never be able to struggle free. Both my mother and father rushed into the room and I tried to tell them between sobs that I only wanted to play with the print-ing set. My father took me from the room but my mother stayed to have a battle of words with the two aunts, stating emphatically that Dennis should now come out into his own room where no more favouritism could take place, with no more toys bought just for him that we could fight over.

With that, Ada started to wail, 'Don't take my baby from me.'

'Don't talk so wet – he's not your baby.'

Ada ran out into the street and began to shout hysterically, 'She's taking my boy away from me.'

My father ran out after her whilst Flo, pointing a finger at my mother, said quietly but viciously, 'If anything happens to our Ada, I'll wipe the floor with you.'

Then they both held onto my brother's shoulders as my mother tried to drag him from the room. She said with sudden fury, 'He shall come out to live with us and I will get him away from you two mad buggers.'

And she and Dad began to pull at his legs, with Ada and Flo tugging at his arms and shoulders whilst Dennis lay there between them, not turning a hair. All this time I was twisting my handkerchief round and round until it was a tight soggy bundle. What had happened was all my fault and as I watched the tussle I felt bad and wished I could stop the loud beating of my heart. Suddenly my mother let go of my brother's legs with a disgusted 'What's the use?' and left the room, with my father following her saying, 'Don't get yerself upset, Nell, my love.'

She gave him a withering and half disgusted look. 'You're a spineless bastard, anyway,' she said.

Dad was silent and bit his lip. It was a terrible thing to say. In those days it was a stigma to have no father, so he walked past her and out into the back yard where, my mother said, he would go into a king-size sulk and not speak for weeks, which suited her just fine. Then she caught sight of me and told me to stop snivelling and get to bed. Nobody was going to put me in a strait-jacket and I must learn not to be so bloody touchy. I fled up the stairs and into that cold white-washed room.

It was peaceful the next day and my mother was making cakes and small buns. The cake smelled delicious when it came out of the oven and she placed it on the dresser with a tea-towel covering it. Ada emerged from the front parlour with two blue tea plates in her hand – could she have just a couple of slices 'fer our Denny'? No answer from my mother, but she nodded her head. Ada wielded the knife with a flourish and cut two huge chunks which rendered the cake to half its size, and then proceeded to scrape up the fallen crumbs between her fingers and stuff them into her mouth.

'My God,' exploded my mother. 'Why don't you take the bloody lot?'

Ada, now with a slight satanic gleam in her large, heavily lidded eyes, turned on her accusingly. 'You begrudge yer own child a farthing's worth of cake!' And as if to emphasise the point she held up her little finger and spat out, 'A farthing's worth!'

Two minutes later Flo appeared and dragged her sister back to the front parlour, with my mother shouting after her, 'What about the other half for tomorrow?'

My dad, coming in from the back yard, enquired what all the shouting was about and Mum, with a scornful sigh and mock derision, replied, 'Only those two mad harpies got loose again.'

Brother Cliff

I was nine when my brother Clifford was born on a cold November day, with the snow falling so thick and fast you couldn't see through the flakes of snow as thick as half-crowns. My mother, dispirited and weary, had carried this baby with the same unwillingness that she had carried me and Dennis except that this time she had been violently sick and ill all the way through. My father had been put on short time at Jackson's: three days on and three days off, which meant that he could not sign on the dole. He could bring fruit and vegetables from the allotment in summer, but there wasn't much to harvest in winter. Twelve shillings a week, with six of that to go on rent, meant that times were very, very hard. Although coke was only a shilling a bag it did mean that sometimes there was nothing to heat the house. We had very little meat, but you could get a pennyworth of pork bones from the butcher and Mum used to put them in the oven by the side of the range with baked potatoes and we would suck on the bones and tear the strips of meat that still hung in delicious fatty layers on them. Pork trotters were another delightful and satisfying repast. As they were brought piping hot from the boiling water, we gnawed happily away at them and used the liquor with a few extra vegetables for stew the next day. Most of the time we existed on bread and dripping, but there were a lot of others in the same boat and clothes and furniture could always be pawned to buy essentials.

I well remember that house in South Road where in winter great gusts of icy wind swept along the cold stone passage through gaps under the front and back doors. The door and window frames rattled in the draught as the wind found entrance to the very room itself. I have images of my father padding along the lino-covered floor, the candle that he held in the blue, chipped holder making weird patterns on the wall. The hiss of the unlighted gas jet, and the sudden burst of yellow flames, would fascinate and soothe me as I lay scared and terrified in my iron bed, for the sudden draught from the door would make the flame writhe in wild gyrations. When the windows rattled, we shoved little wooden wedges between the corded panes; even the thick, faded-blue curtains hung on their fat wooden poles were not enough to keep the cold or draught from seeping through. You sat in front of the kitchen fire with your face and hands and knees aglow whilst your back froze. Most of the house was lino-covered, with here and there the peg mats that we helped to make in the long winter evenings. On frosty days all the windows would be iced up on the inside and you shivered when you had to get out of bed and go barefoot down over the stairs.

This morning there was no fire to come down to and the snow lay piled up against the back door in a high drift, and some had actually blown under the back door and into the scullery. Dad gave me a hot cup of tea and told me to be very quiet and good. He said that my mother was not very well and he was going out to get some coke and half a pound of biscuits for her. I heard him in the yard, shovelling the snow away from the back door and down the back path, and then he pulled out the handcart and put on his trilby and scarf. I heard my mother shout out as if in pain and rushed up the stairs to find her stretched out across the bed, clutching at the bedclothes and shaking with cold and pain so that the bed was jerking up and down.

'Go and fetch Elsie Storey,' she panted. 'And tell her to come quick, the baby is coming.'

I raced over the road and banged loudly on the knocker, yanking it up and down until my wrist hurt. Bert Storey, Elsie's husband, came slowly to the door. He still had a napkin tucked into the neck of his shirt and had been eating his breakfast of bacon and eggs.

'Hello, Joyce,' he said. 'Is there anything wrong?'

I jumped up and down on the step. 'My Mummy is dying,' I said simply. 'And she says the baby is coming.'

'Oh dear, I'll fetch Elsie,' he said.

I was told to stay with Bert until she returned, and then I went into a house so vastly different from ours that I stood in the kitchen with my mouth wide open. The design of the house was the same, but from the moment you stepped through the front door you felt a softness under your feet and you almost sank into thick pile carpets that seemed like heaven to walk on, and as I passed through the middle room on my way to the kitchen the warmth from a coke fire, red hot and piled high, made me take a deep breath and sink into a big brown velvet chair beside it and stretch out my hands to warm them.

Bert began again to tackle his breakfast, eating with quick bird-like motions, first cutting a piece of bacon, then egg, then fried bread. This he would stuff into his mouth and wash down with a swig of tea. Then the whole process would be repeated very quickly as though he was anxious to finish it in case someone came and snatched it away. He looked up and saw me looking at the contents of his plate, disappearing so rapidly whilst I was busy watching. He suddenly finished the whole lot and then with his knife he scraped the remaining bits of egg from the plate and licked them into his mouth, and then he actually licked the plate clean across several times with his tongue. Still looking at me, he leaned over to the plate that Elsie had left, and slapped the bacon and egg between two slices of bread and handed it to me on a plate. 'Tuck in,' he said. 'I shall make some more tea.'

Never had anything tasted so delicious, and by the time I had finished grease and egg had dribbled down my chin and the heat from the fire had burned my legs so that I had to move back. I had another cup of tea before we heard Elsie returning, and she swept into the kitchen closely followed by my father.

Outside the kitchen window in the tiny patch of back yard before the wall of the next house was a mountain of coke. The blank wall had been painted white, which made it a bright spot to look out on, and made the kitchen seem lighter as well, but that pile of coke must have covered five or six feet of the wall. As I'd come through the house, I had noticed a fire in the other room as well. And one more thing – the house was full of flowers. Huge gold and bronze chrysanthemums arranged beautifully in tall vases, and thick velvet curtains with deep pelmets and sashes to hold them back. God, this house was beautiful! I made a sudden and silent vow, there and then, that one day I would have a warm house like this, with carpets and red-velvet curtains. Elsie Storey had made a deep, deep impression on me and although I didn't know it then my life was to be inextricably bound up with hers.

She proceeded to tell my father that he was to help himself to the coke and to light a fire in the bedroom for my mother. She called the boy from next door to tell him to go at once to try to contact one of the nurses who lived at the Nurses' Home in Hanham Road and to tell them it was urgent and someone was to come at once. It was still snowing, and the lad grumbled, but he put on an oilskin and went trudging up the road, not very quickly because the great white flakes still fell silent and heavy and covered everything in a thick carpet of snow which piled in great drifts and made visibility almost nil.

The rest of that day is a memory of hectic comings and

goings. At ten past twelve my mother gave birth to a little boy. He was not a full-term baby, they said, he was a 'seven-month' baby who would need a lot of attention. Elsie kept my mother in hot drinks and soup and kept me informed about all that was happening, but she would not let me go home. She said I would only be in the way. She came over once and then I heard her pulling out drawers upstairs. When she came down, she held a shawl and several items of babywear in her arms. She explained that the baby had come so unexpectedly that Mum had not had time to buy it any new clothes, but I knew it was because there was no money to buy food, let alone the clobber for yet another mouth to feed.

At four o'clock she took me over herself to see the new baby, and all I could see was a red screwed-up little face that looked very old and wrinkled. Two little fists were closed tight with thumbs inwards, and every few minutes he would give out a pathetic little yell as though he was terrified of being catapulted into a strange and alien world. He clung to my mother like a young frightened monkey. I bent down to kiss him, but he let out a stifled squeak and it was then that I noticed he had no nails on his fingers and I guess none on his toes either, and I suddenly lost all interest in him and longed to go back to Elsie's house and the comfort of the brown velvet chair by the fire and the egg and bacon butty that seemed such absolute luxury to me.

Elsie was our fairy godmother and was always popping over with eggs, or pies she had made, or a pot of cream that she insisted must be eaten that very day. Bert Storey worked at Poutney's – the Bristol pottery that was then in Lodge Causeway. He was an accountant and earned three pounds ten shillings a week, compared with Dad's full pay of twenty-one shillings. They were rich and we were poor.

After that, I slipped over to Elsie's quite frequently. Nobody ever asked where I was going. My mother had her hands full with the new baby, who cried a lot and wanted all her attention, and Dennis was locked away in the front room – since that last dreadful scene I was not allowed near them. Elsie always seemed glad to see me and one day she asked me if I would like a book to read. Her only son David was a tall, thin lad, very much like his Mum to look at, but whereas Elsie was vivacious and bright-eyed he was very shy and would stammer and shuffle. He brought me a book that he had been given at Christmas and held it out to me at arm's length. It was *Treasure Island,* and as I took it from him I asked if he had read it, but to my surprise he looked even more embarrassed and quietly admitted that he couldn't read. I asked him if he would like me to read it to him, and he sat the other side of the fire whilst I proceeded to bring to life the story of Jack Hawkins, Squire Trelawney, the *Hispaniola* and that unforgettable character, Long John Silver.

Both Elsie and Bert were surprised that I could read so well. They had hired a tutor to coach David but he hadn't achieved a great deal of success. After that I was a frequent visitor to the house, reading to David. Sometimes I would look up from reading to him about some daring cowboy adventure, and he would be behind a chair, quietly acting out the story as he listened, and taking careful aim at some imaginary and unfortunate Indian chief. When he saw that he was being watched, he would become confused and shy. I think in the end he learned to read in sheer desperation when the tutor told him that his mother or another girl could go on reading to him for ever.

David had a cousin who was a poor relation and who came to stay with him for holidays and sometimes weekends. His name was Bertie. He had brilliant blue eyes and the most shy and disarming smile. He had fair wavy hair and the most beautiful hands I have ever seen – large, capable, beautiful hands with square nails and half-moons showing half an inch long. He was acutely conscious of his shirts, which were always torn or had buttons missing. Elsie used to go upstairs and always produced something of David's for him to change into. Then the three of us played in the parlour, which in Elsie's house had been turned into a study and filled with bookcases, a roll-top desk in the bay window; it had a green Wilton carpet and brown leather chairs. It was Bert's study, but he never minded us being there and he had a quick, dry sense of humour that made everybody laugh. I never thought that one day I would wish that I had never set eyes on the fair-haired boy who looked at me so eagerly. When he took my hand to come and read to him, I followed him, thinking that for the first time in my life somebody needed me. Being able to read was the only thing I could do well. Now David and Bertie respected and admired me, and I felt it was the only worthwhile thing I had done in my entire life.

One day at Elsie's house I picked up a book by Marie Corelli called *The Mighty Atom*, and then found another in the library called *The Sorrows of Satan*. There was a whole series, which I read avidly and which kept me spellbound. In them she wrote about the Ancient Wisdom and I knew I must start on a quest just like the one for the Holy Grail to try to find it. I was like the Watcher on the Tower, or the Seeker after Knowledge. Nothing mattered now except to find this Wisdom, if it took me all my life, then I would have the answer to all my problems. The book and all that was in it could not lie. It was in the book and so it must be right.

When I told Elsie that I had read all Marie Corelli's books, she didn't believe me. She said that it was more than she had done and what were they all about? When I discussed them at length, she was amazed, and I heard her telling my mother that I was a good reader and a very bright little girl.

'She's always got her nose in some book or other,' my mother interrupted. 'I wish sometimes she'd do more for me about the house.'

After that, I had books snatched away from me and I was told to clean the brass or to wash the dishes. Mostly, I had to take the baby out. Clifford as a baby was a very nervous child and cried incessantly, pulling at Mum's skirts until she almost went frantic with agitation. She yelled at him, and then yelled at me to get him out of her way for ten minutes before she did him some harm. If Dad tried to comfort her, then her eyes flashed fire and both of us would beat a hasty retreat, Dad to chop firewood and me with Cliff in the pram going purple with rage and frustration until the motion of the pram lulled him off to sleep. That is, until the pram stopped, then he would start again, so I had to be perpetually on the move. Sometimes I would take him as far as Tumble Fields – a favourite spot of ours. We called it that because right in the middle was a big hill that we rolled down or pretended was an unscalable fortress, and half of us defended the fort, and the other half had to attack it. On the other side was a meadow with tall grasses and buttercups and moon daisies. I thought he would love it there just as I had loved once to be in the countryside, oh so long ago now, but when I unstrapped him and hauled him down into the long grass, he screamed and his face went puce with rage and he kept shaking his head from side to side. I wanted to hold him and convey to him that I loved him. I kept remembering all those lonely desperate hours when I too was desolate like him. I took him in my arms and kissed him and told him that I knew what a strange and frightening world he had come into but that I would look after him and that everything would be all right. Out of sheer exhaustion, he stopped crying, and suddenly his two little arms reached round my neck and I felt tears wet on his face. I brushed the fair wavy hair now damp from his face and kissed the blue eyes still filled with unshed tears. I yanked the pram out of the tall grass and sat with him on the edge of the field. He stuck a finger in his mouth and, still leaning against me, closed his eyes and went to sleep. I went to sleep as well and it seemed on that quiet warm afternoon, with the sound of the rooks and the woodpigeons from the copse away over the meadow, that I dreamed again of that other white bungalow where I had gone to sleep on the verandah to the sounds of the wildlife and the gentle swaying of the trees.

My Best Friend

*V*era Drinkwater was my best friend. Every morning I waited for her to come out of Victoria Street. She would be with three other girls, and then together we all walked to Two Mile Hill School. Vee and I were like twin souls. We liked the same subjects at school and worked hard every term to be near the top of the class so we could sit near each other, usually ending up in the top section as tenth and eighth. We never moved from that top section. We were inseparable.

I was always a little scared of Vee's mother, who was a bit of a dragon and famous for her table-tapping powers. Gran Dark said that Ma Drinkwater would call up something she didn't bargain for one of these days, and no good could come of it.

When I called for Vee, I always went round the back way, because she was usually in her father's den at the bottom of the garden, where he mended shoes in his spare time for a few extra shillings. Vee had a cane basket chair in there which was piled high with cushions and comics, and it was cosy and warm from a small stove which Mr Drinkwater lit when it was cold. He yarned to us for hours and loved to tell us stories about Kingswood in his day when he was a boy. And there were tales his father had told him about the olden days when Kingswood had been notorious for footpads, horse thieves and wife bashers. His tales about Bristol and Berkeley Castle and The Chase thrilled and fascinated me. As I listened, I could hear again the wheels of carriages rumble over the rough, uneven roads. I could see so clearly the velvet coats and lace at the wrists of noblemen and the cry of 'Stand and deliver!' from the masked highwayman. Superstition and the old religion, and even Stone Age man himself, seemed only half buried in those far off days, but I was part of it. I could feel it, and it was my past, and I belonged to a history that was real.

It had grown quite late; Harry Drinkwater had intended to see me home and I was waiting for him to return from delivering a pair of shoes to a neighbour. Vee's mother's table-tapping session began with all the family gathered there that night to try to solve the riddle of some missing money after the death of Vee's grandmother. Vee and I were in the corner of the kitchen reading, and members of the family sat with hands stretched out in front of them and fingers just slightly touching those of the ones sat next to them. One of the relatives sat on one side with a pencil and pad. He was supposed to take the message as it came through. I was reading a serial in the *Schoolgirl* comic and wasn't paying a great deal of notice.

'Is anybody there?' droned Mary. 'Is anybody there?'

The table tilted slightly then came down with a slight thud. It came to me suddenly that if this was a game it was a very silly one. But if, as Gran Dark had predicted, this was not a game and Mrs Drinkwater would call up something one day that she didn't bargain for, then I didn't want to be around when it happened. I began to feel frightened and wished Mr Drinkwater would come back and take me home. I could now no longer continue to read and sat watching the proceedings with ever increasing apprehension. The message had to be interpreted by a number of taps, representing a letter of the alphabet. So far, the table had obliged by giving the letter A, followed by D. I half wondered if the players themselves had manoeuvred the jolt, when suddenly the table lifted up almost vertically and then came to rest with a sickening thud. Almost at once, Mary rose to her feet and let out a shriek. 'I knew it,' she yelled. 'I knew it all the time. It was you, Ada, you took the money from your own mother!'

Ada, looking white and shaken, protested her innocence and her husband verified and backed up her statement. Mary, with eyes blazing, lambasted her sister and called her all the names under the sun. It was at this point that Mr Drinkwater arrived and stopped the proceedings with a few well-chosen words and said, 'I won't have these ungodly goings-on in my house.' Looking over at me, he said, 'Now, my queen, let's get you home.'

The street lights were cool white pools of comfort as we

walked the short distance to my house, but I was surprised to learn it was almost midnight and hoped I would be able to slip inside without waking my parents. The key to the door always hung on a long piece of string behind it, so that all I had to do was pull it through the letter-box. The stairs creaked a bit as I ascended them and I carefully avoided the worst offending ones. The naked bulb at the end of the long piece of flex was swinging slightly to and fro in the draught from the window, which was open at the top. I shivered as I began to undress and remembered the events of the night. I began to feel some unknown evil had followed me home. Vee's mum had been wrong to take things so far. Everybody knew there were some things you could do and things you could not. Just supposing she had called up something evil and it had followed me home. My heart was thumping now. I could hear it as I twisted about in my iron bed. How I wished that I had found the Ancient Wisdom that Marie Corelli had written about in her books! Then I would know everything, even how to banish evil and reach upward to the light.

The clock tower began to chime midnight – the witching hour; this was the time that things went bump in the night. I held my breath and waited for the last chime to die away and just at that split second the light bulb gave a slight click and went out and a great black mass jumped onto my bed. I was suddenly screaming my head off in terror and shouting incoherently, 'I'll be good. I'll be good. I'll be good. Oh please don't let the Devil have me. I'll be good.'

My father appeared from nowhere, wearing his white

longjohns and button-at-the-neck vest. 'Had a bad dream, my babby?' he said, brushing the cat from my bed. 'Shall Dad make thee a nice cuppa tea?'

'Yes,' I said, letting him think it had been a nightmare, yet still wanting to prolong the presence of another human being. 'The light's gone out,' I spluttered. 'The light's gone.'

'Dad'll put in a new one tomorrow.'

'No, now,' I stated firmly.

'If Dad can find one downstairs.' His voice trailed off as he manoeuvred the dark stairs. I heard the steps creak as he made his way down. I heard the kitchen door open and then silence in the darkness. I closed my eyes tight, for it seemed that cold phantom hands still reached out to grab me.

A Bun Dance

An incident happened a few weeks later to convince me that the path of goodness was not an easy one to follow. If I must strive upwards on the way to salvation, I would need all my brains and wits to get there. That morning I met up with Vee and we walked to school. The term had been wonderful and we had for the first time received equal marks, which meant that we were sitting in the same desk together. My joy was complete. We filed into our classroom, where we were fifth and sixth, and sat halfway up the aisle in the top section. I had by now acquired a little knack of tossing back my curls just to emphasise a slight air of superiority. As well as being full of sin, I was puffed up with pride. Well, it was to take a fall this day. The curls bobbed again as I lifted the lid of my desk to take out the English writing book in which we were to have our first lesson of the day, in copperplate handwriting.

Miss Mullan, our teacher, wore tortoiseshell-framed glasses and had a habit of picking her nose. She also had a way of picking up the ruler and thwacking it on the back of your hand the exact number of times she wanted to emphasise something – like history dates, for example. At the same time, she would push her nose and glasses right into your face so that you could see her dilate her nostrils like a bull about to charge. It would go something like this:

'1066 to 1087.' Thwack, thwack. '1087 to 1100.' Thwack, thwack. '1100 to 1132.' Thwack, thwack. A vein on the back of my hand would suddenly appear like a small knot in a rope and cause excruciating pain. She would then command, in sharp, staccato tones, 'What were they?'

Half paralysed with pain and fear, my mind would go blank, and nothing but a wave of relief at the dull subsiding of pain ever seemed to emerge from those encounters, and yet, after all these years that repetition technique has never failed to produce some useless piece of information from those far-off school days.

Miss Mullan closed the register and lightly clasped her hands in front of her. She surveyed us for a minute or two, then, taking a piece of chalk, she wrote the word 'ABUNDANCE' in capital letters on the blackboard. Underneath, she drew two thick lines and then proceeded to transform the same word into beautiful copperplate handwriting, giving the A in 'Abundance' the most extravagant and dramatic tail. My head swirled and the letter seemed to come alive like a courtier in green velvet breeches and a big plumed hat that he now took off with a great wide expansive sweep of the tail of the A.

We had to copy what she had written and later it would be marked according to merit. I loved this flowery writing. To me it was exciting and romantic, a far cry from the untidy and almost indecipherable scrawl you see today. Another lost art (like brass moulding, my father would have said).

I had long since finished and was sitting idly watching the others scribbling laboriously away, some of them leaning over their schoolbooks with pink tongues peeping from the corners of their mouths. I looked at the word written on the board. It seemed to conjure up for me A bun dance, and I began to draw three happy little buns complete with currants and blue bows dancing a jig. 'Tra la la, tra la la' came a little caption out of their mouths, and I beat a soft tattoo on the desktop just to keep time with it. Tra la la. Vee glanced up from her work and saw what I had done. Recognition dawned, she stifled a giggle and the girl behind her popped her head up to see what was going on. Vee passed the bit of paper behind her, and a whole series of sniggers and giggles followed. It had progressed halfway round the classroom before Miss Mullan became aware that the calm of the lesson was being ruffled. Then, with a voice like thunder at the crack of doom, she bellowed, 'Well, what is so funny?'

A tall, lanky girl with buck teeth like a rabbit uncurled her length from her desk, looking awkward and sheepish standing there, holding the offending piece of paper in her hand. She delivered my death knell in one direct blow. 'Please, Miss, Joyce Dark did this.'

She extended my stroke of genius at arm's length, whilst

Miss Mullan advanced to the centre aisle. They met, and the three little buns changed hands. After a cursory glance at it and with a contemptuous curl of her upper lip, she tore it into shreds and committed it to the waste-paper basket. Then her big owl eyes turned on me.

'Come out here,' she commanded, and I wished I was a snail so that I could have retreated beneath the bony structure of my protective shell and defied all attempts at being coaxed or cajoled into coming out. Escape was impossible. I knew her next command before it came. 'Fetch the cane.'

The cane was always kept by Miss Dugdale's desk, which was on a raised dais in the middle of the hall. She was the headmistress. The burning humiliation was, you not only had to fetch the instrument of your torture, you had to carry it back to the classroom and return it to its place after your punishment. And you had to bear the sting of wounded pride by being caned in front of forty pairs of curious and sadistic eyes. When a girl was sent to fetch the cane, Miss Dugdale never asked why. She took it for granted that such matters were justified if the teacher deemed it so. Miss Dugdale had bunions, so she walked stiffly and painfully behind me with an expression that seemed to say, 'This will hurt me as much as it hurts you.'

Not a foot scraped the floor, not a desk banged, not a cough broke the silence as the cane was raised high in the air and then brought down hard. Once, twice, and then for a third time onto my outstretched palm. I gave only a slight gasp as she indicated that I raise the other hand for a further three strokes. I nursed my smarting palms beneath my armpits as she drew herself to her full height and disclosed to the whole class that I was a disruptive influence, a state of affairs that could not and would not be allowed to go on. I could feel the weal from the smack of the cane begin to raise on my hands, and didn't know how I would carry the cane back to its resting place beside the headmistress's desk, where I would have to stand for the rest of the morning as an example for the whole school to gaze upon. With a concentrated effort to control my tears, I took the offending cane she was now wiggling in front of me and followed her. The head girl, Gwen Monks, who was also door monitor, rushed from her seat to open the door, and she sailed imperiously through whilst I followed miserably behind.

As I stood there in that vast hall, I was filled with dark and dire thoughts. Teachers, grown-ups and parents were all too difficult to understand, and if I was as bad as they all made out – well, I wasn't even going to try to be good any more. I would be as bad as they made me out to be. Even God was hard to find, despite the fact that in the Ancient Wisdom Marie Corelli had said that all you had to do was talk to God just like your own father. I thought I ought to give God a chance to intervene on my behalf. Which He did, with the most surprising result.

Ever since the discovery of the Marie Corelli books, I had taken a renewed interest in Sunday school, the Band of Hope and other chapel activities. Sometimes I went three times on a Sunday. I usually went to sleep during the sermon, which went on for an interminably long time, and only woke up with a start when the preacher banged his fist on the pulpit to call on all us miserable sinners to repent. In fact, quite a lot of people woke with a start at this point, and I reckon he did it on purpose. Anyway, I was very pleased that God thought us all miserable sinners because that meant that grown-ups were no better than me. I had also taken to reading the New Testament. I tried starting off with the Old, but got lost in a maze of begetting, which sounded not at all nice. And I had another reason for perusing the Good Book.

At school we had a lesson called Religious Instruction, which I liked. A few weeks prior to my fateful humiliation, the vicar of All Saints just below the school visited us one morning when we were all assembled in the hall and told us that a prize would be presented to the girl who could correctly answer questions about the Bible, and write an essay on a story from the Bible.

On that morning as I stood in the hall with my heart full of dark thoughts, I made up my mind that I would ask my mother to intercede with the teachers on my behalf. Maybe if she would explain to them that I hadn't meant any harm, that I had finished first and was only filling in time, it would be all right. After all, it wasn't my fault that Vee had giggled and then passed those three little buns around the class. I told my mother at dinner time. I showed her my hands where the weals were now turning purple.

'You shouldn't mess about at school. You go there to learn.'

'But will you see my teacher, will you explain?' I pleaded.

'I don't know. I'll have to think about it,' was all she had to say, and I had to leave it at that.

During that afternoon my punishment for being a disruptive influence was completed. I was removed from my coveted sixth place in the top section and made to sit with the dunces at the very bottom of the class. Oh, the bitter, bitter shame of it! How would I ever be able to hold my head up high again? I would rather have had six more slashes with the cane than this crushing and unutterable blow descend upon me.

All the dunces in the bottom section conveyed their commiserations to me, and to their everlasting credit one or two even whispered, 'Aah, what a shame.' A couple of them smiled at me, and Ivy Dickson, who was now my desk mate, whispered kindly, 'Thee kin sit by the radiator if thee dost like.'

In my imagination I wanted some unseen power to rescue me from this dreadful humiliation that seemed like a bad dream. I even sat and fantasised about Rudolf Valentino, complete with black cape flying in the wind and white burnous about his head, who was already galloping across the playground on his Arab steed, and who would presently climb up on to the windowsill and carry me away. To music, of course.

I knew my mother had come to the school because Miss Mullan was called away suddenly by Miss Dugdale herself, accompanied by the frantic leaping of Gwen rushing to open the door. My heart did a mad tattoo and I kept thinking, 'Now it will be all over, and everything will be as it was.'

Miss Mullan returned and there was a sardonic smile on her face. She looked triumphantly over at me and said in cold, calculating tones, 'Even your own mother said she had more trouble with you than her two boys put together.'

God, and Rudolf Valentino, seemed very far away from me at that moment.

When I rushed into the back kitchen that night, I could hardly speak to my mother. She had once again betrayed me and I was filled with anger. She looked at my sullen face and demanded to know what other mischief I had got myself into.

'You didn't have to tell Miss Mullan that I was more trouble than both Den and Cliff put together,' I said. Then recklessly I stormed on, 'You never see Dennis, and you can't wait to get Cliff out of your sight.'

I stopped when I saw the blank expression on her face.

'I meant,' she said, 'illnesswise – I had a lot of trouble with you when you were little.' She didn't continue, but said in a kinder tone, 'Come and have your tea. Nothing lasts for ever, and it will be all right tomorrow, you'll see.'

The next day I made my way to the bottom section, still with a sinking heart. The only people glad to see me were the dunces, who greeted me like a long-lost friend, and one even offered to share her lunch, which consisted of two pieces of cold toast wrapped in greaseproof paper with her name written in pencil on the front. I was told to teach them how to read, a well-nigh impossible task. They laboured over every word and in desperation I produced a comic, sat them all in a circle and read to them the adventures of Tiger Tim. I was defiant now and so reckless I didn't care if I was caught or not. There was nothing more they could do to me now, and the rapt look on all those faces gave me a warm and thrilling feeling. The smell of chalk and dust, cold toast and jam sandwiches filled the classroom and I was Queen of the Dunces and, what was more, their beloved one at that.

There was a kind of freedom down here at the bottom of the heap. No pushing or striving to compete. I found it relaxing and almost agreeable. Nobody bothered you, and high marks were not expected. It wasn't that I didn't care. I cared desperately, but I was gradually coming to the realisation that, if no one else cared, why should I? Events were moving to a climax, though, and all to my benefit.

We were all assembled in the hall, for this was the day the vicar of All Saints was coming to announce the winner of the prize for the best Bible story and the correct question and answer entry from the New Testament. All the teachers twittered and made a great fuss when the vicar came into the hall and made his way to the platform. He wore his long black vestment over which his white surplice and black cross looked so impressive and holy. He began by saying that he wanted to thank all those who had responded so magnificently to the competition and how delighted he was that so many young minds were seeking truth in the Word of God.

With our coming entry into the world of work and adulthood he was sure that this basic religious training would stand us in good stead. 'I know,' he went on, 'that you are all waiting for me to announce the winner of the coveted Bible. But before I do, I want to say one thing about the composition that was so outstanding that it warranted the prize on its merits alone. It was the story of Martha and Mary, told in such a way that it brought tears to my eyes.' He got carried away, and his voice rose to a pitch as though he were delivering one of his own sermons '. . . She who had chosen the better part' (his voice fell again) 'and sat and listened to the words of Our Saviour, the Lord Jesus Christ. I proudly present this Bible to Joyce Dark. A most outstanding achievement and a most remarkable girl.'

There was a moment of almost stunned silence, then applause that carried me forward to receive my prize. God had answered my prayers. I had believed that it would come right and it had. As I passed Miss Mullan I allowed myself that superior toss of my curls as I walked past with my head held high. For who could ever call me bad or disruptive again when religion, and the Lord, and the vicar were all on my side?

The very next day I regained my seat in the top section and all my friends in the bottom section by the radiator waved and smiled to me. I had learned my first lesson in wisdom, ancient or modern. To be accepted as a fine, upstanding and respected member of the community, write a prize-winning composition or get to know the vicar. I still remember the rendering of 'The Lord is my Shepherd' that I sang with all my most dramatic appeal, and the heady feeling of elation when I saw the approval on the vicar's face. When he finally dismissed me with his blessing, the words flashed through my mind, 'And greater things shall ye do, if ye will only believe.'

The Flicks

After that I confided to Vee that I might eventually become a nun. She scoffed at the idea and said; 'Oh come on, Joyce! You wouldn't like it kneeling on a stone floor every day praying for hours. Besides, think of the holes you would wear in your stockings.'

I immediately thought of the darns I had in the only two pairs of black stockings I possessed, and nodded soberly at this practical approach. Then she nudged me confidentially and whispered, 'We're going to the flicks tonight. Coming?'

I nodded. *Ben Hur* was on at the local bug house, and to get a seat for this great epic I would have to bolt down my tea and queue with Vee and her family. If you were lucky you could get into the first few rows of the seven-pences, which came halfway up the hall and just right to be able to see the silver screen without cricking your neck. Right next to the cinema was a sweet shop with bottles of sweets and an array

71

of mouth-watering chocolates for sixpence a quarter. Courting couples usually got the chocs, and they always sat in the balcony seats. Of course, this luxury depended on whether you were lucky enough to be going out with a young man who was in work, otherwise the pictures were right out and a walk round the park would have to suffice. Everybody who could afford it went to the pictures every week. Even the kids went on Saturday afternoon. This cost us three whole pennies and was our pocket money for the week. *Ben Hur* had been blazoned on the bill-posters for weeks. With a cast of thousands, it was supposed to be sensational, and special sound effects had been acquired at great expense.

Although the talkies were about to arrive, the silent films were still with us and those who couldn't read the captions often had plenty of people around them to supply the story they missed. There would be long sighs, and cries of 'Aah' when the villain of the piece did his dirty deeds, and as the film was projected onto the screen, the beam poured down through a thick haze of pipe and tobacco smoke that we coughed and spluttered through in order to see our favourite actors appear on the screen. Janet Gaynor, Charles Farrel, Frederic March, Douglas Fairbanks, Norma Shearer, Noel Beery were just a few of these. They took us into another world of glamour and romance, and escape from the harsh, drab reality of our lives. As schoolgirls, we copied hairstyles and tried to emulate them. The false became the real.

But no film could start before the pianist arrived. He was the most important man in those far-off days of silent movies. When he arrived at the cinema and began to walk down the faded red-carpeted aisle, applause, whistling and foot-stamping would accompany him all the way down to the cinema pit where his grand piano always stood. It was his inspired playing that could bring a lump to your throat when our hero was nigh unto death and our heroine ministered to him, or fill you with fear and trepidation when Indians charged the stagecoach, or prompt you to rise in your seat to urge the hero to sock the villain to death, or kick his teeth in, and to boo and shout until you were hoarse.

The night of *Ben Hur* was one to remember, for as well as the pianist we had a three-piece band. The noise was deafening as the cymbals crashed their way through the great chariot race; drums rolled when the Christians were fed to the lions, and I couldn't help thinking of the vicar of All Saints being among the first batch if he had lived in those dreadful times.

Then the talking pictures arrived. They built a new cinema just down the road at the Kingsway, and Vee and I screamed and held onto each other when the pale horse of death seemed to leap out of the screen and onto us. Everything was now larger than life and full of energy and movement. We raced down to the new cinema before school one morning to gaze at a large poster outside showing Carlotta King dancing in a flame-coloured dress and John Bowles in flowing Arab headgear from the film *The Desert Song*. We gazed in rapt attention, then turned and ran all the way to the school gates with the bell ringing madly in our ears. Out of breath, and just making it to school in time, we whispered to each other as we filed into class that we would go on Friday night, because Saturday would be so crowded we might have to queue for hours. Friday, we could go straight from school as long as we let our parents know. We could take sandwiches, and call on a couple of mates who lived down that way and then we would be ready to be first in the queue for the evening performance.

Oh, the never-to-be-forgotten thrill of that colourful musical, and how our hearts almost stopped beating at the romance and the wonderful songs! We lived in a dream world for weeks afterwards. The books from the school library were discarded. *Anne of Green Gables, Good Wives* and *Little Women* were abandoned, and in their place every week, hot off the press we raced to the newsagent's to get our copy of *Peg's Paper*. This we kept under our desks and sneaked out at opportune moments to read about tragic heroines whose husbands left them on their wedding nights, or about attractive servant girls who were so virtuous and sweet that they married a lord or the boss of a big concern. In the back of my mind, I was convinced that the Ancient Wisdom was at work again, and just as men earnestly believed that there would be a brighter tomorrow, so we as young girls believed that something like a miracle would happen to lift us out of our poverty. So films like *Pygmalion*, which portrayed a rags-to-riches story, became firm favourites with us.

The year of 1930 was a bad one, not only for us, but for everyone. It was the time that Dad was laid off at Jackson's and he looked ill and worried as he travelled from place to place on that heavy upright bike of his, trying to get employment at other local firms. When he arrived home at the end of the day, his face was white and strained. There would be no word exchanged between Mum and Dad, and apart from a momentary enquiring glance she would resume her sewing with just a tired and resigned sigh.

The Wall Street Crash in America had plunged the whole world into recession. The Great Depression, it was called, and it was from America that we got songs like 'Buddy Can You Spare a Dime?'. The dole queues everywhere just got longer.

Of all the memories in those growing-up years, I count as happiest the ones spent with Dad when we dragged our bikes from the shed and started off on a voyage of discovery. On those precious weekends, I would be Dad's companion on long rides into the country. He was no conversationalist, and we rode for long periods without a single word being spoken. Yet I knew that these quiet spells were necessary for him, and although he didn't talk he was acutely aware of what was happening around him. My safety and welfare were of prime importance to him; he helped to shape my values and, like him, I came to cherish a deep love of the countryside. He had a kind of inner strength, and I knew he had the ability to see, to understand and to care deeply. But he could not express the things he saw or felt. Even to write was difficult and painful for him, and my mother did all the correspondence and handled all the money.

It was February, and there had been a slight fall of snow that made the hedges look as if they were covered in a thin layer of cotton wool. Already a thaw had set in and a thin watery sun had melted the snow here and there. Occasionally the branches overhead were loosened of their light burden and the snow slipped and fell to the ground in a white flurry. A small robin, sheltering in the hedge, showed its red breast, peeping out startled by the avalanche, and then shook its wings and flew away. In fact, there was quite a chorus of birdsong on that late-February morning as Dad and I bowled along and the air already held a promise of spring. The twittering of birds and the barking of dogs was like a sudden awakening of something exciting about to happen.

Only a milk cart, with the chink of the metal urn and the cheery whistle of the milkman, and the shrill sound of our bicycle bells, disturbed the silence as we rode along the road, with the wind making a humming sound as it blew through the coloured strands of cord that protected the mudguard of my bike. When we freewheeled down a hill, with my father always showing by example the need for caution, the cold wind blew and screamed through my hair and into my ears. But the mad acceleration finally slackened and left me with wind-whipped cheeks, and almost breath-less I laughed out loud as I caught Dad's expression, for his eyes were shining too. It was as though there was a sudden extra blaze of light that brightened his face, to know I was sharing his love and delight.

There was one other secret that we shared, yet never spoke about, for an unwritten law prevented it. I took the place of his beloved Nell. She was the one who should have been by his side, and as the years passed and I grew more and more to look like my mother, he took pleasure in watching me, as though I perpetuated a dream that he had never realised in life, but played out in fantasy with me. As far back as that crisp February morning I realised that the love he held for me was born out of a longing that he had for my mother, and because I so desperately wanted to reach out for her love myself, I was deeply conscious of the lack of affection that was his cross to bear as well.

That morning, we pushed our bikes up a winding lane and stopped for a while beside a wooden gate shaped into an arch. It led into a garden that was walled with grey stone. The gate was partly open and out of sheer curiosity Dad pushed it open and then stood there transfixed. He stood aside so that I, too, could have a peep and what I saw I shall never, ever forget. By the side of a pond, and growing all around the edge beneath the trees, were masses and masses – millions – of pure white snowdrops with drooping flower heads like gleaming pearls, nodding slightly in the breeze. As we peeped through the half-open gate, a whirl of wings rose from the lawn beyond the pond, as tiny birds fluttered to the safety of the ivy-clad wall, where they set up such a twittering that it was almost as if they were protesting vigorously against this unwelcome intrusion into their privacy. Whilst we stood in silent admiration and awe at the lovely sight, one small bird flew from the shelter of the leaves and perched on the edge of the embroidered border of the pond. Then, emboldened by the long interval of silence, others flew and hopped to join him in tentative little leaps, calling to each other in shrill, high, encouraging notes. The birds flew down again amongst the snowdrops, under the trees and across the lawn, talking to each other in easy familiarity and a kind of

family squabbling that filled the air with a delicious sense of
peace.

We both stood for a long time, deep in our own thoughts,
Dad with his hands in his pockets and his blue eyes smiling.
Then he gave a contented sigh, and tiptoed out softly, almost
reverently closing the gate behind us.

A Courtship

After the death of Aunt Flo, in 1930, Ada became less aggressive. She was always ready to have a go in a verbal battle, and her large, blue, staring eyes still spat fire and brimstone at my mother. However, the long steady stare that Mum returned immediately made Ada retreat to the safety of the door, and it was now Dennis who emerged from the front room to act as her protector and to lead her gently back there.

One evening, just after tea, Ada came through the sitting-room door and into the kitchen. I was startled to see her face covered in powder: it looked as if she had sprinkled the flour dredger all over it, topped off with bright spots of rouge on her cheeks. Her apron was discarded and she had donned a new green crêpe dress with yellow flowers down the front. She reeked of cologne as though the contents of the whole bottle had been splashed on too liberally.

My mother regarded her enquiringly. 'Where's the fire? Have you seen your face?'

Ada wiped at her face and then muttered that it was none of Mum's business.

Later that evening, we heard a loud knock on the front door. We also heard Aunt Ada's voice and the much deeper tones of a man. Then the front-room door closed and, despite the number of times I tiptoed to the door, all I heard was low and subdued voices. At precisely ten o'clock we heard the front door open and close, then silence once more.

It soon became evident that Ada was entertaining a male visitor. Twice a week the heavy scent of perfume would precede the flour-white face and heavily rouged cheeks. The gentle tap at the door and the low conversation would continue until the stroke of ten.

'My God! She's got a man,' exclaimed my father. 'Who would've guessed it?'

'They say love is blind, but a bloke would have to be to fall for a face like that!' said my mother unkindly.

Several months later, Ada sailed triumphantly into the kitchen. It was a mealtime of course. She announced to us, her stunned audience, that she was getting married and Frank, her man-friend, wanted to discuss a few business details with my parents. My father quickly removed the milk bottle from the table, swept away the crumbs, got some clean cups from the dresser and proceeded to make a fresh pot of tea. We hardly had time to tidy round before the figure of Frank burst upon us. Dad shooed the cat from the only comfortable chair in the room and Frank took the seat, obviously very much at ease.

He said he was steward of the Conservative Club at St George. He smoked a lot, for his fingers were stained with nicotine, and his hands shook slightly. He looked then and indeed always – slightly inebriated, and wore the perpetual grin of beer-soaked intelligence. Periodically he would bang his forehead with the flat of his hand, as though he had forgotten something, and finally he stammered out that he was intending to marry Ada and whisk her away. She was a good worker and she would keep the bar and premises at the club clean. Added to that, he had seen how well she looked after Dennis, and he was confident she would supply his every need as well. He thought that she must have been married before, as she had this one son, but when he asked her she would not give him any information. He wondered if my mother could shed any light on this question, but my mother declined to answer.

She told him, 'You know as much as I do. She has never been the one to spill any gossip or family secrets.'

Frank was clearly disappointed and slightly embarrassed, but, as he rose unsteadily to his feet to depart, he said he would merely state in passing that he had a house of his own in Birchall's Green Avenue, so he was not thinking of settling here. Dennis, of course, would be going with them.

My mother, tight-lipped and silent, said goodnight without getting up to see him to the door. Ada came through to the kitchen confident and triumphant. Mother almost leaped at her. 'The boy stays here,' she said emphatically. 'He is my son.'

'He comes with me,' Ada replied, standing her ground and looking defiant. Her two blue eyes glinted madly, and were levelled directly at my mother as she almost hissed out the words, 'He is mine and he comes with me.'

Then my brother Dennis appeared on the scene. He was very white and shaking and he said with obvious emotion, 'I shall go with Ada and Frank. I have had enough of the rows and bothers in this house over me. I want some peace away from the lot of you.'

He then took Ada by the arm and they walked into the front room and closed the door. A fortnight later they moved out, and a strange silence fell on the house. Nobody went to the wedding, which was a quiet register-office affair. I moved into Mum and Dad's old room, and the front bedroom was for the very first time occupied by my parents. All the years that I had contrived to enter the front parlour by kicking on the door or screaming blue murder on the stairs were over. I could go in and out at will. But the room never appealed to me again, and the ghosts of the two aunts haunted it all the while I lived there.

My mother often stopped her machining or washing to cry. Large tears rolled down her cheeks and when I overheard her talking to a neighbour she sobbed uncontrollably to think she would never see her son again. I was amazed and startled, for my brother had rarely exchanged more than a few words in passing, and she had never wholeheartedly enforced her demand that he should be with us. I wanted to reach out and tell her that I, too, wanted her love, and there was Dad as well, who would have done anything for a look of interest or concern. Once more I was on the outside struggling for attention that would have made all the difference in the world, but as the days went by I began to almost hate my brother for the virtues she suddenly bestowed upon him. Dennis did things so much better than I could ever hope to; his handwriting was a joy to read whilst mine was a spidery scrawl; he could spell, I could not; Den tackled things in a quiet, methodical way, whilst I was untidy and tore things up if they didn't come right first time. Dennis had never been any trouble. He had never had a day's illness in his life. That was why the two aunts loved him and fussed over him, and she had been glad of their help because of all the trouble I had been.

She went out one day and did not return until tea-time. She told Ma Saunders she had been to a fortune-teller to ask if Dennis would ever return. She had been told that he would return suddenly and be extremely sorry for the sorrow he had caused. I blurted out in anger, 'He will come back when he wants something, all right. But the bit about sorrow is just what you want to hear. He doesn't feel anything. He only knows what he wants.'

She turned on me then in spite and anger. 'Don't you talk about your brother and his feelings. You had none for me when you returned from Painswick.'

I felt suddenly sick, for there was a growing antagonism between us that seemed to develop in intensity every day. As I grew more like my mother in looks, it seemed the attention my father gave me infuriated her, and on the days I spent riding with him he often seemed remote from me. I was apart from him and apart from her and felt so cut off, lonely and sad. I was confused and unable to understand what was happening, and certainly at a loss to know what to do.

My First Job

It was a day like any other when I walked for the last time out of the playground of Two Mile Hill Girls' School in 1931. No friends milled around to wish me good luck as I ventured into the frightening world of adult life. My fourteenth birthday had coincided with the beginning of the end-of-term holidays. Everybody was eager for the long break. The leavers had been handed long brown envelopes, and once outside the gates I ripped mine open to read my mind-shattering school testimonial. This precious slip of paper would go with me on every job I ever applied for. I glanced down at Miss Dugdale's sprawling handwriting. On a twelve-inch-square piece of vellum paper it stated simply:

This is to certify that Beryl Doreen Joyce Dark has been a pupil of this school for the past seven years. Having reached the accepted standard her general work is good.

Her regularity is good. Her conduct is good. She is clean
and neat in appearance. She is honest and truthful.

Not much, I thought bitterly, to be armed with out there
in the big world and the great workforce that I was about to
join. I guessed that the ability to get up at some unearthly
hour and clock in on the dot was far more important than
any academic qualification.

Before coming out into the freedom and sunshine, I took
one last look around the hall and at the Honours Board with
the names of girls who had won scholarships, their names
emblazoned in letters of gold for all to see. From the whole
school perhaps only one would be clever enough to gain a
coveted place, and for a whole year she would be placed on
a pedestal as a shining example of what we could all achieve
through our wonderful education system, which was the best
in the world. I had made no such mark of distinction. Little
Miss Average, along with a million other little Miss
Averages. No one would ever know we had ever been inside
these walls.

I stopped only once on the way home, at the forge at the
top of the lane, where old Tom Pillinger was making the
sparks fly as usual, and I listened to the chink of hammer on
steel as he shoed a horse. Now no more would I stand and
watch, fascinated and silent, as the horse waited patiently for
her new shoes. The stopping and running on again to school
had been part of my everyday life, as important as the four
Red Indian eyes you got at the tuck shop for a ha'penny.
Over now. I felt tearful and sad, tossed about with emotions

I didn't understand and couldn't cope with. At fourteen I didn't feel grown-up and, what was more, I didn't want to.

On the following Tuesday morning my mother informed me that Lottie Collins, who kept a drapery store next door to Williams the vegetable shop, wanted to see me. She had told my mother when she'd popped in for half a yard of reversible cretonne at sixpence three farthings a yard that she knew of a job that would be 'just right for your Joyce' and I was to go down to see her right away.

The Collinses were respected businesspeople in Kingswood. Old man Collins had a grocery store and was astute enough to know that if he gave good service to his customers he was only looking after his own bread and butter. He had four children: three girls, all in drapery shops scattered about the city, and a son. This son was now married with a small child and was about to set up business in a modest little shop in Bedminster along the Cut. This, I discovered, was where I came in.

Lottie made much of the job, glossing it over so that it sounded like the chance of a lifetime. I was to receive five shillings a week. She mentioned the five bob first. She was quite right – I had never had five bob in the whole of my life. My duties would be simple, she said, merely helping in the house with a bit of cooking and light cleaning. There was the little girl to be fetched from school, but I would be very happy there; she just knew that I would get on with her brother Harold and his wife, and of course I would get good food, the best. My mother made me a blue velvet holdall with brown bone handles. She also made me a flannelette nightie and a skirt with two warm blouses, and I started my duties the following Monday.

Harold Collins was tall and freckly and he had a boyish face. Like his father, he respected his customers and wanted only to do the best he could by them, so he had a friendly and pleasing manner. His wife was different. She also was tall and slim but with a haughty attitude. She looked down on me now, and although her smile was as bright as a sixty-watt lamp, I could tell she was asking herself if this tiny slip of a girl could get through the rota of duties she had in mind for her. She quickly made a decision and spoke to me.

'I shall require you to help with the preparation of the meals, the washing up and clearing away. There will, of course, be a certain amount of cleaning to be done and I shall allocate your various duties daily. I have a daughter who needs to be fetched from school and you will be required to play with her until bedtime. There will be a small amount of mending and sewing to be done, but shall we give it a try, say for a month? See how we get on?'

She then showed me a little box room that contained a bed and a small bedside cabinet, but outside on the landing was a cupboard, which she said I could use to hang my things, and a shelf above was also at my disposal. The cupboard had a musty smell.

I found nothing difficult in the work I had to do in the days that followed. I loved the little girl and read to her and played with her for hours. Only one thing worried me. I came down one morning to find that Mrs Collins had put a duckboard down for me to stand on to start the washing.

The big tub stood on a long bench. Even with the duckboard, I could hardly see over the top, and the heat and steam made me feel hot and faint. At home, I might have helped turn the mangle, or held the sheets and helped my mother hang things on the line, but I had never actually had to do all the washing by myself. It was all done by hand, of course, shirts, overalls, tablecloths, towels, sheets, the lot. That night I fell into bed sick with exhaustion.

Every Thursday afternoon from two to eight-thirty was my 'half-day'. I sometimes walked along the riverbank and then had tea in a café somewhere, feeling very lonely but grown-up and quite a woman of the world. One day I took a walk down Castle Street, and then I saw it: a coat with a great fur collar that would make me look like a film star. The more I looked at it, the more convinced I became that I must have it. I hardly needed the shop assistant to convince me that she was sure that if I came inside there would be something to suit 'Modom'. I said I wanted to try on the coat in the window. She said she was sorry but they didn't take things from the window until it was due to be dressed. I was not going to be put off that coat.

'Fetch the manager,' I said curtly.

She looked very frightened at that, but he came. A short, dapper little man in pinstriped trousers and a thin Ronald Colman moustache. He confirmed what she had said, but in the end it was agreed that I should start paying for the coat and, as soon as the last instalment was paid and the window redressed, it would be packed and my name put on the box ready for me to collect. Every Thursday after that, I went to the shop and paid my five shillings off the two-pounds-ten-shillings coat. One more payment only now remained and this Thursday I would be collecting it.

I skipped through the bedrooms. I sang as I flipped the duster lightly over the ornaments. The vegetables were ready and standing in salted water and the meat was in the roasting tin surrounded by the potatoes that were to be baked for supper. Lunch was cold meat and salad, which I intended to miss because of wanting to be out on the dot. It was just ten minutes to two when, in my best black stockings and grey jersey coat, I presented myself for my wages.

Mrs Collins hesitated, and then looked at her watch. As if to reassure herself that she was absolutely sure of the time, she glanced up at the big clock on the wall. Under my breath I said, 'Damn!' I should have waited until dead on two.

'Ah now,' she said, and my heart sank. 'There is a small job I would like you to do before you go. It shouldn't take long and then I will have your money ready for you and you can be away. Now there is no need to be too fussy, but I would like the coal cellar washed over. Put the house flannel on the end of the broom but give it a good sweeping first.'

It never occurred to me to refuse her. I just stood there in abject misery, knowing it would mean having to take off all my decent clothes, and then afterwards I would have to wash before I could go out. It would be three o'clock before I would be out of the house on my precious half-day.

I suddenly became very angry and a red mist swam before my eyes. I would wash her bloody floor like it had never been washed before. To this day I cannot remember getting the pail or the water, but I began to scrub each patch slowly and methodically. I didn't feel the stone floor tear and ladder the only pair of black silk stockings I possessed. The adrenalin poured into my bloodstream, giving me all the energy I needed. My face was smudged with coal dust and tears; my black dress, where the water had dripped down the front, was stained and filthy. It was only when I came to the final patch that I looked up and swore a terrible oath.

'This is the last time in my entire bloody life I will ever be on my knees with my nose to the ground, for I belong up there with my eyes to the light, and walking upright and tall.'

I emptied the pail and washed it clean with cold water. I washed the scrubbing brush and the house flannel and, putting both in the bottom of the pail, I climbed the cellar steps and quietly put the pail away for the last time. I picked up my coat from the peg where I had hung it before that wild rage had overtaken me, and walked upstairs. Mrs Collins opened her mouth to say something when she saw the state I was in, but took a step backward when she saw the wild glint in my eyes that held the clear message that our paths would never meet again. She held out my five shillings and I passed her without a word. There was just one more thing I had to do. I ran upstairs to collect the blue velvet holdall that my mother had made for me just ten short weeks ago. I had worked blindly and solidly for this woman for ten weeks, for a coat I was now going to collect, come hell or high water.

I must have looked a sight, with my coal-black face, my stockings all torn and my hair dishevelled, and with that dreadful, determined look on my face. Even the shop assistant ran to collect the package when I demanded to have it now and not a moment later.

I never saw the long stares of passers-by or the other passengers as I sat huddled in the corner of the tramcar on its way back to Kingswood. When I opened the door of the sitting room, my mother as usual was on the sewing machine. She looked up, but stopped when she saw my face and the utter misery and dejection so clearly etched there. She watched me fling myself into an armchair and sob, hard sobs that tore at my insides and made it difficult to breathe. She waited until I had quietened down, then with a long sigh she said, 'I'll go and make us a nice cup of tea, girl.'

The Corset Factory

It was Elsie who once again came to my rescue, but first she took the coat to renovate completely. She told me I must never buy a coat with a big fur collar because only tall girls with long, elegant necks could wear them effectively. Little shorties like me had to be content with a tiny band of fur for a collar, and wear boxy jackets. I received this news with downcast heart, for I had dreamed of this great fur collar ever since I had seen the huge fur collars of my heroines on the screen. However, Elsie went off to buy several yards of astrakhan and this she sewed around the neck and all down the front of the coat and around the bottom as well. The bottom was a flared skirt, which she shortened, and the end result was a replica of a skating outfit. She made a small fur hat from the collar, and I also had a muff. When it was completed, I looked a treat, and I had stares of envy from the other girls. When they were catty, I just knew they were jealous and I tossed my curls and felt good.

Elsie also found me my first real job. At the local corset factory, called Langridge's, she personally knew the manageress, Miss Joy. More formally, her name was Mrs Blackford and both she and her husband worked for Mr Ryall and his son Charlie, who owned the family concern. Elsie always went to Miss Joy to be measured for her corsets. For these, she paid a sum of money that made my mother gasp, for she would never be able to afford such luxury, and had to wait until Elsie finished with her old ones and handed them over to her. Elsie enquired from Miss Joy whether any vacancies existed and mentioned me. The following week, I received a letter telling me I was to call at the offices in Waters Road.

My first glimpse of the inside of a corset factory filled me with fear and trepidation. The noise of the machines, all whirring incessantly, and the white-aproned girls with arms full of half-finished garments, and other girls bent low over the machines, hardly daring to lift their eyes for fear of losing precious seconds in piece-time rates, dismayed and appalled me. I was led through the workshop and into a tiny office at the far end, where Miss Joy was deep in conversation with a young man from the cutting department. Miss Joy was red-faced, with grey hair that was strained back from her face and wound in a bun at the nape of her neck. She looked severe, and her thin lips did nothing to soften the contour of her face. She invited me to sit down and scooped a large pile of cloth from the chair to allow me to do so. The young man from the cutting department eyed me for a few seconds then, with an audacious wink at me, he went out and we were left alone.

Miss Joy eyed me for some time, then shot a question at me: 'Have you ever used a machine before? We use electric ones here.'

'No,' I said simply. 'I have not.'

She leaned towards me, and touched my hair admiringly. For a second it seemed as if her mouth would soften into a smile, but in the next breath she said quickly, 'You will be required to put your hair up and wear a protective cap.' Then she murmured something inaudible and sat there deep in thought for what seemed like ages. Finally, she seemed to make up her mind, for she said briskly, 'Follow me!'

We came out of the building and into a kind of warehouse situated on the opposite side of the road. We went up a flight of stairs and entered a packing room, which was a hive of activity, but without the incessant noise of the machines. A happy babble of voices was going on all around us and, although the pace of work never faltered, I was much more comfortable here than in the factory that we had just left. Down the centre of the room sat about twenty or thirty girls, snipping at thread-ends on the corsets. With nimble fingers they twisted and turned the finished garment, which was then collected by a foremistress and put into a pile where three pressers skilfully ran a cool iron along the creases and then piled the finished corsets onto a table. Another girl then sorted the piles into sizes and checked the numbers against a pile of orders. Finally, three more girls took the completed piles, rolled them in soft paper and put them into boxes. The girls at the end tied up the boxes and marked each one with the appropriate size.

I was handed over to Phyllis Baxter, who was in charge of the girls, and was introduced to Mr Woolrich, who was foreman of the packing department. Everybody stared and I felt awkward and strange until a pretty girl called Barbara stepped forward and began to show me how to fold some Tea Rose brassières and put them into their bags. Later that afternoon I was given a long green overall and cap, and Mr Woolrich handed me a red note-book in which he had to insert the hours per week that I had worked. He also informed me that I would be starting on one penny three farthings an hour for a forty-eight-hour week, with a rise of one farthing an hour every six months.

So now I really had joined the ranks of the great working class. I went to work at seven-thirty each morning, and worked until six or six-thirty each evening. By the time I rushed home and had my tea there wasn't much of the day to relax in. Yet we found time to go to the pictures, to visit friends and go dancing. On Saturdays we caught the tram and went into Old Market Street, which was filled with stalls and where the barrow-boys shouted their wares, and for one and thruppence you could have three pictures taken by a photographer called Jerome, or we could call in at the Lyons Corner Shop in Castle Street and, to the clatter of china and the happy chattering of people, while away an hour over a cuppa that cost no more than a penny ha'penny. Yes, I was happy then. The years that lay ahead were full of promise. I was young, I had a job. Life was as good and uncomplicated as I could reasonably expect it to be. But not for long.

Patrick

Mrs Baker, our next-door neighbour, had a new lodger. We had both noticed him, my mother and I, when we were hanging out the washing. He opened their gate and glanced our way over the three-foot wall that divided the houses. I know that I stared because he was outstandingly different from the men I knew. When he spoke to my mother and raised his hat, she giggled and dropped all the pegs in the peg bag. He was in uniform when we first caught sight of him, a sergeant walking stiff and upright as though he was still on the parade ground, with his cap well down over his eyes and carrying his cane under his arm. We were all a-twitter to find out about him, and Mrs Baker told us he was her son's old army sergeant, who was retired from the army now but was staying with them until he could look around and see what he wanted to do.

His name was Patrick O'Hara. He was in his early forties

96

and his black hair, only just sprinkled with grey, served to give him an attractive and distinguished air. His eyes were blue and roguish and when he laughed, which he did often, they shone and crinkled a little at the corners. He had a habit when he was talking to you of moving his feet in a little kind of tap-dance, and I always felt that he was about to whisk you up and dance away with you. That Saturday morning when he stopped and talked to us, although he was looking at my mother, he kept looking at me, and I was amused when at length she asked me to run indoors and pop the potatoes on for dinner. Clearly, she was impressed with him.

As the days passed, he became a popular and familiar figure, especially with the kids on The Patch. He'd give the younger ones a ride on his bike when they saw him coming down the lane. And he would stand outside the gate and invite them to test his strength when he held out his arm to let them swing on it. I also noticed that my mother might stop whatever she was doing to stroll down to the garden gate and watch these exploits with interest. He'd casually walk towards her and engage her in conversation, but always looking down at his feet, finding something very amusing there.

Once, when I was coming down the lane, he pulled up beside me on his bicycle. He stopped right there in the lane and looked intently at me. There was nobody else around, and I felt uncomfortable with him looking so hard that his eyes seemed to flash. I made the excuse that I could hear my mother calling, waved to him and ran into the house. Mum glanced up quickly at my flushed face and her look was hostile, especially when she heard the Bakers' gate open and close at that precise moment. I felt guilty and angry at the same time, but nothing was said and I was glad to have my dinner and get back to work.

The following Saturday, I noticed Mum wearing a new dress in green flowered silk. She was always neatly dressed and she could run up anything on that old treadle. Yet it was mostly skirts and blouses that I saw her wearing. The green silk suited her and her dark brown eyes and dark hair with the green velvet band made me realise how attractive she was. She had strong off-white teeth – when she smiled they showed wide and even – and she had a motherly, matronly appeal you could not fail to notice. I often wanted to put my arms around her and be close to her, but ever since the day of my return from Painswick I had never broken down the cold reserve that had grown up between us. Nevertheless, I was surprised to see Mum in that green silk dress, and more surprised still when she announced her intention of taking a walk as far as the lane and Fry's Farm.

She applied some lipstick as she passed the mirror in the hall, and when she looked up I was shocked that the colour was too harsh for her and she had gone too high on the lip contour, which gave her a clownish look. I said nothing but, as I was returning from the shops through Halls Road and down into the lane, I was positive that I caught a glimpse of a green silk dress just behind the pavilion of the tennis courts at the top of the lane, and hurried home as fast as I could.

The days and weeks passed and were fulfilling. To my utter joy, Vee was now working at Langridge's, although she was working on a machine on piece-time rates, which didn't even give her time to glance up from the endless stream of corsets that she fed into the great mechanical monster. We got together at weekends, and some weekdays when work was done, and enjoyed our limited leisure time together. We went to the Hippodrome to see David Hanson in *The Student Prince*, to hear him sing my favourite song, 'Golden Days', and we also enjoyed artistes like Ann Zeigler and Webster Booth.

One year we went camping at Uphill with four other girls who worked at Langridge's. My uncle took us all down in the back of his van and we camped in a small paddock that belonged to the local farmer. Two lads, who called themselves Bill and Cody, helped us erect the heavy canvas tent, and it was they who came to our rescue that night when we were all flooded out in a summer storm. The farmer made available one of his hay barns, where he put down fresh straw for all of us. When Elsie Philips realised that we were all going to doss down together, boys and girls, she got upset and said she was going straight home. The farmer said it was the best he could do for the moment and told the lads to be on their best behaviour and to look after the girls. Meanwhile, in the morning, he would make other arrangements.

Both Vee and I enjoyed the situation very much. Blankets were thrown over makeshift lines to divide the boys from the girls, but nobody slept much that night and we sang into the early hours when Bill produced a mouth organ from his jacket. Never had we been so taken care of. In the morning it was the lads who went outside and lit a fire and later brought us steaming mugs of tea. And, when the farmer offered to let us take it in turns to use his kitchen, they offered to be the cooks and brought us plates of beans and bacon that tasted delicious.

We decided to be pioneers and brave out the week. It was no hardship really – the boys took care of that. The barn with its litter of clean straw was warmer and roomier than any tent, and the lads took up their own quarters in a hay loft about twenty yards away. We used the kitchen and the bathroom at the farm and that holiday was a very pleasant memory to look back on.

We found an old wreck of a boat half buried in the baked mud and sand just off the shore at Uphill. Most of our time was spent on this old wreck. The lads tied me to the mast, and they were pirates. I rather suspect that they found it easiest to catch me and tie me up, as I was the littlest girl of all of us. At sixteen, I was five foot and weighed about six and a half stone. I could race them all up the hill to the chapel at the top; I could climb as well as any boy and run like the wind. Best of all, I loved to roly-poly down the hill. I longed to learn to swim, but was terrified of the water. And, much to my dismay, I remained as flat-chested as any lad. But I felt and loved the wind in my hair and the freedom of not being fettered in tight restrictive clothing. I was as wild and free as the wind which whispered to me in the dying of my childhood, 'You and I are one, stay a while longer yet, not yet, not yet . . .'

When we returned to work the following Monday, I was eager to relate the events of the holiday, but Elsie Philips begged me not to tell the incident of the barn. She said that if her father ever found out that she had spent the night with two boys in a barn she would be thrashed within an inch of her life. It had never occurred to me that any father would take such drastic action over such an innocent matter. Elsie said her father thought she had spent the week with a married sister, and I did get the impression that it was not the holiday she was anxious about, but the guilt at having to tell lies. I was always feeling guilty about something, so I knew just how she felt.

So nothing was said about the holiday, but I did tell my mother about the night of the storm, rolling about with laughter at the comic sequence of it all. My mother's face did not move a muscle and she stared hard at me as though I was making the whole thing up. There was condemnation in her eyes, as though at sixteen I was capable of every seductive device to bring a man to my side. Like Elsie, then, I did not enlarge on that holiday. But, unlike Elsie, I was not afraid that I would have the living daylights belted out of me. My father had never physically chastised me, and I had had a lot more freedom than most girls, but how I wished I could have talked to my mother about so many things to do with growing up. Instead, her looks did more to hurt and defeat me.

She had been very quiet of late, and I had even caught her crying as she sat and sewed. Plainly she was unhappy, but she always got up and left the room the moment it came upon her. There was a new girl called Katy James I used to bring home with me at dinner. She brought her sandwiches and together we'd make a cup of tea. She was empty-headed and vain and would often sit giggling at nothing. She had a round face and a rash of pimples on her chin, and possessed the most beautiful fringed eyelashes that swept onto her cheeks. She fluttered them coquettishly every time she dimpled a smile. She irritated me.

Katy's sister, Pet, worked in Miss Golding's haberdashery shop in Regent Street and Katy boasted of her, 'She's the most beautiful creature in the world, you should just see her.'

I couldn't wait. Anything had to be an improvement on Katy. So, after we finished our dinner, we decided to take a stroll as far as Regent Street and I would see for myself that she was not telling lies. We ran up the lane and into Halls Road and across into Regent Street right opposite the Maypole. On the other side of the pavement was Golding's. There stood Pet, bearing a striking resemblance to her sister, with the same round moon face and large, long-fringed lashes. When they giggled together, it reminded me of the two ugly sisters in *Cinderella*. Pet was prancing up and down, giving little jumps like a cat on hot bricks, when Katy looked up, saw someone and shrieked, 'Oh Pet, he's coming, he's coming!'

I turned round and there was Patrick O'Hara, wheeling his bike and grinning at the two girls, who clamoured round him, almost swooning and slamming their eyelashes. Patrick did his little tap-dance routine and looked very pleased with all the attention he was getting. The look he gave me warned me to stay clear of the dark back lane, and I decided that he was an outrageous lady-killer – the younger the better, in fact. Katy and Pet were having a whale of a time. Soon they would both be boasting that it was self-evident that Pet was attractive, she could already draw a man. I felt slightly bored with the whole affair and said I was going to carry on walking back to work. I left them both and turned to go. As I glanced towards Halls Road I thought I caught a glimpse of my mother peeping out behind the houses, but I thought no more of it and went on to work.

That night my mother was weeping again and my father was visibly upset as well. For the first time ever, I heard them having a row, and finally my mother ran upstairs and I heard her crying. She was pregnant again and I heard Dad telling her he was sorry that it had happened. I felt a great wave of sickness come over me. Why was it that all the women who became pregnant wore that totally resigned face? She hadn't wanted me or Dennis; she had no patience with Clifford now; and she wasn't happy with the news of the new baby. Why did men give women babies they didn't want? Life certainly was not simple.

My mother emerged the next day with red eyes and announced that she didn't want Katy to come home with me at dinner time any more. She also made a bitter attack on my behaviour outside the Maypole.

'Right there in the middle of Regent Street,' was her scathing comment. 'Three giggling females all asking for trouble, and you were the worst from what I saw and what Patrick said.'

'Well,' I retorted angrily, 'he would have to say that, wouldn't he? He'd have to make me out to be a liar in order to establish his own innocence. And with his Irish blarney, he shouldn't find that at all difficult.'

'He doesn't like you, either.' Mum's eyes were bright and defiant. 'He says you stop him in the lane and encourage him.'

We stood there facing each other and I said sadly, 'Is that what you believe then, Mum?' I didn't wait for a reply. Somehow I just knew that I would never get close to her, not ever.

Towards the end of the year, Mum gave birth to a baby boy who she called Brian. He was a handsome little fellow with brown eyes like his Mum's, a chubby, chuckling, happy little baby that my mother adored. She cooed and crowed over him and left us to fend for ourselves. It was Clifford who suffered the most, for he was still only seven and a very nervous child who needed a lot of attention. Now the responsibility of Cliff was thrust upon me, and I often had to mother him and pacify him to get into bed, and stay with him until he slept.

My father fared no better, for it seemed as though, with the birth of Brian, my mother became her own woman. She did what she wanted to, and the Devil take the rest of us. It wasn't that she stopped doing the things she'd always done without murmur; rather, it was as though she was released and we just had to do more.

Patrick O'Hara vanished from our lives as quickly as he'd come into them. He had gained a reputation with every young girl in Kingswood, then a schoolteacher finally caught and married him. She was a quiet, demure little mouse of a thing, who one would think couldn't say boo to a goose. But teachers have to know how to control a class of unruly youngsters if they are worth their salt and I think she knew just how to control Patrick. At any rate, he suddenly disappeared from the High Street altogether and settled down in peaceful retirement somewhere in the country.

Meanwhile, mother and son joined forces and ruled our household. Brian could do no wrong and as the days passed I felt a growing awareness that even my presence was superfluous, and I felt apprehensive and afraid.

Saturday was the day that all the brass had to be cleaned. That was my job. Dad had the whole house filled with brass ornaments that he had lovingly brought home for my mum. There were candle-holders and brass crosses of all sizes, horse-brasses and ashtrays. The companion set in the grate was brass and the great brass fender had been bought to match. Even the lion-head knocker was brass. The handles on the doors were brass, below brass finger-plates, and over the front door was a sheet of brass that had to be continually cleaned. Two solid brass horses either side of the mantelshelf were a work of art and my father's pride and joy, but the bane of my life. It took the whole of a morning to complete the task of cleaning and I – along with my mother – hated it. I merely loathed the task in itself; my mother hated the ornaments. There came a time when she warned Dad not to bring another single brass ornament into the house. Pointing to the brass horses over the mantelshelf, she said, 'They must weigh half a ton. If they fell on anybody's head he'd be pulverised!'

Dad looked with pride at the two rearing horses, with a young lad pulling at the reins, and then began to sing quietly. This only served to enrage her further and she burst forth in angry protest, 'D'you hear what I'm saying, Chas? I want no more of the bloody stuff in my house!'

In the weeks that followed, I noticed when I was cleaning that several little items seemed to be missing. I said nothing, for the very simple reason that if they weren't there then I had less to clean, and my task would be finished all the sooner. However, something happened one morning that shocked me and made me feel a bit sad. The ashbins were collected every week, and in those days the men actually used to open the back gate and walk up the path to collect them. They wore some kind of leather protective apron over their shoulders and down one side. They would skilfully twist the bin onto a shoulder, and walk with it down the path and into the lane, where, with one more twist of dexterity, they tipped the contents into the waiting lorry. They then returned the bin to its rightful place and replaced the lid as well. As a final gesture, if the woman of the house was around, the dustman would doff his cap and quietly close the gate behind him.

This morning, my mother was standing silently behind the curtain in the sitting room, where she had an uninterrupted view of the garden path right down to the gate. She made a sign for me to keep quiet and get away from the window where I might be seen, so I sat on the box fender and looked puzzled. I did not have long to wait. The young man from the Corporation made his way up the path, and without looking inside the bin removed the lid and went to hoist it up on his shoulders. When he found that this familiar and simple task was impossible and he had nearly done himself a nasty injury, a look of sheer surprise came over his face. At this point, my mother was bent almost double with suppressed amusement. Meanwhile, the young man had found out the reason for the rigid immobility of the bin and the look of surprise had now given way to a lot of sly and furtive eye-darting, up and down the path and in all directions. Finally, when he had established that not a soul was about, he whistled to his mate, who came to his side and for a few seconds engaged him in low conversation. The two of them advanced cautiously up the path again and stood looking into the depths of the bin. Then, looking at each other as though they couldn't believe the evidence of their own eyes, they took a handle on either side of the bin and together they carted it triumphantly away.

All this time, my mother was almost choking with uncontrolled amusement. She hung onto the side of the table and shook with laughter. I looked on in shocked silence, for I knew that half the precious items that Dad had so lovingly crafted for her had now gone from the house and were the dustmen's perks.

'Mum,' I said, 'how could you? Dad made every one of those things for you.'

Her face and mouth hardened and she almost spat out at me, 'I hated every one of them. And now you won't need to moan and groan because your precious Saturday is disrupted.'

107

Before five years were out, there would be a war. Nobody knew it then, but I often wonder, when the price of brass rose to a staggering figure, whether she ever looked back on that incident and would ever be ashamed enough to admit that the last laugh was on her.

Reunion With Dennis

At seventeen, Vee was courting. I was devastated. Everything seemed to change overnight and now there would be no more cosy evening chats and weekend jaunts to the cinema. I'd lost my mate.

'Vee,' I said, 'you must be mad.'

'I love him,' she replied, in a tone of total conviction.

'What utter rubbish,' I shouted at her. 'How can you possibly be in love in the five minutes you've known him?'

I was utterly devastated and dejected, and hated Cecil Garland. I hadn't met him, but if I could have eliminated him I would have done. Vee was my best, my closest friend, and for the first time in all the years we'd known each other someone had come between us, and nothing would ever be the same again.

'Be happy for me,' she said, and put her hand on my arm. 'What if it had been you instead of me?'

I just clung to her and cried.

Cecil Garland was a dish. He was blond and blue-eyed and worked on the buildings. That night I went to Morris's School of Dancing by myself, although we had arranged to go together. I thought that if from now on I had to do things on my own, I might just as well hurry up and get used to it. I had a new pink taffeta dress and a deeper maroon bow for my hair, and a black velvet cape. I felt and looked good. If only I could have developed a bosom I would have had all the confidence in the world.

Morris's School of Dancing was in Deighton Square and I had to catch the tram to get there. The hall seemed to be filled with potted palms, and the doorways were hung with long strings of coloured glass beads that made a swishing sound as you passed through. The coloured lamps in the shape of lanterns gave the hall a faintly oriental look. There was a three-piece band consisting of a drummer, pianist and saxophonist. I was surprised to see that the drummer was my brother, Dennis, who immediately came down from the raised platform to welcome me warmly, and continued to talk to me in the interval and again at the end of the evening. We were pleased to see each other. He introduced me to his friend, Roy Coombes, who played the saxophone.

Roy was a slightly built young man with serious, deep-set eyes and the unhealthy pallor of someone who lived his life indoors. The three of us found a lot to talk about and I found myself laughing easily with both of them. Dennis had a wicked sense of humour to match my own, and at times we laughed uncontrollably at stories we shared with Roy about little incidents that had happened in our strange family circumstances way back in the past. Den was interested to know about Mum and Dad, and was surprised to learn that he had another brother. He told me that he was now a conductor on the buses, and played in the band with Roy for the Saturday dances. I asked him about Ada and Frank, and then he was serious when he spoke about her.

He lowered his voice a little to tell me she was having some kind of treatment for depression. 'Frank and I have to do everything for ourselves now,' he confided.

'That's hardly what he had in mind, was it?' I said tartly.

It was evident that he wanted to be loyal, but also plain that things were not all as they might be. 'She often talks about you,' he said at length. He bent lower and smiled confidentially as he repeated Ada's words. 'I wish I was like your Joyce, she ain't scared of nothing. She's strong, she'll always get by.'

'I have bravado, not bravery,' I corrected him.

Roy Coombes called me 'Little Joycee' and offered to run me home on his motorbike. I urged Dennis to come and see Mum and had a mental image of Ma Saunders assuring her that the fortune-teller was right and he had returned to the fold after all. Dennis promised to visit my mother, and I got on the back of Roy's bike and we roared off with the biting November wind stinging icily into my face. After that, he called regularly for me every Saturday.

Dennis kept his promise and had a tearful reunion with my mother, although he never did come back home to live, and Mum was too taken up with the new baby to grieve for long. She said that to cry for a whole day and a night was long enough to howl over anything, and that whilst she was weeping over other people they were not crying over her. She directed this piece of logic at me, but I know if I had asked her whether she meant me or not, she would have concluded the conversation with the classic remark, 'If the cap fits, wear it, my girl.'

On Saturday when Roy came to pick me up, his bike coming to a shuddering halt outside the house, she saw me all dressed up and waiting and cryptically remarked, 'Your boyfriend's here on his flying bedstead. If you land up in a field tonight, don't leave the gate open or you might catch cold.'

Dad raised his anxious eyes in my direction and told me to be a good girl and not let him down. I used to think he meant that I must always be nicely dressed and not look common. I always brushed my shoes, giving them an extra brush around the back, and made sure that my coat length was the same as my dress. I stood in front of him and asked if I would do. My mother smirked and Dad coughed and went outside. Mum said, 'Now don't be late home, and no mischief, my girl, you know what your father means.'

It was some time before I found out. That was the night I'd gone to visit Katy James, who was now married and had a baby and was living in rooms in her parents' house. My way necessitated negotiating a dark but gas-lit alleyway, and tripping along brightly I had only been dimly aware of a man in a light raincoat coming up behind me. Danger signals flashed through my head too late to prevent the man from suddenly grabbing me and pushing me up against the wall, where his great hand disappeared up under my clothes and into my knickers. The shock was electrifying and I felt violated and very angry. The anger burst forth immediately and I used the same tactics on him that I used on the enemy who was Ma Saunders when she tried to stop me climbing The Mountain as a child. I screamed as loudly as I could into his ear.

With his eardrum obviously shattered, he took a step backward so quickly that my knicker elastic slapped my legs with a whack that made me wince, and I began to bash him about the head with my handbag. He put both hands over his head to protect himself and began to back away.

'How dare you,' I heard myself saying, beside myself with fear and anger. 'How dare you even touch me. My father will kill you.'

Several people began to arrive on the scene and the man in the raincoat vanished into the night. Only then did the anger subside and I was left white and shaken. When I finally related the incident to my mother she said without hesitation, 'Fancy going through the alleyway at all at that time of night. I thought you would have had more sense.'

Well, I couldn't win, could I? From that moment on I became very alert in dark shadowy places and made damn sure it wouldn't be my fault next time. I still wondered about the Ancient Wisdom and wondered if it involved the lessons that I seemed to learn so painfully.

It was on a warm August morning that I came into the packing department with a few minutes to spare before starting time. I found the overlookers and the pressers standing around all engaged in happy and light-hearted chatter, leaning over the table and all gazing intently at something bright and colourful. All around were little gasps of wonder and delight.

Iris Webster was a quiet, friendly enough girl who employed a limited and monosyllabic form of conversation. For the last eighteen months she had been courting a soldier who was stationed in India, and from time to time he sent her small trinkets, which she displayed to the other girls with obvious pride. I moved over to the section, my curiosity aroused at this tantalising display of the exotic colours peeping from the parcel, and was intrigued to discover four exquisite silk handkerchiefs displayed in rich splendour on the shiny surface of the table.

'Oh, how lovely!' I burst out. 'Did your pen friend send you these?'

'Yeah,' was her only comment, but she was obviously delighted at the interest her gift provoked, so she added, 'He ain't my pen friend, 'ee's my chap.'

This added information, from someone who never gave very much away, sent a buzz of interest through the group clustered round her, and eager voices now demanded to know how long this had been going on. Very shyly, she produced a small ring box and displayed a solitaire diamond ring, waving it around with the smug air of someone who had finally acquired a ring and a man. Her chap, she then informed us as we looked on in rapt admiration, had sent her the ring the week before. She said it was a bit too large, but the man at the jeweller's had made it fit by putting a small metal clip inside it.

'Was your young man in the army when you met him?' I asked.

'Yeah,' she answered in her usual, irritating monosyllabic drawl.

I was puzzled, for if he was in the army, and still in India, I couldn't see how she could have met him.

'I wrote to 'im,' she volunteered. 'A friend of mine who already had a chap in India sent out my address to 'im, and 'ee passed it on to 'is mate.'

'Do you mean to say you've never even met him?' I was so shocked that she almost laughed in my face.

'My friend ain't never seen 'er bloke, neither, but when they both comes 'ome on leave, we'em goin' to 'ave a double weddin'.'

I couldn't find any answer to that one. I couldn't imagine how anybody could contemplate such a foolhardy action as to get wed to a man they had never seen. It seemed the world was full of stupid females prepared to do anything rather than be left on the shelf. However, the bell rang out loud and shrill, breaking up the groups of girls who dispersed to the various places.

There was barely time to whisper to Iris, 'Well, I hope all goes well for you. Meanwhile, if there are any more handkerchiefs to be given away like those, just send my name and address to your chap and see what happens.'

I completely forgot the incident. I certainly had not meant what I said, and only wanted to say something complimentary about her gift and to wish her well. About a month later, a letter addressed to Miss Joyce Dark slipped through the letter-box and onto the mat, bearing an Indian stamp. It was from a Gordon Robinson, who wrote that he was twenty-one years of age, five foot ten with grey eyes and dark brown hair. A mate of his had passed on my address to him and he would appreciate a letter from home, and any items of news that I cared to tell him about. He said he'd like a photograph and in return he would send one of himself to me.

I thought about it for a long time and then decided that writing letters in the long winter evenings to come might be an interesting hobby. He could be a pen friend, no more. Just a pen friend, and I would have something to tell Iris the very next day. I suddenly remembered the silk handkerchiefs and wondered, if I played my cards right, whether I might get some of them as well. I wasn't so sure about the ring that didn't quite fit; and of course I must never forget the picture in my mind that now went everywhere before me, the wall-to-wall carpets and the red-velvet curtains, the solid security that only money could bring. I would settle for nothing less.

I pushed the letter behind the clock on the mantelshelf. I would reply, but not tonight, for I had something better to do.

Sailing Too Close to the Wind

*I*t had rained heavily all weekend, so that as I set out for work on Monday morning the roads were still wet and shiny. I crossed the road at Fears the Bakers and joined a queue already forming there. From the interior, there came the most delicious smell of freshly baked bread and cakes. On Mondays and Fridays they sold jam and cream doughnuts, and I eagerly exchanged two pennies for one cream and one jam doughnut. As I hurried on to work, I could feel the warm doughnuts inside their white-paper bag, and I had to resist the temptation of sliding my fingers into that interior. I closed my eyes in anticipation that today's lunch would be scrumptious to the last morsel, when I would fold the corners of the bag into my mouth and, tilting back my head to an angle level with the ceiling, let the sugar from the doughnuts slide into my mouth.

I entered the warehouse and called a friendly greeting to

Mr Blackford as I bounded up the stairs two at a time. Those few moments in the packing department before the bell rang to commence work were friendly, cosy ones and already there was the hum of noisy chatter. Bags of doughnuts were being handed round, and the chink of coins exchanged. Those girls who couldn't get to Fears had arranged for their friends to bring in doughnuts for them; the fame of those hot buns was a Kingswood byword. Even Mr Woolrich had left the lift, where he was stacking an order, and was joking with the girls and waiting for his Monday-morning treat to be extracted from a shopping bag that contained at least a dozen other white-paper bags, still warm, and with just a trace of mouth-watering grease and sugar.

We turned as we heard noisy footsteps on the stairs, and stood in shocked silence as a rosy-cheeked and friendly girl from our section called Barbie rounded the corner and came into view. She screwed up her face just like one of the Bisto kids as she smelled the buns and came over to collect hers. But it was what she was wearing in her overall lapel that made us all stop in shocked silence, for she was wearing a large red rosette that people only wore on election days.

'You'd better not let Mr Ryall see you wearing that thing,' Miss Baxter said grimly, walking away and looking troubled.

Barbie picked up her bag of doughnuts and with a defiant toss of her head walked to her place further down the room. Mr Woolrich walked quickly down the rows of packers who were already busy at work. He walked to where Barbie was folding Tea Rose brassières deftly into cellophane bags and spoke to her firmly and quietly, and as her face reddened, she suddenly capitulated when she saw us staring at her, then she took off the offending rosette and stuck it in her pocket.

When break time came and we made room in the long racks behind us to sit and eat or read whilst we relaxed, Barbie was the first to speak and volunteer the information herself. Ella, who was a much older girl, was seated a few feet away, with her nose deep in a novel. Barbie burst out with some heat that she was not ashamed of being a social-ist, and she was angry that she was not allowed to wear the party colours. She was wearing them because there was a meeting that night at the Labour Hall and she was going straight from work. I couldn't see any harm in what she was doing, and said so. After all, it seemed to me to be a matter of simple choice which party you belonged to, and working people should support the party that did the best for them.

At home, my father still cherished the dream that when Labour got into power all would be well for the working man and woman. The Great War had left Britain impover-ished but it had been the poor who really felt the pinch. The warmongers had made untold wealth and our young men had died to pay for it. Part of the socialist dream was the abolition of war, and an end to the glorification of mass-slaughter and the class struggle ended for ever with equal opportunities for all. My mother's views were not so lofty. She was cynically convinced that there was no party that was one hundred per cent for the working class. On the eve of an election, she maintained, they'd promise you all sorts of things for your vote, but when they got in somehow it was all changed and they never carried out their grand promises.

Barbie cut across my thoughts. 'Have you realised just how many hours a week, a month, a year, we work for old man Ryall, for a pittance?' she asked. 'If we all joined a union we could demand less hours and more money.'

Ella now glanced up from her book and called down, 'On your soapbox again, Barbie?'

Barbie turned on her with eyes blazing. 'We don't all run with the hare and hunt with the hounds. You're despicable.'

'I know which way my bread is buttered,' Ella continued. 'And I won't stick my neck out.'

I turned to Barbie. 'Is that what your meeting is all about?' I looked from her and back to Ella. 'Do you think, then, that Mr Ryall could object to the girls joining a union?'

Ella gave me a withering and half-incredulous stare, as if I was either mad or too naïve to be believed.

'Join a union in this Tory stronghold? Just you organise one and find out. I've worked for worse bosses and I don't intend to rock the boat.' Ella straightened up and brushed the crumbs from her skirt. Pushing her book under her bag in the rack, she proceeded to take her leave, as much as to indicate that, as far as she was concerned, she had nothing more to add to this useless argument. She disappeared down the steps.

There was something familiar about her line of reasoning, and I suddenly remembered the look of almost terrible resignation on my mother's face when Dad came home with the news that there would not be a full week's wages to put on the table. How men would twist their caps round in their hands with a pitiful look of complete servitude and stand in long silent lines to queue for one of the few jobs, or receive a few shillings' dole money.

Dad had told me about the miners from South Wales who walked all through the Dean Forest and down to Bristol through the Gloucestershire coalfields looking for work. They had even offered to work shifts, undercutting the men at the Bristol pits. Fights broke out in the Chequers pub on Soundwell Road and finally everybody had joined together in a peaceful march down to Old Market. They had chanted on the way, 'Not a penny off our pay. Not a minute on the day.'

The women of almost every house in Kingswood gave a screw of tea or cocoa to make hot drinks for them as they passed by. Even Fears the Bakers handed over a sackful of stale bread, cakes and rolls to the women to fill with anything they could spare to give to the miners. My father marched with the miners of Speedwell down to Old Market Street and there on the cobblestones encountered the mounted police, who charged them, with truncheons bashing and slashing into them right, left and centre. It was a sad day and the men suffered badly. Dad staggered home with two of his mates; he had a broken nose and blood poured down his face.

'Bastards,' he said. 'They were waiting for us.'

'What do you think we as women can do that the men have attempted and failed to do?' I asked Barbie.

'Emmeline Pankhurst tied herself to the railings so that women could have the vote and a say in the running of the country,' she commented. 'Look,' she said at last. 'You must make up your own mind about it, but you can't stay on the fence for ever.'

'I'll come with you,' I said on the spur of the moment.

Later that night, it was still raining as I set out for the hall. The rain beat a tattoo on my umbrella and trickled down the silk-covered spokes and dripped into my shoes. I was glad to arrive at the hall, which was beginning to fill rapidly. I spotted Barbie almost immediately. She was giving out leaflets by the entrance and looked surprised and pleased when she saw me. 'Well,' she said with a wry smile. 'I was sure you wouldn't turn up, especially in this weather.'

I sat down at the back. I took off my coat and draped it over the chair and with my handkerchief tried to wipe a few splashes from the back of my legs. It was impossible. With a tut of annoyance, I knew I would have to wash my stockings when I got home that night. The meeting was a noisy one, with a lot of heckling from a crowd of youths at the back of the hall near the door. Several speakers expressed in their own way what they thought was an immoral system that extracted huge profits at the expense of the working class, and until we all had the strength of a union around us the capitalists would go on exploiting us. We must all stick together, for unity is strength. There was much thumping on the table, which made me think of Dad when he was trying to be explicit. The audience cheered and clapped and stamped their feet in agreement.

The meeting finally broke up and they asked for volunteers to distribute the leaflets urging men and women to join a union. I noted at this point there were only a few who eventually picked up the piles of white printed flyers and Barbie was one of them. I put on my damp coat and slipped through the door. The rain had ceased and the sky was full of stars. As I turned to walk homewards I gave a sigh of relief that it was all over. How wrong I was.

The next day I was a few minutes late and the bell had already gone. When I arrived in the packing department the girls were busy at their work and Miss Baxter said in mocking, stern tones, 'You'll be shot at dawn.'

Ella glanced up half enquiringly, but carried on working. I suspected that she guessed I'd gone to the meeting, but I was not going to let on. As I moved past her to continue working with Barbie, I noticed the great pile of leaflets in the rack, and knew that Ella had seen them too. I thought idly how wilful and fraught with danger this action of Barbie's was, and it was like asking for trouble to bring them into work after the events of yesterday. My discomfort deepened, and I said to her, 'What are you thinking about? Why don't you hide them or something?'

Barbie startled me by replying, 'Why should I hide them? You are going to help me distribute them outside tonight.'

'I am?' I said, with my mouth open in both fright and surprise.

'Well, aren't you?' she said, and laughed.

I looked into those merry eyes, and then saw Ella's grim, disapproving face as she glanced our way, and I threw all caution to the winds. I would strike a blow for socialism. What could anyone do to us? We could do what we liked in our own free time after working hours. But why was I so scared? And I still wasn't sure, even when I turned to Barbie and said with forced resolve, 'Oh, all right then.'

At five to six that night, we both made our way out into the evening twilight and took up our positions. I posted myself by the door of the machine shop on the opposite side to the warehouse. Barbie stood on the pavement outside our works to catch the familiar figures of all our workmates in that building. I shivered as I waited for the shrill notes of the bell. We had escaped a few minutes early in order to take up our positions, but at last, after what seemed like an eternity, one of the cutters emerged from the door. He looked up in surprise to see me waiting there with a huge pile of white forms in my hand, but the smile of greeting froze as his eyes took in the printed message, and with an oath he screwed it up and threw it in the gutter. They were coming out now in a long steady stream, and as they did I thrust leaflets into their hands. Some turned their shoulders slightly, so that they would not be able to take one. Others thrust the leaflet deep into their pockets and glanced furtively this way and that, whilst others read what was written and, half ashamed and embarrassed, let them fall to the ground and hurried on. I sensed a wave of fear that matched my own. Not many folded the leaflets and put them in their pockets without alarm. Most everybody dropped the leaflet like a hot potato.

A ripple of fear passed from one to another, and they vanished quickly and silently into the night. The leaflets lay scattered and motionless in the gutter until a last bicycle whizzed out of the factory gates, its black tyres defacing the whiteness of the forms, obliterating the words printed there and rendering them useless in the still night air.

I awoke on Wednesday morning with an air of impending

doom. As I walked to work, I had a premonition that all was not well in my world. Now, as I again turned the corner into Waters Road, my heart thumped a little and my feet dragged themselves up the dark stairs and I came into the lighted and noisy room of the packing department. Miss Baxter gave me a half-scared look and said almost at once, 'You're in trouble!'

At that moment, another pair of footsteps sounded on the stairs and Barbie's expressionless face appeared. She walked straight to the rack where her bag and personal things were stored. She picked them up, then undid the buttons of her coat overall and laid it across the table. Without another word, and looking neither to left nor right, she passed us for the last time. Her footsteps clattered down the wooden stairway and faded away, out of our lives for ever.

'She's got the sack,' someone whispered in shocked amazement.

'Instant dismissal,' Miss Baxter confirmed and looked vaguely troubled. She suddenly remembered something, and looking directly at me she stammered, 'You're wanted in Charlie Ryall's office.'

My legs felt like lead weights, and I began to tremble violently. The time it took to descend the steps and cross the road seemed endless. As I stood outside the office door, I had a sight of the long rows of whirring monsters, the girls bent double with heads held low, hardly daring to raise their eyes for fear of losing a precious second. They reminded me of my mother, sitting by the window and trying to earn a few shillings to help out with the money that Dad gave her. Just then a voice called out to me to come in, and I turned the handle and went in with my heart in my mouth.

Mr Ryall and his son Charlie were standing by the window. They did not immediately turn round when I entered and I stood there, white and shaking, by the table that was both work bench and desk. I suspected that their turned backs and the silence was a ruse to make me feel totally cowed. It certainly succeeded. Then they turned and indicated a chair that I almost fell into, to stop my shaking limbs. They both towered over me then, which if anything made me feel even smaller and more insignificant, so that I sank lower into the chair to try to hide my misery and shame.

'Tell me,' Mr Ryall senior said at last. 'Are you not happy working with us?'

'Oh, I am, I am!' I cried from the depths of the chair.

Mr Ryall continued. 'Miss Dark, we are a small family concern and we do our best to ensure that the working conditions are as congenial and comfortable as possible. We adhere strictly to the wages as laid down by the Board. Sometimes we even agree to pay more than the Board suggests. Having our employees' interests always at heart, at Christmas we lay on a party – at no mean expense, mark you – at the Berkeley Café in Park Street, and I am sure we have all benefited from this relaxing and stimulating evening. On those occasions we mix happily amongst our workers and I am sure you must agree that we try our best to make our firm one big happy family.'

He broke off here to give me time to reflect on the happy

time we had that last Christmas party, and I recalled miserably how Charlie Ryall had danced with me and I had been the envy of the packing department for weeks afterwards. Ryall Senior leaned closer over me and his voice now held a sterner note. He breathed heavily, as though the effect of his words would hurt him more than me. 'I doubt if a union would bring about any more benefits than the ones you enjoy already,' he said. 'I'm sure you agree with me on that point, eh?'

I mumbled something inaudible and wished that the interview was over so that I could crawl away to lick my wounds.

'However,' and he stood back as though to brace himself for the final onslaught and humiliation. 'Your colleague was a disruptive influence and I could not allow her to lead weaker minds astray. I'm afraid it was necessary to dismiss her to ensure the smooth running of this establishment.'

Now his tone was conciliatory, and he moved back to the window and stood there with Charlie, looking out onto the road where two carrier vans filled with corsets from his empire were being dispatched to large department and retail stores in the city.

'I have spoken to your manager, and he tells me that you are a good worker and this little episode is completely out of character. In his considered opinion you were sincere but misguided, and I respect this assessment of you. I will say no more about it, although I do not, of course, expect a repetition. Now get back to your work.'

He dismissed me with a curt nod and I fumbled for the door catch and left the room. Once outside in the street, I gulped great breaths of air until the frantic shaking stopped and I retraced my steps to the packing department. I found the rack where Barbie and I had talked about striking a blow for socialism and I suddenly burst into tears. I couldn't believe it when Ella left her work to kneel by my side and put her arms round me.

'Oh Ella,' I wept. 'Oh Ella.'

'I know,' she said simply. 'I understand. But don't forget, he who fights and runs away, lives to fight another day.'

'I feel so guilty,' I said. 'It should have been me as well as Barbie who got the sack.'

Ella's face was grim and hard and she was looking somewhere beyond the window when she said in a low voice, 'They only needed one to make an example of. The other serves to remind the rest of us not to sail too close to the wind.'

We were silent for a few seconds. Then I caught Miss Baxter's eye and knew she had already overlooked too much time-wasting that morning. I stood up and squeezed Ella's arm.

'I shall never forget this moment, or Barbie,' I said.

'It's not intended that you should,' she replied. 'Or the dream of a Utopian tomorrow. They're not scared of the dream, only the reality. That's why they make it so hard.'

I began folding Tea Rose brassières into their little cellophane wrappers. The dream I held before my eyes returned to the deep-pile carpets and the red-velvet curtains. I had survived. I breathed a big sigh of relief.

Gordon

*F*or a whole year I wrote to Gordon. His letters were something special, just like chats by post or long conversations. In imagination he took me on long train journeys in India, and he had this wonderful knack of being able to describe in vivid detail places and events that he had been to and seen.

His letters were long, wonderful epistles that came in exciting thick brown envelopes often marked *Part One* and *Part Two*. They plopped through the letter-box down onto the coloured tiled floor with such a thwack that made me come rushing down over the stairs just to collect them. I read and re-read them. Nobody before or since has ever written a letter like Gordon. I loved him even before I saw him or knew what he looked like. He also sent me funny little drawings of army life that made me laugh, convincing me that he had a sense of humour that matched my own. The days that I waited for those letters were full of eagerness and pleasure.

Oh yes! I did get my embroidered silk handkerchiefs from India, plus a string of cheap soapstone beads. They came accompanied by a photograph of Gord haggling with an Indian, who in his long white robes reminded me of Gandhi. So now I had a sketchy picture of him, five foot ten, slim but well built, with a mop of dark hair and a pair of very respectable legs that looked good in shorts.

In March of the following year, he wrote to say he was going to be released on extended leave. He expressed the wish to drop off at Bristol on his way home, to come to see the girl who had cheered up his lonely sojourn in India. As the day of his visit grew nearer, I was in a fever of excitement. He never knew just how my heart gave a big leap when I first saw him standing there grinning, looking so tall and beautiful and tanned, like an Olympian sun worshipper.

That spring and summer will be for ever green in my memory. That was the length of time that he stayed with us. We rode on bikes to all the places that I loved. We rode to the top of Tog Hill, then free-wheeled all the way back down again with our legs off the pedals and Gord shouting, 'Yippee!' in a loud voice, and the wind rushing past us and blowing our hair about our faces. We found a pub towards evening and I had my first taste of cider, with cheese sandwiches and pickled eggs from a large jar on the side of the bar. I was a bit reticent about the cider at first until Gordon roared with laughter at my wry face.

'You drink and swig your mother's home-made wine from a bottle like a veteran, yet you hesitate to drink cider,' he said.

'Home-made wine is different; how can you get drunk on that?'

Again, he laughed at my absurd logic, shaking his head in bewildered mock severity. We laughed aloud at silly things. One day we carved our names, *Joyce* and *Gordon*, on a big oak tree after a sharp shower of rain had sent us scurrying beneath its mighty branches for shelter. Another day, we found a stream and lay down on the bank and went to sleep. The sun burned our faces on opposite cheeks to each other and we giggled about that. We spent hours curled up by each other's side reading books, for Gord was an avid reader, just like me. Sometimes when he was deep in a book I would inveigle him into taking me out somewhere. He'd suddenly throw the book to one side and chase me, and I'd squeal with laughter and excitement when he caught me.

We went to Dawlish Warren on the train. I had never been further than Weston-super-Mare before, so that when the train ran along the miles of track right by the side of the ocean I thought I had never seen anything so beautiful in my entire life. The sun was shining on the water, turning it to magic, breaking it up into millions of tiny sparkling diamonds. When we returned late in the evening, I stood in the corridor watching the moon making a silver path over the same expanse of water. Gord laughed at my quaint attempt at poetic description, but held me close and tenderly kissed me.

On the Pathé Gazette news at the films, there were disturbing scenes of Hitler's Storm Troopers at the great rallies in Germany, with Hitler shouting and gesticulating beneath

the swastika banners and the crowds roaring their approval.
Gord said a war was inevitable. But that summer of 1938
was so warm and peaceful, people were still lazing on the
beaches, totally and blissfully unaware that soon everything
would change for ever.

So far he had not even been home to see his parents. I
knew they had written to him several times about this, and
that they were upset about it. I urged him to go home to see
them and he agreed to leave the following week. We rode on
our bikes for the last time to our favourite spot by the stream.
We had to cross a wooden bridge and, as we stood there
looking at the water gurgling and splashing over the rocks,
the words of a poem by Tennyson flashed into my mind, and
I began to speak it aloud. I was surprised and delighted to
hear Gord join me and we both shouted the words out loud,
holding hands and calling into the soft breeze.

'I chatter over stony ways, in little sharps and trebles
I bubble into eddying bays, I babble on the pebbles.
I chatter, chatter, as I flow, to join the brimming river,
For men may come and men may go, but I go on for ever!'

When the poem was finished, we laughed and ran to our
special spot by the side of the stream. It was right there that
I kissed Gord and held him so tight and told him that I loved
him and would go on loving him until the day I died.

At last his case was packed, the lid closed and a leather
belt tied round to make it doubly secure. A label was written
out in block capitals addressed to his home town all the way

to west Hartlepool. It seemed so remote and so far away, like part of another land.

Walking up the incline to Temple Meads Station the next day, Gord had to change the case from one hand to another because of its bulk and weight. We didn't speak much, now that the actual time had come for parting, for there seemed so little to say. I was far away, immersed in my own sadness. We passed through the barrier and onto the platform. There was just ten minutes to wait and ten minutes was so shockingly short a time. The train rumbled round the curve, snorting smoke and hissing to a halt after spreading its great length along the platform. Doors opened and a stream of people trailed from the carriages, all making for the exit. The low buzz of conversation mingled with the calls of the porters, and the banging of luggage being piled high on trolleys. Gord found a seat and put his case up on the rack, then he came and stood by the open door. He took hold of my hands and kissed me.

'Write every day, promise?'

He didn't hear my answer, for I had pulled him close to me as though I never wanted to let him go. Then I heard the guard blowing the whistle and caught a glimpse of the red flag waving and a voice calling, 'Stand clear of the doors!'

Just a second of silence, then the brakes released and the rush of steam and the train moving slowly at first and then gathering speed with Gord waving from the open window. I ran along the platform, still waving but as it gained in momentum the great iron monster rounded the bend of the platform and Gord was lost to sight.

The platform had emptied and I felt lonely and very forlorn. A sudden vision of another parting flashed into my mind and with it a dreadful premonition. Just like that day when I had rushed to the white gate and my parents had deserted me. How many times had I gone to that gate in the days that followed, to see if they would be coming back to fetch me? Now, once again I couldn't breathe. I found a seat and staggered onto it, feeling the same mad panic I had felt then. The pain in my chest slowly relaxed, but still I sat there feeling scared and afraid, for it seemed that someone else who I loved and relied on was being taken from me.

Presently I began to walk through the barrier. I surrendered my platform ticket and walked out into the bright sunshine towards the city centre. When I reached Bristol Bridge, I stopped to look at the swans on the river. That's when it came to me in a moment of revelation, when I realised that nobody could take anything away from me. How could the memories of that perfect spring and summer ever be erased? Gord and I were special people; how could a love like that ever die? I had been right to choose Gord as my first love, for he had given me so many things that were good, and in loving him I had become a woman.

I never saw him again.

Bertie

*I*t would have been impossible to survive the following months without some kind of drastic measure. Retracing my footsteps over familiar ground where Gord and I had been together filled me with the same dreadful feeling of suffocation. In the end, I sublimated all my feelings and drew a black curtain across the thing that hurt so much. In order to survive I had to do or die. Get up, go on again, the voice within me whispered. And when I prayed I heard the voice remind me that we search so eagerly for God, only to find ourselves.

I saw Barbara get married to her soldier lad. I stood on the edge of the pavement outside Kingswood Church as she came out of the door and walked towards the waiting car, and I called out congratulations to her and threw rose petals. She did not have her double wedding after all, and I thought she looked heavy about the waist. She was whisked away, and did not acknowledge my cheery greeting. I thought she looked strained and anxious and she seemed to have trouble with the frothy lace of her headdress: she was holding it tightly as she stooped to get in the car.

When I got home, my mother called out that Elsie wanted to see me as soon as I came in, so I made my way to number 35 across the road. The door was open, and so was the glass inner door. I called out, and a cheerful voice told me to come in from the kitchen. A tall form detached itself from the chair, and a pair of bright blue eyes that I recognised as belonging to Bertie smiled into my own. He stood and held my hand in an affectionate manner. He was wearing the uniform of the Royal Air Force, and the dull blue of his clothes made a brilliant contrast with the brilliant blue of his eyes.

Elsie bustled around, making tea and saying she knew how much I would like to see Bertie, who was home on leave before flying out to Ceylon. It was his birthday, and they had given him a watch because he was twenty-one. On cue, he stretched out his wrist to show me the watch, which he said was shockproof and waterproof, and I made suitable sounds to show I was impressed. I noticed how he'd grown since I had last seen him, so that he stood nearly six foot tall, and good-looking in that boyish way of his, in his RAF uniform. When he asked if I'd like to go to the pictures, I was on the point of making an excuse when I suddenly remembered that there was a good film at the Regal I wanted to see. So I said on the spur of the moment that he could take me.

That night, we sat in the best seats in the balcony, with a quarter-pound of chocolates that I nursed on my lap and forgot all about until they began to go soft and melt and make a sticky mess. Bertie seemed to look at me with rapt attention throughout, running his hands through my curls and whispering that he had always wanted a girl with dark, wavy hair. I was becoming increasingly annoyed at having the sequence of the film interrupted and began to wish that I had come on my own. I was glad when the curtains finally closed for the first performance, and we could emerge from the smoke-filled atmosphere of the cinema into the cool outside air.

Bertie suggested a walk and did his best to entertain me. For a full hour I was treated to details of the fuel consumption of a Catalina flying boat, and the make and home-town registration plate of every car that passed us during our stroll. I was bored, tired and irritable by the time I reached home. I pulled the key from behind the letter-box where it hung on its piece of string and said that the walk had made me tired, and that I certainly wouldn't take much rocking tonight. Completely oblivious to the snub, Bertie almost fell up the steps to prolong what to him had been a successful venture. Optimism was always one of his strong points, his boyish charm another, but neither helped him much that night. He mentioned that he was thirsty, and wasn't I going to ask him in? I answered firmly that I wanted to wash my hair and I was sure Elsie would still be up and would be delighted to get his supper. He looked disappointed, but accepted the situation with good grace.

Then he suddenly blurted out, 'If you married me, you would be coming to Ceylon!' He cupped my face in those beautiful hands of his and kissed me very lightly. He stood away from me for a second, then turned and walked over the road and into Elsie's house. I stood watching him and a picture came into my mind of warm sunny places and sun-soaked beaches where I could lie and become like a bronzed goddess. Escape from all that hurt and heartbreak. Run away and start again. I heard a door close and the dream faded, for my hurt was already safely buried under a black, black cloak deep inside me. And if I travelled to the ends of the earth I would take it with me as it lay forever buried there. Bertie was just a nice young man. I too went indoors and forgot all about Ceylon.

By the time Vee was twenty-two she had been married for five years and had three children and was a widow. After the birth of her third child she had been very ill and they had sent her into hospital where they did a hysterectomy. I tried to get to see her as often as I could and was shocked at the change in her and the weight she had lost. She still lived in the little terraced house in Worcester Road. Then came the news that Cecil had met with a motorbike accident and had been rushed to hospital. Coming home, he had swerved to avoid a cyclist, had come off his bike and fell, hitting his head. At first, he seemed all right, and with only a slight headache to show for his spill got back on his motorbike and rode home.

The pain in his head had become worse by then and he went to bed, where he lapsed into unconsciousness and Vee sent for the doctor. He was rushed to hospital, but he died the next morning. Cecil had been dead for a couple of weeks before I heard the news at work and rushed over to see her.

Vee's mother had the children for her, for Vee herself was still far from well. She was almost bent double, and looked like a very tired old woman. I immediately went into the kitchen to make some tea. When I returned she was lying on the settee, but patted the place by her where she wanted me to sit.

'Vee,' I said at last. 'How will you manage?'

'Like everybody else has to manage,' she replied without hesitation, but her voice held a note of defiance. 'I'll have the generous sum of twenty-six bob a week widow's pension for me and the kids to live on. At least I'll be able to count on getting it – they don't have any lay-offs or short weeks.'

I was lost for words of comfort and support and could only lean over and take both her hands in mine.

'After this lot got better,' she giggled and patted her stomach, 'we could have had a good sex life with no more shocks or worries.' Then she leaned forward to pick up the cup of tea by her side and to whisper confidentially, 'Do you know, Joyce, there is one thing I am happy about that dreadful morning. I am so happy he went from here for once without a row.'

I looked at her incredulously.

'We rowed about sex all the time,' she said.

I looked down at the floor. The awful doubts that had assailed me before came flooding back. And now even Vee. I wanted to ask her so many things, but I knew the timing was wrong. I could only hug her and tell her I would come again soon. It was only when I was walking home that I remembered I had not told her my news.

Bertie did not go to Ceylon. He was still stationed at Southampton and so able to make several trips to Bristol to visit his Aunt Elsie and so pursue me. He made a habit of walking down to the works about five-thirty, just before knocking-off time. His presence was revealed to me long before I saw him by one or other of the girls in the packing department.

'Your airman chap's downstairs waiting for you, Joyce. Bit of all right. Got lovely blue eyes. I should hang onto him if I were you.'

It was all good-natured fun, but I was not ready yet for Bertie, or anyone for that matter, to rush me into a committed relationship, however friendly. I was slightly annoyed, not very sociable and certainly embarrassed, when the nods and grins still carried on along the road. When we got home, Elsie was talking to my mother and didn't help matters by saying, 'Here's the young lovers, then.'

She immediately invited me to have tea with her and Bertie. I was being rushed along and I felt angry at all this matchmaking. I resolved I would speak to her about it at the first opportunity.

The following Sunday Bertie pleaded with me to come and visit his mother. 'Just a flying visit,' he said. 'As I have to get back on the six-ten train.'

I didn't think it would do any harm, so I consented to go. Bertie lived in Brislington, several districts away, and we walked there down through Hanham, along the Netham, up Newbridge Road past St Anne's paper mills until we came to Wick Road and Sandy Park, and into Repton Road where the houses huddled together in one long terrace. Bertie's mother opened the door of number 90, and ushered us inside saying, 'Come on in, kid!'

She had the same piercing blue eyes as her son, the same wide, shy smile. Her hands were large like his as well, but years of toil had knotted and reddened them. She led the way into the front parlour and beckoned me to sit down. Everything in that room had seen better days, from the faded upholstery of the chairs and couch to the worn carpet and discoloured drapes. All wore the mark of an earlier era, of a more prosperous time of ease and plenty.

This then was Minnie Alice. I had heard all about Bertie's mother, because Elsie had told me endless stories. Her father had been a wealthy merchant in Bristol and he and his partner Mr Barnard owned a chain of tobacco shops that dealt directly with Wills the tobacco people. Elsie had shown me photographs of Minnie with her sister in the garden of the big house in Totterdown. They wore long, beautiful dresses and carried parasols. Minnie and her sister went to a private school, driven there each day in their own carriage, and she was every inch a lady. While she was in the kitchen making tea, I looked at the photographs of three other members of the family in gilt frames on the mantelshelf, and Bertie told me that these were her three other children, his half-brothers and -sister, from her first marriage.

Over tea and cake, I enquired where Mr Storey was. Bertie looked uncomfortable and embarrassed, but Minnie said directly, 'He's gone back to his mammy!'

She then rummaged in a big black bag and produced a

small silver box filled with snuff. She pushed her finger and thumb into the box and took a liberal pinch, which she proceeded to shove up her nose. She offered me the box with an encouraging 'Take a pinch, kid!'

I declined, but she only laughed, sneezing and rubbing her nose and wiping flecks of brown dust from the lacy frill of her white blouse. Again she dived into her handbag, this time to retrieve a tattered bar of Fry's Five Boys chocolate cream. This must have lain amongst her other treasures for ages, for where the silver foil was rubbed and torn there were little smudges of snuff and dust from the bottom of her bag.

'Have a bit,' she offered, holding out the sagging chocolate to me. I took the proffered piece in my hand rather gingerly, then burst out laughing. She was the oddest, warmest character I had ever encountered and I loved her immediately. When it was time to go, she whispered again as if in confidence, 'Come again, kid. Consider yourself one of the family.'

Bertie looked pleased that I had passed the test, and it wasn't until I got home that I remembered that the one thing I hadn't wanted to happen had indeed taken place. Bertie was now even more pleased and confident. I was less and less sure. Life was very complicated. Men that you loved did not love you, and those you could not work up any enthusiasm for pursued you with craft and cunning.

'You are rushing me,' I protested that night when Bertie again pleaded:

'Come with me to Ceylon. I promise you won't regret it.'

Marriage

People were now signing petitions in the street protesting that England should not intervene in a European war, and an uneasy feeling of change prevailed. My mother was unsettled too; she often talked about going into business, and I got the impression she would be glad if I were living my own independent existence away from the family, so that I too felt a pull towards change. As much as I hated and kicked against it, I knew that the time was coming when I would have to make a decision.

If only I had been able to see all the choices. If only it had occurred to me that there *were* choices. If only my parents had counselled me, or shown me the alternatives. I needed only a parental hand on my shoulder to direct me away from the path that, even then, I knew I should not have taken. But the only escape seemed to lie in going to Ceylon with Bertie. It was time for me to leave home and it seemed the only way was through marriage. Two months later, when war was declared, young single girls across the country rushed to join the services. How I envied them, and how I wished I could have gone. My life would have been full and exciting; I could have learned new skills and become a different person. The possibilities were endless. But it was not to be. I had already made my choice.

I was awakened early on the morning of my twenty-second birthday, the 23rd of July, by the sound of gravel being thrown at my windowpane. Rushing to the window, I saw Bertie down below waving a piece of paper. I opened the window and he called up to me that we could get married that day as he had a special licence and the Reverend Cousins would marry us at two o'clock. I came down to let him in and to wait for Mum and Dad to get up before breaking the news to them. Mum's only comment was, 'I hope you know what you're doing, my girl.'

Dad didn't even glance my way, only enquiring from my mother if his best shirt was ready. I went up to my bedroom to search through my wardrobe for something special to wear. The choice was easy, for I had only one navy two-piece which I kept for high days and holidays, so I wore the skirt with the bolero, and a blouse covered in embroidered pink rosebuds. Navy shoes and white gloves completed my outfit.

We all walked up the lane together, Dad in front with Bertie and Mum and I behind. There was little conversation, except that I was informed, at the very last moment, after the service, that Bertie would have to get straight back on the tram and head back to Calshott. He was already absent without leave, and would have to do Jankers, whatever that was, when he got back.

It was a strange day. And a strange feeling; and not at all how I had imagined that my wedding day would be. No white bridal dress and no friends. We reached the church door, where the vicar was waiting for us in his white surplice with a gold-fringed ribbon around his neck. He held a black prayer book and smiled a welcome, looked at his watch and then waved with his book for us to follow him.

'Dearly beloved, we are gathered here in the sight of God and this congregation . . .'

I felt a sense of loss and loneliness, for two people only were seated there in the front pew on this great venture into a new part of my life. I felt cold and I shivered and remembered how I had experienced the same feeling of aloneness that day I had left school with just a brown envelope containing a few inadequate words about me from someone who didn't know me at all. There had been no handshake then, either, no good wishes.

Here I go again, I thought. The ring was on the book and I vaguely remember my father stepping away from me. The gold band was on my finger now and the gold-fringed ribbon tied loosely and symbolically around our wrists.

'Those whom God hath joined together, let no man put asunder.'

From somewhere deep inside of me, I heard a door bang shut. For better or worse, we were man and wife. I closed my eyes and felt Bertie kiss me. There was no wild exciting

'Wedding March', only phantom listeners as we turned aside to sign the register. Joyce Dark, spinster of this Parish, and Bertram John Storey, of the Royal Air Force. I saw the open doorway and the sun shining outside.

As we made our way to the door, my footsteps echoed hollowly all the way down the aisle.

From Miss to Mrs

Now in our weekly visits to the flicks there were disturbing reports on the Pathé newsreel about Hitler, but by the time the big film started the thoughts of Europe faded and war seemed far away. However, there came the day when all that changed.

Our radio sat squarely in the middle of the sideboard in the recess by the side of the fireplace. We had taken down the glass cupboard just above, but had retained two shelves. The lower one now housed a battery and this was what my father was changing on that fateful day. He rushed up to the garage to get the recharged battery and was twiddling with the mass of wires when I came into the room. Our neighbour Mrs Baker and her daughter Barbara were already there sitting on the settee. She did not have a radio and always came in to us to hear the King's special Christmas message. Mrs Baker was very patriotic and loved tradition, pomp and the royal family. She had sat and cried when we heard Edward VIII's abdication speech. Dad was twiddling the knobs now, trying to find the station. In the midst of all this, there was a knock on the door. Mum went to answer it and returned with Elsie and Bert and their son David from across the road. Elsie was flushed and agitated, and explained hurriedly that Bert had forgotten to put their battery on charge and now their set was as dead as a dodo. Elsie hugged me, and we all moved up to make room for them just as the chimes of Big Ben solemnly rang out. Our other neighbour, Mrs Saunders, poked her head round the door as we all simultaneously hissed, 'Sshhh!'

She sat down obediently on the arm of a chair, trying to retrieve hairpins that had slipped from the straggly and untidy bun at the nape of her neck, occasionally brushing back wisps of wayward hair from her forehead with the back of her hand. Everybody listened in silence to the voice of Neville Chamberlain as he began to tell us that Germany had been given until eleven o'clock that morning to undertake to withdraw her troops from Poland.

'I have to tell you that no such undertaking has been received,' he said in serious tones, 'and that consequently this country is at war with Germany.'

Mrs Baker cried openly and clung to her daughter, who wept with her. Mrs Saunders said, 'Oh my Gawd, oh my Gawd,' convinced that they would use poison gas this time. Elsie said that she had spoke to Mr Fry, the local councillor who lived next door to her, and he had told her in confidence that the first consignment of gas masks due to be delivered the following week would be far from adequate and it was a question of distribution – whoever got there first would be lucky.

Elsie was quite right about the gas masks, and several weeks later there was a kind of mad panic for these frightful-looking things at local schoolrooms and village halls where they were distributed. Some people reacted in the most uncivilised way, driven of course by fear and the conviction that the Germans would use poison gas. But eventually we all got them, and carried them everywhere with us. In fact, it became a kind of ritual to say each time we went out, 'Don't forget, gas mask, identity card and torch.'

The identity cards had to be carried in wallets and hand-bags at all times. There was a brisk trade done with identity bracelets and necklaces, and we bought special ones for loved ones and friends. Air-raid shelters were erected in back gardens. Ours took up the whole of the small dirt square, with the opening coming right up to the edge of the path. Each street had its own air-raid warden, part of whose job it was to go round and make sure the blackout was complete, with no chink of light showing at night. My father was the warden in our street. He had no flowers to look at now, but spent hours looking up into the sky.

Towards the middle of September, I received a letter from Bertie, which seemed to be the crowning blow. All leave had been cancelled, and the crew of High Speed Launch III were to proceed forthwith to Grimsby, where they would be patrolling the Humber and the North Sea in liaison with the Royal Navy. Bertie was negotiating with Flying Officer Bowen the possibility of obtaining a sleeping-out pass. As soon as possible he would find digs, and send for me. I was to stand by and await instructions.

I had never thought for one moment that I would be deprived of my trip to Ceylon. It had simply never occurred to me that even a war would prevent us from taking the journey to another, more exotic place and the start of a new life. The whole reason for saying yes to Bertie was on account of the glowing picture he had painted of how our life together would be in that warm and delightful place.

But Grimsby – where on earth was Grimsby? As far as I knew it was somewhere 'up north' on the cold east coast. I had dreamed of tropical beaches and the warmth of the golden sun, now all I was going to get was the cold North Sea and bitter winds. I felt angry and frustrated.

'I might just as well stay here and earn myself some money. That way I might get the deposit for a house,' I said angrily to my mother. To my surprise, she told me rather sharply that I could forget that idea.

'Your place is where your husband wants you to be. You made your bed, my girl, so now you go and lie on it.'

She then implied that she was also entitled to a life of her own. She and Dad were thinking of moving, and buying a little business together. Now that I was married, it was my husband's responsibility to provide a home for me. I could no longer regard South Road as that.

'Come upstairs, I have something for you. It's a present from me and Dad.'

She knew that her words about South Road never being my home again had sobered me so that I was crestfallen and sad, but I followed her up the stairs and into the small white-washed back room. There, by the side of the single iron bed, was a neat little brown tin trunk that she confided to me was her only possession on the day that she had left her home in St George to start her new life in South Road. Inside the trunk was a pair of new white wool blankets with blue borders.

I had but two gifts to start me on my way – the woollen blankets from my mum and dad, and half a tea service from Elsie and Bert. It was in a beautiful orange colour. Because I was afraid it might break if it was packed and taken with me, I asked Mum if I could leave it behind and collect it later. Perhaps it was just as well that I had no way of knowing then that it would be nine years before I had a real home of my own.

The letter from Bertie finally arrived. He wrote to say he had found some nice digs and enclosed a railway ticket for Grimsby Docks. He emphasised that I was to be sure to get out at Grimsby Docks, where he would be waiting to meet the train, not Grimsby Town. The tin trunk was taken down the stairs, where I packed the rest of the things I would need. When it was carefully locked and strapped, I sent it via the railway carrier to Grimsby, where Bertie would collect it and make sure it was delivered safely. My transition from maid to married woman had begun.

Stirling Street

That first morning, the sounds of coal trucks awakened me. Our digs were in one of a row of houses facing the railway siding, at the very top of the house where we had a view of the goods yard. Bertie was nowhere to be seen, but a note propped up by the alarm clock said that he would be home for lunch at twelve-thirty. I stretched in the comfortable bed and could easily have dozed off again, but hunger nudged me into activity and I got up to go in search of food and to explore my new surroundings. Except for tea in the caddy and a half-jug of milk on the drainer, I found nothing to eat. Clearly my wifely duties commenced from that moment and I would have to get a move on to do the shopping for a meal by midday.

As I sipped my tea I looked around the room. It was well furnished and everything was new. There was a dining suite, two comfortable fireside chairs and a sideboard to match. On the landing outside was a small stove, a sink with a right-hand drainer, and a cupboard above. A tiny box room revealed a toilet. No bathroom. This, I discovered, was on the floor below. Since we occupied the two rooms on the top floor, our bedroom faced the railway siding at the front, and our lounge-cum-diner faced the gardens at the back.

I went downstairs to investigate who else lived in this quiet house. A pint-sized woman was brushing down the steps and moved aside to let me pass. She nodded to me, smiling brightly and showed a large, loose tooth that protruded over her top lip. Wanting to make friends as well as needing information, I sat down on one of the lower steps and asked where the local shops might be. She told me where all the best and the cheapest shops could be found, and that there was a market, a place that everyone frequented, on Tuesday mornings.

She became very chatty and informative, telling me that she had heard us come in late last night but had not wanted to bother us, knowing we must be tired. Her name was Mrs Eden. She and her husband owned the house, and she had one daughter who was married but had gone and joined the land army and was now somewhere down south. ''Tis a nice flat, is that,' she said with a nod towards the top of the house. ''Tis the daughter's,' she explained. Then, leaning forward confidentially, she whispered, 'Thought I'd do meself a mite good while the army straightened our Gloria out.'

Here the loose tooth waggled up and down and Mrs Eden chuckled. Mr Eden was a trawlerman and was away for long periods at sea. She walked with me to the door and pointed the way to the market.

I enjoyed the walk and found the market. I lingered longer than I meant to, but I was happy that morning and I bought a record and a pot of bright yellow chrysanths to brighten up the room. I completely lost track of the time and was horrified to find that it was well after twelve and I still hadn't got anything for lunch. Bertie would be there and waiting when I got home. I bought some apples from a barrow and then saw some yellow crumbly cheese on another stall and then rushed back the way I had come from the still-crowded market. At the baker's, I recklessly splashed out on six jam doughnuts, and dismally reflected that the twelve shillings I had started out with would now have to be very carefully juggled if it had to stretch right till the following Tuesday when my housekeeping was due. Perhaps Bertie would give me a little extra, I thought hopefully, as I let myself in and bounded up the stairs, all three flights of them. He was already in and waiting, had made himself a cup of tea and was sitting expectantly at the table.

I placed the flowers on the table, hoping they might brighten him up as well as the room. I must be careful at this stage not to strike a wrong note.

'Crumps!' Bertie exploded. 'You know I only have an hour.'

I quickly placed an apple on a plate and stole a glance. I really wanted to laugh because he was sitting there holding a knife and fork in eager anticipation. His eyes followed mine as I slowly brought the cheese into view and set it on a plate by the side of the apple. So far there wasn't much evidence that he was going to enjoy anything as substantial as a cooked meal. Without looking at him, I began cutting slices of bread in the hope that he would resign himself, as first days are often fraught. Perhaps the doughnuts might just clinch the deal. I even muttered something about a cooked meal later and then he could hear my record.

He almost choked on a piece of cheese and shouted, 'Record, woman! Do you mean to tell me that you have been spending my allowance on records?'

Before I could say another word, he had grabbed my purse and made for the door, muttering something about needing some money for a proper meal and not being sure what time he would be back. I sat down, nibbling at an apple and contemplating my next move. Without any money, there was nothing to be done. I walked to the radiogram and put my new record on the turntable. 'Tales From the Vienna Woods' came loud and clear into the room. Nobody heard me cry as I ate my apple and cheese.

Mr Eden was home. The house seemed to come alive as soon as he stepped through the front door. He was both good-natured and noisy and went about banging doors and singing sea-shanties at the top of his voice. He was skipper of his household as much as his boat and bellowed right up from the basement to me, 'Come down to t'kitchen, lass.'

When I arrived at the kitchen door, a middle-aged bearded man in a striped butcher's apron, brandishing a sharp-pointed knife, greeted me. He was skilfully and deftly slitting open plaice and lemon sole and filleting them. Then with a quick flourish the fish was flopped back and forth in some creamy white batter. A large pan full of bubbling fat covered the whole of the top of the stove and into this went the fish, sizzling and turning a lovely golden brown. Periodically, he pulled the handle of a small chip machine, feeding in whole peeled potatoes. The chips slithered out the other end and into a bowl of cold water. When enough chips were done, he put them into a sieve and then straight into a massive chip pan on a special gas ring by the side of the stove.

Mrs Eden darted about laying the table for dinner. With dancing eyes and her front tooth wobbling, she explained, 'It's a right good day. Mr Eden is cooking fish and chips all round. Go and fetch that young man of yours and bring him down for dinner.'

I rushed back upstairs, where I had been going to do sausage and mash; now he could have that for tea. My mouth was already watering in anticipation of eating such deliciously fresh fish. I opened my new book: there might be time to finish the chapter before Bertie came home. I was so absorbed that I didn't hear him come in, and he had been standing in front of me for some time when I looked up.

He spoke at last. 'Well. Where's my dinner?' He snatched the book from my hands.

'It's downstairs on the kitchen table, all ready for you to gobble up.' I wanted to laugh at the puzzled look that came into his eyes, and wanted to prolong this cat-and-mouse game. But I made the mistake of laughing as I tried to explain that it was fish and chips for everybody because Mr Eden was home. So instead of being pleased he got angry, childishly accusing me of getting so lazy I expected other people to do my work for me. My look of dazed incredulity was broken by Mrs Eden calling to us, 'Come on down before your dinner gets cold and is spoiled.'

Bertie got stuck in to the excellent meal and some of his surliness melted. He even managed a grunt of satisfaction by way of thanks as he laid down his knife and fork to hurry back after his break. 'See you tonight,' he said.

Mr Eden eyed me after he had gone, especially when I began to thank him profusely for the lovely meal he had prepared for us all. To tell the truth, it was the first time in my entire life I had seen any man cook a meal.

On impulse, I blurted out, 'Would you show me how to fillet and skin a fish?'

He leaned over and gently ruffled my hair. 'Eee, lass,' he said. 'I'll do just that. You'll learn to cook, lass, long before your lad learns his manners.'

'He finds it rather difficult to communicate,' I said breathlessly, rushing to Bertie's defence. 'You see, the ancient cavemen developed a well-defined set of grunts and groans which covered most things, including table manners and marital rights.'

Mr Eden's face puckered in a puzzled frown until he saw that I was joking. He thumped the table and gave a hearty chuckle and the pair of us burst out laughing. 'He's very young.' I smiled. 'And I'm working on him.'

The time spent at Stirling Street will always be remembered as a happy one, especially when in the company of Mr and Mrs Eden. We looked forward to the periods when he returned home from sea. There was always plenty of fresh fish and seafood, including lobster and crab, the most delicious stuff I had ever tasted. We certainly ate like kings when Skipper Eden came bounding home.

It was a sad day when Gloria, their daughter, came home to find that her flat had been invaded. One night we heard her angry voice shouting indignantly, 'If I had a bloody room I'd go sit in it.' Sadly, we knew it was time for us to move on.

Clyde Street

On the following Monday I went into the town to collect my allowance from the post office. I collected my money from the counter, and exchanged a greeting with the counter hand. Turning round rather quickly, I collided with a young girl right behind me, almost knocking her over and, much to my consternation, spilling my money on the floor. She laughed and mentioned something about chucking my brass around, but gave up her place in the queue to bend down and help me find all the coins that had rolled away. After that, I waited for her and we stood outside in the sunshine, talking easily and laughing about the incident. She told me that her name was Margaret Burton. She had two boys, Tommy who was four and an older boy, Georgie, who was at school. Her husband was abroad in the army.

'Eee, you're right bonny, lass,' she said. 'Come and have a cup of tea.'

A number of small streets led off the main road. The houses on these streets had no front gardens so that the front doors came directly onto the pavement. They were tiny, cottage-like buildings, two up and two down, squalid little houses built for the dock workers in the poorer quarter of town. The range and the flagstones of her home reminded me of South Road, but she had made that small kitchen bright and homely. I felt I had at last found a friend and was happy. And when I looked around this bright little room I felt the faint stirrings of a need to own something permanent like it for myself.

'Do you know of any rooms to let around here?' I asked her.

'Tom Bradley's sister wants to let her house. Her husband got killed at sea a while back. She's gone to live with her mother, but Tom has got the key if you're interested.'

I couldn't believe my luck. I sat and stared at her.

'Nice warm little place is that,' she said, nodding towards the house two doors down. 'Finish your tea and I'll take you across to Tom. Five shillings a week is what he's asking for it.'

Then she said, with a smile that lit up the whole of her face, 'We could be friends.'

Tom Bradley eyed me suspiciously. I was not local and, what was worse, I was a southerner. Margaret, however, assured him I was a friend of hers, which apparently made things a bit better. He led the way over the road and inserted the key into the lock of number 7 Clyde Street. The tiny front room smelled damp and musty. A faded carpet covered a stone floor. There was a radiogram in one corner and a three-piece suite of doubtful origin taking up the rest of the space. The kitchen was the same in design as Margaret's and reminded me so much of home. I wanted to sit in front of the range with the fire halfway up the chimney. I wanted to hear a kettle singing on the hob.

I glanced towards the scullery, which was a glass-covered lean-to. I noted a black stove and a cold tap with a sink and drainer. A dolly tub complete with a wooden basher stood in the corner. The drains didn't smell so good. A great air-raid shelter took up the whole of the square of garden, and Margaret explained that it was for the whole rank of houses. Tom Bradley was the air-raid warden.

'I'll look after you, ducks,' he said confidently.

I said I would take the house and returned to hug Margaret, who seemed as pleased as I was that our friendship should be cemented in this way. Once more, the small brown tin trunk was transferred, this time from Stirling Street to Clyde Street, and we moved into that tiny house. A whole house, however tiny, was better than rooms. It was here that I began to think of myself as a real housewife. Bertie, too, was more relaxed and settled, and together we would sit by a roaring fire that he became adept at lighting. Members of the crew sometimes used to drop in for a chat, and I proudly showed them into the parlour and felt very married and happy.

Margaret remained a loyal friend. Most days we'd have tea and biscuits together. One day we had a heavy storm when the drains blocked and the filthy water came right up to the lean-to kitchen. The smell was awful. Margaret assured me that it had been happening for as long as she could remember. Laughing at my look of disgust, she helped me sweep out the evil-smelling seepage. She didn't laugh in the weeks that followed, when her youngest lad went down with diphtheria. Tommy was flushed with a high temperature when we wheeled him to the doctor, who immediately admitted him to the fever hospital. We went to see him every week, but were only allowed to wave to him from the window. His tearful little face looking down at us made us both cry.

I'm sure she appreciated my tears. We made a cake on the day he came home. It was my first attempt at icing, and I proudly placed it on the table in front of him, with *Tommy* written in pink. He promptly told me it should have been in blue, but he said the cake was still good, and he kissed me.

The sirens wailed that night, but it was like a party, with everybody singing and the women taking it in turns to make jugs of hot cocoa. Tom gave us a minute-to-minute account of the damage the bombs were causing in town. Such and such a building was blazing away, or parts of the docks were their objective, he explained.

We became familiar with the low throb of enemy bombers. Tom had a real sense of humour and kept us all happy by telling jokes every time the dull thud of a falling bomb could be heard. We sang songs and played cards down in that shelter in Clyde Street. Afterwards, the whole street met to talk about the events of the night before. We all helped each other and commiserated when a relative became a casualty, or a telegram arrived with the news of the death of a loved one in the services.

On the nights that Bertie went off to the pub with the boys, I stayed with Margaret. In the evenings we sat knitting or sewing or just talking. So far I had never been out with him and his mates, and one evening Margaret commented on this and said I ought to insist on going with him sometimes. Bored with the long hours on my own, I pleaded with him to take me to the pictures. He thought for a minute and then said he would perhaps be able to manage it next week. He also said he envied me my freedom – after all, I could spend all day exploring the town, get to know people and sit and drink tea with Margaret. I told him I was not impressed with Grimsby and that unless he could spend some more of his precious time with me I was packing up and going home.

He thought about that for a moment and then said, 'You can't. You haven't any money.'

I instantly regretted the next remark, when I stupidly confessed that I had been saving two shillings a week so that I could go home for a visit.

'Man and wife should have no secrets from each other. Where have you hidden it?'

'No secret,' I said innocently. 'It's in one of the china bowls on the dressing table.'

'Get your coat on,' he said at last, putting the money in his pocket. 'But don't think I'm going to make a habit of taking you to the pub every time I go out with the boys.'

The other members of the crew were already in the pub by the time we arrived, seated around a table that was swilling with beer, but room was made for us with a great scraping of chairs, and another round of drinks was called for. A look in my direction and a hurried consultation finally brought a dainty, tiny narrow-necked glass filled with a thick yellow substance which Bertie whispered to me was called egg-flip and had to be sipped slowly, not tossed back in one gulp.

The members of High Speed Launch III were a motley crew. Bertie was one of the deck hands, together with Billy Davis, a Cockney whose favourite expression was 'Cor blimey, stone the crows!' Wally Walsh was a leading hand, which was another step up the promotional ladder. He didn't speak much, and gave the impression of being somewhat surly and withdrawn. In complete contrast was the coxswain, who laughed at everything and especially his own jokes, and was appropriately nicknamed Smiler Smithy. These four stuck together like glue and formed a boozing quartet, asserting that, as they were fighting and bleeding for their country, they were entitled to drink and be merry today, for tomorrow they might all be dead. To my surprise, they called Bertie 'Jack' or sometimes 'Fred'.

The room was smoke-filled and noisy. A blond lad was playing the piano. Small knots of airmen stood around singing bawdy songs in half-tipsy voices. A dishcloth came whizzing through the air. Catching it expertly with one hand, Billy Davis began mopping up the beer that lay in pools all over the table, and amidst loud laughter he wrung it out into an empty beer mug and threw it back towards the bar, where it just missed the barman.

I sipped my drink and found it very pleasant. Every time another round of drinks was called, another tot of egg-flip was added for me and I now had six of the things lined up like soldiers in front of me. By the time I had consumed a third tot of this delicious stuff, I was amazed to find that the whole room was taking on a brighter dimension. As I looked around at Bertie's friends, I found their company fascinated me and every word they spoke seemed to hold a deeper meaning. I found myself leaning forward so that I could catch every word. The whole room became enhanced with colours, which emphasised the swaying figures, and everything seemed to hold a special meaning for me.

When I heard Billy calling my beloved 'Fred' for the third or fourth time, I had a sudden impulse to set the record straight. I leaned across the beer-soaked table and said in a very loud voice, 'His mother calls him Darling Bertie.'

A great roar of laughter went up from the crew around the table but Bertie looked uncomfortable. His face reddened, and his quick glance in my direction let me know he was both embarrassed and cross. In my happy state, I became convinced it was about time I gave him a proper name, a real man's name.

'Well, you can call him what you like, but he has a very nice second Christian name of John and that's what I shall call him from now on.'

The crew looked on, still grinning, but I think they approved. From that moment on, he was John to me, Fred or Jack to his mates, Darling Bertie to his mother and just plain Bert to his sister and two brothers.

Out of the corner of my eye, I saw Flying Officer Bowen and Sergeant Brodie making their way to our table. By the state they were already in, it could safely be assumed they had visited most of the pubs in a five-mile radius. They were of the same stature and build, both about the same age – in their early thirties – and where one went the other followed. Flying Officer Bowen was definitely public-school. He had a smooth, round face on which he had cultivated a rather fine moustache, which reminded me of a colonial officer from the Boer War. He was a charmer, oozing it like cream from a doughnut. Brodie, on the other hand, looked surly and sulky and lacked charm of any kind. He was as battered as a bruiser boxer. With his cap pulled well down and a cane under his arm, he would have been at home on the parade ground drilling raw recruits and bawling, 'You might break your mother's 'eart but you won't break MINE!'

They were as different in character and background as chalk and cheese, yet surprisingly enough these two were inseparable.

John got to his feet to introduce me and also to offer Brodie a chair, because it was evident that he was swaying so unsteadily that it was safer for him to sit down.

'This is my wife, sir,' John began.

Flying Officer Bowen waved his hand airily around, trying hard to focus on me, whilst holding onto the table for support. 'Welcome aboard, little lady. Welcome aboard.' Then he addressed the crew, his face now wreathed in smiles. 'This calls for drinkies, what?'

John went with him to the bar and he ordered yet another round of beers and of course one more soldier tot of egg-flip for me. Meanwhile Brodie was sitting there, looking slightly glassy-eyed and foolishly trying to reach out to grasp a pint mug of beer that was directly in front of him, yet not quite making it because of his blurred vision. I watched him intently, and presently he leaned back in his chair and without warning slid effortlessly down to the floor and under the table.

Bowen returned a little while later and stupidly looked around for his drinking partner. The look of bemused anxiety on his face when he beheld only the empty chair made me almost choke with mirth. I stole a look at Brodie's inert form under the table and vowed I would not tell a soul where he was. This would be my great secret. Bowen is so drunk, I thought, he doesn't even know where he left Brodie. At this point, it became urgent for me to go to the loo. As I made my way to the door I was surprised to find that I was not walking properly. However, as the room was so crowded I didn't fall over and got to the door without mishap. Then I tried to manoeuvre the four steps to the Ladies. The step instead came up to meet me. This, I thought, was a novel experience, with the world going up and down several times before a sudden urge to be sick prompted a dash to the loo. There, with my two arms embracing the pedestal, I was horribly and revoltingly sick.

I became conscious that I was sitting on a dirty floor strewn with pieces of toilet paper that had been pulled from the china holder on the wall. With shafts of pain going through my head, I pulled myself up from the floor and made my way to the tiny sink outside in the corridor, where I washed my face in cold water.

A door at the rear of the corridor revealed a small enclosure or back yard and I leaned against the wall to take in a few deep breaths of night air. It seemed, as I stood there, that I became aware of shadowy figures who stood facing and talking quietly to the wall. I giggled when I realised that these silent bods were, in fact, relieving themselves. It was here that John found me. I could tell instantly that he was displeased with me by the way that he tutted and said, 'Oh crumps!' when I was sick again. 'Can't take you any-where,' he grumbled.

I couldn't answer him because my head felt like bursting and, what was worse, the sky never seemed to be where it ought to have been.

'Never again!' I vowed, as John tried to extricate me from a lamp-post that seemed to get in my way. I sat down in the gutter feeling I badly wanted to die. 'You can only reach a point,' I wailed miserably into the night. 'And then you have to come back.'

John eyed me grimly. I knew I would never be asked to the pub again.

But, to my surprise, he did take me to the pictures. 'Be ready at six-thirty sharp,' he said as he left home that morning. I couldn't wait for the evening to come, and the afternoon dragged on and on. I was ready on the dot with my hat and coat on. My gloves and torch lay on the table. To venture out in the blackout without a torch would present a hazard. John was ten minutes late, despite the fact that it was he who had insisted on my punctuality. As we hurried along the darkened streets I grumbled a little. It was very cold, and the wind blew in sudden icy little gusts that made my face smart and my eyes water. I shivered and pulled up the collar of my coat to help shield my face. John pulled me closer to him and then covered the whole of my face with his big warm hands. I was now warm, but quite unable to see where I was walking. He was guiding me, telling me how to negotiate kerbstones to cross the road. In a devil-may-care mood, he played a trick on me, telling me quietly and earnestly that we were coming to a flight of steps.

'Up, up,' he directed, so that I immediately complied by lifting my foot from the ground. When I discovered I was not making contact with any kind of step, but almost losing my balance, whilst my high-stepping antics threw him into hysterics, I gave him a well-deserved thump. The pair of us were laughing so much we had to stop in a doorway to recover our breath. Then we both ran along the road to the cinema because John whispered, 'It's a Bette Davis film and she's got such a sexy voice.'

The cinema was Bible black. No bright neon emblazoned the names of the stars and the feature film revolving round and round in an endless square of light. These had been extinguished at the start of the war. Gone too the all-important figure of the commissionaire, with his grey uniform with the gold epaulettes, shouting on the steps the number of seats in the balcony or stalls. A very full, pleated blackout curtain now draped the great doors at the entrance to the foyer. Once inside its voluptuous folds, you came face to face with a high plywood partition forming a corridor along which we all shuffled. A sharp turn to the right at the end of this makeshift and temporary entrance led at last to the pay box, but so low was the light in that gloomy, dimly lit area that it was wise to have the right money for the ticket – you couldn't see if your change was correct.

The Pathé news had already started, and we found ourselves seats right at the back where we took off our coats and snuggled up to each other. I was surprised and delighted when John placed a bag of sweets on my lap. They were on ration now and we usually gobbled up the two meagre ounces we were allowed each week. The fact was his boyish charm made him a firm favourite with the older women who worked in the NAAFI, and they often gave him their sweet rations. I was relaxed and happy and, snuggled up by his side, I was soon immersed in the great escapism of the film.

We blinked when the lights suddenly went up in the middle of the feature film and a message was flashed on the screen announcing that an air-raid warning had just sounded. All those wishing to take advantage of the shelters across the road could now do so as quickly as possible, through the exits provided. The film would continue for those wishing to stay behind, who were reminded that they did so at their own risk.

I pulled back the red plush seat and began putting on my coat. I knew that in the event of an air raid John would have to make his way to the docks as quickly as possible. I watched the hunched figures making their way out through the exits. When they had turned on the lights, it seemed not just to have interrupted the sequence of the film, but shattered a fantasy. Through the endless yards of celluloid, reality had once again intruded, reminding us that outside a war was still going on, and we must not forget it. Not even in the cinema could we dream, perchance to sleep.

Once again outside, we shivered in the cold night air. The beams from dozens of searchlights criss-crossed, searching the skies. In the distance, we heard the menacing low sound of bombers. Holding hands, we ran as fast as our legs would carry us through the darkened town until we came to Clyde Street. John grabbed his bike from the shed and I had only time to call, 'Take care!'

Tom Bradley almost pushed me into the shelter as the first stick of bombs fell very, very close with a sickening thump! thump! thump!

I knew I was pregnant that first morning I was sick. The previous week I'd had my suspicions, because when I walked through the market with the stalls piled high with fruit the smell had brought on a faint feeling of nausea. Feeling wretched, I confided in Margaret. She only laughed and told me that the shop at the top of the road sold the best selection of baby wool, and that one cure for the baby blues was to get the old needles clicking. I yelled at her that I was not happy about the patter of baby feet in pale blue booties, especially right bang in the middle of a war. I personally thought it was the dumbest thing imaginable.

That night, I confronted John and told him what I thought and how I felt. He said that women had babies all the time and didn't make half as much fuss. And if nobody had babies because there was a war on, the world would be in a sorry state. I replied coldly that in my considered opinion women had no control over their own bodies, and if only he had used the 'thingies' that the services dished out so easily, and had a bit more respect for me, none of this would have happened. And if we could have discussed more rationally how and where a child could be born with no home of its own, we would not be standing here now like a couple of fighting cocks.

Margaret came with me to the clinic. It was October and I had been in Grimsby a whole year. As we set off to catch a bus into town, the air was crisp and cold. The leaves on the trees were already falling, and the wind blew them along in front of us and piled them against the shelter of the wall. I have always loved this time of the year – the colours of the leaves, earthy browns through to shades of gold, harvest time and the month of the long shadows. This was the month that my parents had married. I remembered that my mother had told me about the pots of yellow and bronze chrysanthemums in the chapel windows, and how the sun had shone on the altar rail. I felt very homesick and wanted to cry.

The clinic confirmed that I was about twelve weeks pregnant.

Towards the end of October we had a howling gale with gusts of wind up to fifty miles an hour. Tiles and chimney-pots were blown around and came crashing down. The wind shrieked as though all the fiends in hell were abroad that night. Miraculously, the only damage sustained by our little glass lean-to was five missing panes of glass, leaving a hole about five feet wide in the centre.

Tom Bradley assured us that he could obtain the glass

quite cheaply and it would only be a matter of a few shillings if John could fix the glass back in. He was so convinced that he had settled the matter amicably and with the minimum amount of fuss. He was therefore amazed when John adamantly refused to pay for the damage, saying that any replacement costs should be met by the person who owned the house, not the person who paid the rent. It was Tom's sole responsibility.

Tom was furious. He thought John's attitude was unhelpful and arrogant. Damage as negligible as this was trivial, and in his opinion he had suggested a compromise between two civilised men. John would not budge from his position. In a man who was so often gentle and easy-going, this sudden obstinacy always came as a surprise. He would dig in his heels and refuse to budge. It infuriated me, and made the sparks fly – although I did admit that he was entitled to his point of view.

As for Tom, he was so angry he said we could vacate the premises, and in due course we received the notice to quit. For his part, John felt sure he could find other accommodation just as good, if not better, than this. The drains would not be good for the new baby, anyway. I clung to Margaret and wept whilst John took his bike and went in search of fresh lodgings. So sadly I said goodbye to the first little home that I had known. I hugged Margaret and told her I would come back to see her often. I pulled the tin trunk from the cupboard under the stairs. It was heavier now, for a few more things had been added to it. It was ready and waiting for one more move.

Mill Lane

Clyde Street had been a humble place and the people in that small terrace of seven houses generous and willing to share the little they had, all eager and ready to help a stranger. Though poor, the houses were decent.

In comparison, Mill Lane was situated in the poorest part of the dock area, and my first impression was that it left a lot to be desired. A fat, squat, round gasometer, painted a dirty dark green, stood out stark and ugly against the skyline at the far end of the lane, which ended in a mud track and led into the premises of the Gas Board. On this particular day, the wind was in the wrong direction and the smell from this silent monster was truly dreadful. Only six houses remained, and these faced a boarded-up bombsite, behind which was the rubble and remains of the facing terrace that had once housed people who had lived and loved and laughed. Now only a wooden hoarding hid the silent bricks scattered around. No life there now; the devastation could be hidden, but not the depression that seemed to brood over the whole lane.

With a sinking heart, I let my gaze follow the boarding to where a single gas lamp leaned crazily at the end of the pavement. I smiled, for it was apparent that the bomb blast had not quite succeeded in dislodging it completely from its cemented moorings. Ironically, neither had it touched the pub on the other side of the pavement. This stood intact and untouched with its wooden sign swinging in the slight late-autumn breeze: the Rising Sun.

John led the way to the very last house in the row.

Miss Robinson owned the house. She came down over the stairs to greet us. Very tall and thin, she had grey hair and slate-grey eyes. There was a grey pallor to her skin, and she panted and wheezed alarmingly, for she suffered dreadfully with asthma. She had to sit on a chair and recover from the effort of descending the stairs before she could speak to us. But when she smiled, her whole face lit up. It was like an April sun sweeping over a field, transforming the day to mellow gold. I always loved seeing that smile light up those slate-grey eyes of hers.

Our room faced the yard. From the french doors we could see a path extending down about fifty yards to the back gate and a wall dividing the house from next door. A bed-settee took up one side of the wall. We had a grate with an oven one side. In the recess by the window there was a sideboard, on the top of which had been placed a piece of flowered oil-cloth and now it housed cups and saucers and a tray with a teapot and a jug. Underneath was an assortment of pots and dishes. She breathlessly assured me that I must ask for anything that she had omitted to provide. She showed me the tiny scullery that she said we had to share.

'Not that I shall ever be in your way,' she smiled. 'I have my own bits and pieces upstairs and don't come down unless I have to.' She looked across the room. 'I guess if your name is on one of those whizz-bangs you've had it,' she said stoically, then pointed to a deep cupboard under the stairs where she'd put a mattress. 'I've no need for a shelter, and would die trying to get in one. You'll be as safe under here as anywhere.'

I wanted to ask her why she stayed in a place that was so dangerous, and so obviously bad for her asthmatic condition, but she was already tiring and heading for the stairs. She called over her shoulder for us to make ourselves at home and to make ourselves a cup of tea. When I called after her would she like one as well, she could only nod. She was sitting on the top stair, trying to get her breath, but shook her head vigorously when I asked if there was anything I could do to help.

When the bed-settee was pulled down that night, it took up the whole room and even extended into the grate. The mattress was lumpy and hurt my back. When I wanted the toilet in the middle of the night, I had to crawl over John, negotiate the dark scullery and unbolt the back door into the cold yard. The sky was full of stars and there was no raid that night. I thought of Margaret and knew I would miss the crowd from the terrace. Tom Bradley and his warm-hearted humour had given us the confidence to laugh in the face of danger; the jugs of steaming hot cocoa and the cards that we played helped to take our minds off things. Sometimes, though, even this was forgotten when a stack of bombs falling much too close for comfort made us hold our breath.

I realised I was not only lonely but unhappy, and I resolved to go and see Margaret. She was overjoyed to see me and said we should take the boys into Cleethorpes on the bus. I'd never been to the beach and although it was November the sun was warm when we set off, despite the tang of winter in its pale rays. When we arrived at the long stretch of sand, the boys raced on ahead to find flat-topped pebbles that they could skim across the surface of the water.

A colder wind now blew off the murky grey waters of the North Sea, whipping up the tide's wavelets so that they splashed angrily on the beach, staining the mud-coloured sand an even darker shiny hue. I had a sudden mental picture of the softer contours of our own south coast, with its tiny inlets and sheltered bays, rock pools and walks along cliff paths. And once again I felt sick with longing for home.

To keep warm, Margaret said we would race the boys to the sand dunes; it would give us an appetite for dinner. When we got there, Georgie and Tommy started digging and scooping out a large hole whilst we hid behind a great wall of sand to shelter us from the keen wind that would sometimes blow the sand particles and sting our faces. I watched the two boys for a while, playing their fantasy games in the big hole they had now converted into an imaginary speed-car. Sometimes they sparred with each other on the sandy slope and rolled over and over like two young wayward puppies.

'Do you want a boy?' Margaret interrupted my thoughts to ask.

'No,' I replied without hesitation. 'I want a girl to make up for the sister I never had. A sister just like you,' I went on impulsively, and we both giggled and hugged each other.

Autumn slipped into winter, with high winds that whipped up the green-tipped waves of the North Sea so that they pounded the harbour wall and sent spray high into the air and over the roadway, making the way impassable. Traffic and pedestrians were diverted via another route. During the summer months, this was a favourite walk of mine. I loved the salt breeze, the cry of the gulls, and all the activity that a busy harbour brings. Most of all I loved the vast expanse of sea and sky, one great space where my imagination could soar and go on for ever.

There had been a day when two planes appeared from behind a feathery, frothy white cloud. The sun was glinting on the wingtips, making both planes look as though they were shot with silver. A crowd of us stood there by the harbour walls, shading our eyes with our hands to watch this drama being enacted over the water. As one streaked away, veering sideways to avoid the staccato bursts of gunfire that could be plainly heard by those on the ground, the other again zoomed upwards. There was a moment when both planes blotted out the sun so that they seemed like purple shadows against the sky. In that momentary silence there was a tiny cough and splutter as if the engine of that plane was emitting a half-strangled death cry before finally bursting into flames and beginning its spiralling descent into the cold waters below.

Witnessing this tragic episode affected me deeply. I watched the bystanders who were beginning to disperse, some shaking their heads sadly before walking on to continue with their own affairs. I suddenly felt very cold and empty. I wanted an answer to all this insane killing and aggression. I was very aware of being pregnant, and creating life while men were wasting it. Women were the creators and carers, men destroyed. I found myself praying desperately that my baby would be a girl, then hopelessly wondering if, one day in the future, she too might be praying for an answer to how she fitted into this ceaseless, futile round of warfare and aggression and senseless human sacrifice.

John had joined a branch of the services that saved lives instead of taking them, and I always admired him for that. Whether it was one of ours or the enemy made no difference to the crews of the Air Sea Rescue Service. And when Jerry had been fished out of the cold North Sea and wrapped in blankets and been given a warming cuppa, even the language barrier could be broken by smiles and handshakes and the exchange of photographs of dear ones.

One morning, Sergeant Brodie called round to the house. John was shaving and his face was still covered in lather when I showed Brodie into the drab little room.

'Posting's come through,' he said to John. 'You and Smith are to proceed to Southampton on Friday. You will be kitted out there for a posting to Gibraltar.'

He hardly glanced my way and only just managed a nod of recognition as he made his apologies and went out again. John saw him to the door. The lather was still on his face. I heard them talking for a while and when he returned to the room he looked anxiously at me, wanting to be assured that I would be all right. He wiped his face and then came over to where I was standing looking out of the window. He put his arms around me and whispered, 'I'm sorry, sweetheart.'

I remained passively in the circle of his arms and made no attempt to give him the reassuring kiss he needed. I was eight months pregnant, scared and frightened but not wanting to let him know. I waited to hear him utter the same old remarks that I knew would come.

'You'll be all right, sweetheart. You're strong, you'll get by.'

'Of course I will,' I said with an enforced conviction that I did not feel, and disengaged myself from his arms. He was already whistling as he pulled out his kitbag and began to pack.

Motherhood

March came in with high winds that blew slates off roofs, and dustbin lids and debris everywhere. The clinic had given me the 7th of March as the approximate date of my baby's arrival, but the day came and went and left me feeling tearful and distressed. Another week dragged by until one evening a kind of rhythmic pain sent me over the road to the landlord at the Rising Sun, who called the ambulance for me.

At Nunsthorpe Nursing Home I was finally admitted to Labour Room 4. In the corner was a kind of surgical trolley onto which they told me to climb, but I thought they must be joking. I was not very good at acrobatics, and I shoved one leg up onto the contraption, hoping for a helpful leg-up from behind. No help came. Instead, a pain that made me gasp for breath and grasp the steel of the trolley and which kept me in this position for several minutes. 'Ooh.' I bit my lips and felt like tearing my hair. A squat little sister waddled over to where I was standing, still with one leg on the trolley, and demanded to know what I was making all the fuss about.

'You've had the sweet, now you must have the sour!' she said vindictively, and gave me a shove up onto the trolley so hard that I arrived face-down on the cold surface with nothing but a cold pillow and a cold sheet to cover me. After a cursory examination that must have told them I would be in that stage of labour for some time, the sister and the two nurses went out of the room and I saw them disappearing into the corridor outside.

The sounds of the babies crying in the nursery nearby came to me, and there were sudden little bursts of activity and laughter as footsteps hurriedly passed by Labour Room 4, where I lay trying to cope with the rhythmic contractions that seemed to come all too frequently now, with hardly any respite in between. Towards morning, I saw the grey dawn break. I don't know how long I had been there on that cold trolley, but I knew when the contractions became urgent and different that somebody ought to be around. I tried to call out but all I could do was make horrible noises like some animal and grapple with a pain that threatened to squeeze the heart out of me. Then, without warning, there was someone by my side and a voice said, 'Are you all right? How long have you been in here?'

Footsteps echoed in the corridor, mingled with the sounds of frantic and concerned activity. I was being told to push, and I thought that I couldn't do much else.

At eight-thirty in the morning of 15 March 1941, I gave

birth to a baby girl. She was born twenty-two inches long and weighed barely five pounds. She gave one agonised little wail and went to sleep. I guess her journey into the world was not exactly a joyride and sleep was her only way to recover. As for me, I was glad when they wrapped me in warm red blankets, placed two hot water bottles on either side of me and wheeled me into a ward and put me to bed.

I too wanted only sleep. Before I closed my eyes, I felt happy that I had my baby girl: Patricia Joy was the name I'd already chosen. I turned my head towards the window and saw a big bush of yellow forsythia in bloom. I sighed contentedly and drifted off to sleep.

I awoke the next morning to the sound of a trolley being wheeled along the ward and a cheerful voice offering me a very welcome cup of tea. I eased myself up in bed and made a wry grimace, for I felt as if I'd been flattened by a steamroller. Every part of me was stiff and sore. Looking round the ward, where every bed with its neatly enveloped bottom was in line with its neighbour, I noted an air of expectancy from all the eager new mothers, who were now sitting up in bed, arrayed in bright colourful nighties and crisp new bed jackets. I snuggled closer into my warm flannelette nightdress, which was long enough to wrap my feet in if they were cold.

In the next bed to mine was a huge woman who was a bit of a celebrity. At the age of forty she had given birth for the first time to a bonny, bouncing ten-pound baby boy. When I first caught sight of her she was kneeling up in bed, trying to retrieve some misplaced article from among her bedclothes. I thought that she looked just like one of those fat little fertility goddesses that people used to worship in olden times. She had enough milk in her swinging udders to be surrogate mother to all the babies in the ward. Matron, along with all the nurses, thought she was wonderful, the embodiment of motherhood, and at the amazing age of forty years.

It was now time for all the infants to be fed. Sister Blood came into the room like a ship in full sail. Matron led the way, with the nurses in full attendance and each carrying two babies, one in each arm and firmly bundled around in a tight blanket. These they distributed to all the fond mothers now sitting bolt upright in bed, ready to do their proud duty to their offspring. Let guzzling commence! I thought, and gritted my teeth.

Now it was my turn to see my little specimen and to rouse myself from the comfort of my bed to do my bit. Sister advanced to our beds with the last two babies in her arms. Ten-pound Billy Buster in the bed next to mine already looked about six months old. His wide blue eyes took in everything and when he was slipped into his waiting mother's arms she cooed and clucked, while he grunted like a large suckling pig. Her little treasure made immediately for the teat and began to gulp away with two chubby, tiny fists on either side of her great appendage. Pausing only to burp, he then went on sucking madly away.

Meanwhile, on Sister's other arm was a small scrap of humanity, still asleep and taking no notice of the proceedings whatsoever. 'You will need to fatten this baby up,' Sister said with a disapproving look in my direction. 'Matron won't let her leave until she is five pounds at least.'

More humiliation was to come, because as I sat there eyeing the neat little bundle that was still fast asleep, Sister Blood sat down on the bed, whisked the baby up and pushed her small face into my breast. She tried it from all angles, even pushing the tiny mouth under my armpit.

'Inverted nipples!' she roared, and the whole ward looked up, hearing the disapproval in her voice. Patricia's lips shut tight. A stubborn streak plainly indicated that this was not her favourite can of milk. She promptly went back to sleep.

Sister Blood was not about to give up. Again the infant's head was pushed into the teat in a vain attempt to encourage the sad little nipple to rise from its crumpled state long enough for my babe to get the hang of it. Neither babe nor nipple responded. While Sister Blood fumed and I howled, the ward looked on amused, and I was left in no doubt that I was a pitiful failure.

During the whole time I was at the nursing home, I had but one visitor. When I looked up and saw Margaret coming down the ward, her cheeky face wreathed in a wide grin, my spirits soared immediately. We spent the entire visit giggling together. She opened the locker by the side of my bed, looking for a container for the small bunch of violets she had brought for me, and pounced triumphantly on a little fish-paste jar. She washed the jar and filled it with water and placed the violets on the locker beside me. They were such a heavenly blue colour, and I pressed my face into them. They reminded me of cool places in the woods where we went when we were kids. It's funny how the fragrance of flowers lingers like memories.

Matron was concerned that there was no one at home to take care of us. Later the next day she came and sat on my bed and explained that she wished it were possible for me to stay for a few days. She looked relieved but not wholly convinced when I said I would be all right.

'I want you to go and see the doctor about that cough of yours,' she said. 'And as soon as possible get to the clinic for the free National Dried Milk. I doubt if you are going to be able to feed this lass of yours.' She leaned forward to touch my arm and pressed it reassuringly. 'Persevere though, my dear; you will find it so much more rewarding.'

The following morning as I stood on the windswept steps of the nursing home, waiting for the taxi to take me home, Matron handed me my baby wrapped up in the shawl I had so painstakingly made for her. Then she pulled up the collar of my coat and walked with me down the flight of steps to where the cab had pulled up. As I waved her goodbye, I felt a slight pang of regret that now I really was on my own and realised I would miss the dull but reassuring routine of the ward. From now on there would be no nursing staff to wait on me, or take the baby at night, to bath it and change it. These duties would be mine. I leaned back further in the taxi so that my ribcage was clear of the armrest because the pressure was hurting my side.

The taxi manoeuvred the maze of little streets and finally turned into Mill Lane. On this blustery March day, the smell from the gasometer was worse than ever and as I opened my purse to pay him I saw the taxi driver wrinkle his nose in disgust. He quickly reversed onto the dirt track by the side of the house and was gone. I sighed and inserted the key in the lock. Carrying the case and my baby, I found this simple feat alarmingly complicated, and was glad to reach the dark hallway and shabby stairway, where Robbie was almost halfway down to meet us, her laboured breath loud and rasping.

I set down the case and stood waiting for her to reach the last step. She looked at Patricia and her lovely grey eyes lit up when she pulled aside the shawl to gaze at her. I sank down on the bottom step with Robbie, and sat for a while telling her all about the nursing home and making her laugh with the saga of the goddess and Billy Buster in the next bed.

She got up and went into the tiny kitchen to make me a cuppa, calling out to me that she had taken an extra pint of milk from the corner shop only that morning just in case I came home. I gave her the baby to hold and pulled down the bed. I placed a rubber sheet and a folded flannelette blanket on one side and, carefully removing the woollen shawl from her, I put my precious bundle in the bed. I couldn't wait to crawl in beside her, for I felt so ill and tired and ached all over.

The next time I awoke was to see the sun through the partly opened green blind, dancing on my bed. I lay there, not wishing to move because I felt so weary. I heard the sounds of the day's activities going on outside, and the sounds of people further up the street talking. The wind was still high, and from time to time blew in gusts, rattling the windows; where the window was not closed, I could feel the cold wind on my face, but I was too weary to get up and close it. The baby was well below the bedclothes so there was no fear of her being in a draught. After a while I drifted off again.

It was the morning of the third day when I awoke and felt hungry. I knew this was a good sign. When I put my feet on the cold lino, I shivered, for the room was icy cold. Today I would have to light a fire and give Patricia her first bath, but first I must find something to eat. I thrust my feet into old slippers and pulled on a coat. Kneeling in front of the sideboard, I prayed fervently that I would find a box of Shredded Wheat, then I could warm up the last of the milk to pour over them. Alas, there was nothing except a handful of Quaker Oats at the bottom of a box and in desperation I stuffed them into my mouth, swilling them down with the last of the milk. It tasted a bit sour, but I took no notice and finished off the oats. I was breathless by the time I finished, but the hunger pangs had abated, and I got up slowly to make a pot of tea and to pinch a drop of Robbie's fresh milk.

Fortified and feeling better, I set about raking out the dead grey ashes from the fireplace and soon had a bright fire going. I pulled up the green blinds so that the pale yellow shafts of March sunlight shone through the window and filled the room with the promise of spring. I glanced at my daughter, who was now wide awake, not making a sound but staring round the room, with her big clear eyes seeming to take in everything. She had been so good these last three days, hardly moving or making a sound, but now I must bath her and freshen her up. I wondered how I would score on this, my first operation. When the bath was ready, and I had made sure everything I needed was to hand, I went to lift her gently and felt a wave of guilt when I discovered she was wet through right up her back.

When her little body touched the warm water, she gave a convulsive little movement but soon relaxed and seemed to enjoy the soaping and soaking. I was glad when the towelling stage was reached, as it had been an ordeal for both of us. Tomorrow it would become easier, I told myself, and laid Patricia on the bed to dress her. As I did so, I felt a flow of milk rush through my breast and trickle down my chest. I was so surprised. I guess it was all that resting in bed.

'No cold milk for you this morning, miss,' I laughed, and held her close to me, trying to encourage her small button mouth to take a firm hold of that stupid little nipple. She began to suck almost immediately, pulling with strong, swift gulps that seemed to stimulate nerves right inside me. I felt the pressure go right through to my back, so that I winced with the pain of it. She lay there afterwards, just looking up at me, and I felt a strong surge of mother love rise up within me. I pulled her to me so that I felt the warmth and sweetness of her.

'I'll make it up to you, Patty,' I said. 'I promise I will make it up to you.'

The Mauve Pram

I started out to collect a pram that Margaret had promised me. She told me it wasn't up to much but it would keep the baby warm and dry and be better than nothing. The baby was bathed and all ready, wrapped up in a warm shawl because, although it was April, the sky was grey and occasional flakes of white snow blew in my face. I was glad when I finally arrived at the row of neat little houses in Clyde Street. When I cuddled up in the big wooden chair by her blazing fire, I thought back with nostalgia to the happy days I had spent with her and wished we were still neighbours.

The boys went wild with delight when they saw the baby and demanded that their mother have another baby. She didn't answer. She just winked at me and told Tommy to get the pram out of the shed. Tommy looked at his mother and cried out in protest, 'What, give our pram away? What will you do if you have another baby?'

'Can't think about that till your dad comes home,' she laughed, and shooed him outside.

I went to stand by the back door but was unprepared for what I saw. As the pram finally emerged from the shed, very dusty and covered in cobwebs, I blinked at the colour of it. Margaret laughed aloud when she saw my face and with twinkling eyes explained that her husband had painted it mauve when she had to use it for her second little un.

'A good clean-up will work wonders,' she assured me. 'And the hood's not torn, neither is the apron. She'll be as snug as a bug in a rug.'

And the two boys thought that so funny that they giggled uncontrollably. There was a great deal of rubbing down and polishing. It was true that the pram would be better than trying to carry Patricia around in my arms. I did not have any money for a pram, and if I could have afforded the carriage of my dreams for this first baby of mine, it would have been a high Silver Cross carriage that I would have been so proud to have wheeled around.

The bottom end of the pram could be let down to make a pushchair. Two little silver clips kept that section of the pram in position and formed a deep well in the bottom of the pram when upright. Margaret said that it was great for holding all your groceries and would even take a bag of coal as well. I put the baby in the pram on a blanket that Margaret had found for me and pushed the pram out onto the pavement. I never did tell her that every time I manoeuvred a kerbstone, I lost the babe as she slid down into the great well at the bottom of the pram.

I had to go to the clinic to have Patricia weighed and collect my two tins of National Dried Milk and free cod-liver oil and orange juice. The hall was full of mothers and babies, and nurses busy placing infants in a big weighing scoop and then recording it on a card. There was a general hum of conversation, young mothers excitedly discussing the new weight of their offspring with other mothers. Some were showing off their little darlings and discussing the latest knitting patterns and complicated stitches.

I was tired, for I had pushed the pram a long way. I didn't want to undress my baby in front of everyone. As yet, I had not got used to all the jerks and strange noises that came from her. I wanted only to collect the two tins of dried milk and be gone. Alas, a tall uniformed nurse curtly told me that I was late and might have to come back next week. She glanced at the small bundle in my arms and enquired if this was my first time. I nodded, and was then told to undress the baby and hurry and put her on the scales. Not feeling very pleased, I began the complicated task of extricating the matchstick arms from the clothing of my little fledgling. Ten minutes later, I was still there, trying desperately to avoid her slipping out of my arms and onto the floor. At home, I was used to dressing and changing her by putting her on the bed. The nurse standing impatiently beside me directed her remarks to the whole room and I was now the object of their amused stares. She picked up the baby and with a quick expert movement placed her on the cold weighing scales. Patty let out a howl of displeasure at the loss of her clothes and the coldness of the scales. At the same time, the nurse let out a stifled screech, which turned every eye in our direction and made me go hot under my armpits.

'This baby, this baby,' she repeated, 'has not gained an ounce.' And turning to me she demanded in the same tone, which struck terror into me, 'What have you been doing to this baby, starving her?'

There was an audible intake of breath as every pair of eyes now focused on me, the knitting patterns discarded. Here was a real live scandal. What self-respecting mother would want to starve her baby? What an unforgivable sin, when the government was already doling out free National Dried Milk and orange juice and cod-liver oil.

I saw the open hostility in their eyes and I was all set for flight. I had a hunted feeling and realised that this great institution could actually take my baby away from me. I removed the protesting scrap from the scales and began to dress her. I laid her on the floor where I knew she would be safe and where best I could handle her. I was on my knees beside her, feeling my face red and the tears very near. I ignored the nurse and her scathing remarks, and when I had finished dressing Patricia I wrapped the shawl very tightly round her and marched up to the tiny counter, where a young girl, leaning on her elbows, was taking in the whole procedure. When she saw me coming, she straightened up with an insolent stare. No doubt I was already condemned in her opinion. Of all the articles that passed for mothers, no doubt I took the biscuit.

I placed two round blue tokens on the counter and said in a calm, clear voice, 'Two tins of National Dried, please, and

I will take the cod-liver oil and orange juice only if they are free.'

I walked to the bottom of the hall where I had left the pram right by the entrance. All the brand-new prams were lined up against the wall in neat rows. Woollen pom-poms, beads and satin ribbons graced the fronts, and expensive eiderdowns and coloured blankets lay folded back waiting for the fortunate babies to be laid in them. The mauve monstrosity stood away from the rest, looking more like a garden wheelbarrow than a pram. With my nose in the air, I put Patty in the thing and the dried milk in the well. It was true what Margaret had said, a whole week's groceries could be stored in the bottom. I could even pick up a bag of coal on the way home.

The line of eyes that had followed my progress up to the counter had reversed whilst following me down the room. A silence fell and the hush continued as their eyes followed me making for the hideous lilac-colour pram. Nobody moved as I pushed open the door and the pram, baby and I made our exit. Then a great burst of laughter, disturbing and mocking, came through an open window. I leaned over to hang onto Patty and prevent her slipping into the bottom of the pram again as I let it down over the kerb, and then I ran as fast as my weary legs could carry me all along the road. When I was out of sight of the clinic, I stopped for breath, filled with humiliation and rage. I stood there white and shaking, and knew that I was the only one who could make things change for me. Suddenly I was filled with a great longing for Bristol and all that was dear and familiar.

'We are going home,' I whispered to Patty. 'You and I are going home.'

I dropped my first two shillings towards the fare home into a chipped cup and set it resolutely away in a cupboard. I knew that I could not take immediate flight, and it would mean saving a few precious shillings each week for months yet.

I had not seen Robbie for some time. On the brief occasions when I saw her on the stairs or in the scullery, I was always busily getting ready to go out for the day. Today we were going again into Cleethorpes with Margaret and the two boys. Robbie's eyes brightened when she saw Patty and she stopped to talk to her. I thought nothing of the unusual pallor of Robbie's white face or the blueness of the thin lips drawn so tightly in one thin line because of her difficulty in breathing. I had seen her so often gasping on the stairs. Often she stayed in her bed all day, only emerging for brief periods to enquire where we had been that day and to view the progress of the baby with that bright smile of hers.

I had heard from John, who was now in Gibraltar. He said he'd like some books as they were difficult to get, hoped I was well and that I would write soon to let him know if he had a son. Now I had an address, I could write. It was six weeks since I'd seen him and he had become a vague figure standing somewhere in the background. Like so many other women in those war years, I had to carry on alone; the whole burden of bringing up the children fell on us. I wrote to tell him that a baby girl was now very much alive and kicking and that her name was Patricia Joy. I hoped he would approve, both of the baby girl and the name I had given her.

I arrived at Margaret's. She excitedly told me that Tom Bradley, my former landlord, had acquired a whole roll of material on the black market and was letting it go cheap for two bob a yard. I was full of interest, for Margaret had told me many a time that she could easily run up a dress for me on that treadle machine of hers. She was a wizard on the machine and I could do with a new dress. I thought about the little cracked cup that held my cash to get me home.

The next moment she was showing me a pattern that she insisted would be just right for me. I capitulated and urged her to get it for me as soon as possible. The next few days found us busy laying out the pattern on the material. I raided the cup with a slight feeling of guilt, knowing that such extravagance would set me back many weeks from my goal. Still, I argued, it would help to make the waiting all the more bearable. As Margaret snipped away with the scissors, I could almost see myself in that finished dress. It was going to be cut on a princess flare, with a Peter Pan collar and cuffs, and buttons all the way down the front. I would buy a cord-tasselled belt and daringly leave the top button undone.

'Brazen hussy,' Margaret laughed, with her mouth full of pins. 'You'll have all the old men falling off their bikes looking round at you.'

I couldn't wait for the dress to be finished.

The house was strangely quiet when I entered it that night, and I became aware that I hadn't seen or heard Robbie for the past few days. I called up the stairs to ask if she would like a cup of tea, but there was no answer and I suddenly became alarmed. It was not only the sombre silence of the house that alarmed me, but something else that made me race up the stairs two at a time to pound on Robbie's door. It was a kind of inner knowledge that I had seen her lovely wistful smile for the last time when she had followed me to the gate and waved bye-bye to me.

Oh, why hadn't I shown Robbie some concern? Why hadn't I called out last night to make sure she was all right? My mind had been too full of that damned dress, so eager was I to sit by Margaret and watch the material speeding under the needle and those active hands of hers transforming the soft green jersey into a dress that would be exciting to wear. Having that dress meant so much to me, a kind of reward now the long months of pregnancy were over, and I wanted to feel attractive again.

After Patricia was born, there had been no one to come home to, there had been no cuddles, no one to make a fuss of me and the baby. Just the two of us in that cold little room with no one to confide in that I was scared as hell with the weight of responsibility of a baby to look after, and feeling so ill. When Margaret bought the length of material I had come home and daydreamed about the finished dress. I saw myself swinging easily and confidently down the road with those two top buttons undone, the belt with the tassels tied loosely at the side, bare legs in white sandals, giving a toss of my dark curls to all the women staring so enviously at me. It made me feel better, somehow; a good old fantasy dream helped all the mundane things, and life was eighty per cent mundane.

When I pushed open the door, I knew instantly by the deathly silence in that shadowy room that Robbie was no longer with us. She lay propped back against the pillows, her half-closed eyes now focused on something beyond any mortal scene. Her mouth had fallen slightly open as though caught unawares in one of those painful intakes of breath she had borne uncomplainingly in life. My tears that fell were tears of self-pity because she was such a gentle soul and I loved her so. Now, never again would I see her grey eyes light up with pleasure and her features soften when she saw Patricia.

Once again the landlord of the Rising Sun came to my rescue and phoned for the ambulance and for Robbie's sister, who lived at Loughborough. The ambulancemen came and took Robbie away wrapped in a white sheet. Robbie's sister arrived the following day. She was as plump and stout as Robbie had been thin and tall. She had none of the gentleness and humility of her sister; she was businesslike and brusque.

'The house is unsafe,' she said with finality. 'And I have no wish to continue with the letting of it. No doubt it will be earmarked for demolition. Despite all our pleading and attempts to get her to give up this house and come and live with me, she insisted on remaining here on this awful bomb-site. And all because she said she wanted to remain independent. Sheer lunacy, I call it!'

She made this last statement with such scorn, as though being a spinster and independent should not go together.

'Not all women choose marriage,' I said. 'Because Robbie chose another road, you should not be contemptuous of her. She was a very brave person.'

She did not pursue this line of argument, although it was very obvious she had no sympathy with it. 'I have a very limited time in which to settle my sister's affairs,' she went on. 'I have to be back in Loughborough by next week and intend to leave after the funeral. Shall you be happy with a week's notice, then? I am sorry it is all such short notice, but you see how it is.'

I wheeled Patty round to Margaret's on the day of Robbie's funeral, so that I could go to the service. There was just Robbie's sister and myself there. We sang Robbie's favourite hymn, 'Oh love that will not let me go, I rest my weary soul in thee.'

Later, when the coffin was being lowered into the earth, I pulled a red rose from the wreath that her sister had sent and that was now placed by the side of that gaping hole. I threw the rose onto the shiny bright wooden casket and whispered my own goodbye to Robbie. She had reached her final destination. I walked thoughtfully back to Mill Lane for the last time and the silence of an empty house.

Going Home

A few days later, I stood on the platform of Grimsby Docks station once more. I had been away from Bristol for almost two years. As I stood there, I recalled the foggy November night when I arrived and I caught sight of John under the solitary lamp on this very platform. Was I the same girl who had run to that dark figure, full of excitement, waiting for those arms to reach out and hold her, assuring her that she had been wrong to have doubts? I stood by the lamp alone now, and that same young girl seemed to mock me from the shadows.

I waited for a lull in the lines of people queuing for tickets and finally approached the ticket booth. My heart was beating so fast and the uniform-clad figure of the ticket clerk did not even look up as he called, 'Next, please!'

I hesitated before blurting out, 'I want to get to Temple Meads, but I haven't got any money. But I promise I'll send the money as soon as I get home, honestly I will!'

His head jerked up then, for this small chit of a girl he couldn't even see properly had shattered the smooth routine of his morning. He peered over his glasses to get a proper look at me whilst I burst into tears of nervous agitation, and the people in the queue behind me began to shuffle uncomfortably. The reaction to my tears was electric. A young soldier in the queue behind me fumbled with his wallet in the back pocket of his trousers and reached forward to thrust a folded note onto the pay box, whilst several people stepped out of line and craned their necks to see what was going on.

The man in the ticket box coughed, then waved the back of his hand over the money as if to tell the young man it would not be necessary, and motioned me to come round to the side entrance. The young soldier picked up his cash and accompanied me to the door of the tiny office and helped me into a swivel chair. Filled with abject misery, I snivelled loud and long. The soldier handed me his handkerchief and finally the ticket clerk got rid of the queue and handed the soldier a cardboard ticket for me. Pointing towards a train that had pulled up on the other side of the track, he told the young man to help me on the train and make sure I was all right. I allowed the young man to take Patricia from me, and he piloted me over the bridge and onto the train.

Once seated on the train, he came in and sat opposite me, holding Patty easily and effortlessly in the crook of his arm. He looked at me with deep concern, then reached into his pocket with his free hand and brought out a flask. Handing it to me, he urged me to take a sip. 'Go on, it will calm your nerves.'

201

I did as I was told and took a big sip. The brandy burned my throat and took my breath away so that I coughed and spluttered, but I could feel the warmth spreading all over me. Some twenty minutes later we reached a station and the soldier rose from his seat and gently returned Patricia to me. 'Will you be all right now?'

'Of course. And I shall be eternally grateful for what you've done for me today.'

He squeezed my hand, opened the door and was gone, swallowed up in a sea of nameless people. The carriage seemed empty without him and I wished he could have stayed.

At King's Cross, I collected my luggage and expertly pulled Patricia onto my left hip so that I could have one hand free. I took out my purse containing the precious six shillings that I had managed to save and not surrender to the ticket man and walked confidently to the cab rank and calmly asked for Paddington.

More memories filled my mind as I neared familiar countryside and we finally puffed into Temple Meads Station. What changes would I find here, and how would I be greeted, after an interval of two years? Then I started to notice the bomb damage; the buffet and the waiting room were no longer there. I missed the friendly station that had housed all those bright seaside posters along with the bustle of porters struggling with great cases and trunks denoting holidays. All of that was gone, replaced by a kind of austere politeness, like a quiet acceptance of what was lost.

Outside, I noticed that the clock and all the façade of Temple Meads had been damaged. At the bottom of the incline there had been a paint warehouse where a pile of rubble now stood – that must have been a blaze. I stopped again on Bristol Bridge. I saw the gaping hole in the roof of St Peter's and stood gazing in abject misery at the devastation of my beloved Castle Street, now barricaded off because of the dangerous buildings and the piles of rubble where it had almost been razed to the ground.

I had to retrace my steps and cross the bridge again, skirting Castle Street and coming out at the end of Tower Lane, and entered Old Market, the old tram terminus before the war. On Saturdays the stalls were piled high with fruit and vegetables and flowers, packed with the crowds who chatted and laughed and carried home their bargains on the open-decked trams.

No tramcars now. Instead a solitary bus to Kingswood stood by the Shepherd's Hall. *Greyhound Bus Service,* it said all along one side, and I made my way to board the vehicle. I prayed that nothing would have changed at Kingswood. I didn't know what sort of reception I would get and hoped that my absence would have mellowed my mother. I was desperate for a relationship with her, and had only received three letters from her since I'd been away. I hoped she would be glad to see me, for where else would I stay?

When I alighted at Downend Road I saw the damaged Odeon Cinema. With apprehension I realised how near that had been to home. Then I had my hand on a new green gate with a black-painted latch. I remembered the old one with its peeling paint and the dented brass handle with the loose spindle that Lady pulled at with her teeth so that the whole lot would fall on the ground with a clatter.

Everything else was the same: the privy door right next to the back kitchen, and the tin bath still hanging on the wall by its six-inch nail, but the middle room window and the top bedroom window were boarded up – bomb blast, no doubt, from the bomb that had fallen on the cinema at the top of Halls Road.

I opened the back door quietly. The old tap was still dripping and the great iron stove still stood along the wall. The dresser was bare and pictures taken from the walls left pale spaces as reminders of their former friendly splendour. My mother was busy on her knees, wrapping china in newspaper, and her head was half hidden in the interior of the wooden packing case. She glanced up, startled at my quiet entry into the room, and peered through the semi-darkness to where I stood with Patricia in my arms. She stopped to look more closely, as though she could hardly believe the evidence of her own eyes.

'Our Joyce? What are you doing home?'

I came further into the room and sat on the arm of the old faded velvet chair. I was so tired. I wanted to wake up and not see all the changes that I could not cope with, not today and not here. My mother sighed a deep sigh.

'Well, you've chosen a fine time to come home, my girl. Another hour and we should have been gone. We're moving today.'

'Moving?' I repeated stupidly. 'Why? Where?'

'We've bought a business.'

She broke off suddenly to turn to my father, who had just come in from the front room, to say to him, 'Look what the wind has just blown in. It's our Joyce.'

'Well, well, well,' was all my dad could say, but he came over to the baby, now asleep in my arms. 'Nice little thing.' He continued to look at the baby, obviously at a loss to know what to do or say. 'Look, we can't even offer you a cup of tea. Everything is packed, and we are waiting for the van to arrive.'

'It's all right,' I now hastened to assure them. 'After I've seen Bert and Auntie Elsie, I'm going to Gwen's. John's sister, you know. She's expecting me.'

The relief on their faces made me smile. The lie that had come so glibly had even taken me by surprise. I had expected many things, but not this.

'When we turned out the understairs cupboard we found nothing but doll's arms and legs.' My mother was looking at me accusingly. 'That right, Chas?' She shot this question at my father, who was now helping her finish packing the last pile of plates.

'Aah,' he assented and laughed at the recollection. 'All those lovely dolls your mother dressed for you and you pulled all their arms and legs off.'

'Hope you don't start pulling her limbs off in the same way,' she shot at me, and I stood back at the open hostility in her voice.

'There's one complete dolly left; you might like to have it for her,' said my father, and he went over to where a very dishevelled doll with matted hair lay propped in a corner.

'It still says, "Mama",' he said, and turned the doll over so that a sad and pathetic little 'Maa-maa' came from it.

'I must go,' I said, for I wanted suddenly to run from the room. I knew in that instant that the enmity between my mother and me would always be there. The precious bond between us had been severed the day when I left that very room as a child for Painswick. I had hoped when I returned home with Patty that the broken relationship would be replaced with a friendship between two women. But it was never to be.

I picked up the doll for Patty. It bent over as I did so and uttered again its mournful cry. From somewhere deep down inside of me where all the heartbreak was buried I heard the cry echo and re-echo.

'Maa-maa,' it wailed. 'Maa-maa.'

Nightingale Valley

*T*he sun was just setting and birdsong could be heard in the orchard when we turned down the slope into Nightingale Valley, where Gwen and Harry's cottage was situated, right by St Anne's Station. Elsie and Bert insisted on driving me over to Brislington in their little Jowett car, and stayed long enough to hear Gwen declare that she wouldn't hear of us staying with anyone else but them.

Oak Cottage was one of a pair that stood squarely facing up the valley so that the cottages with their gardens full of flowers were the first things you saw. On one side there were woods and fields and at the bottom of a steep bank on the other side ran the main railway line with the tiny halt of St Anne's. On the other side of the railway line and over the bridge was an avenue of bungalows and private houses with mature trees that graced the gardens and lined the entire length of the road. And beyond that again was St Anne's Woods.

Harry reminded me of a pilgrim father. When he had occasion to chastise his brood of two boys and a girl, he would look very grim and stern as they stood in front of him and he delivered his lecture. After they had been dismissed, I detected a light chuckle, but he always turned aside so that the telltale smile did not show, and I suspected that he was a softie at heart. However, he was both firm and just, and his children accepted the telling-off, knowing it was justified. Gwen never interfered with her husband's authority as head of the household and, if the running of it was slightly Victorian, I could not oppose it. For here in this cottage I found a sense of love and stability that I never found in that loveless house in South Road.

A tin of sweets was kept on a top shelf, as a reward for jobs well done. Nobody was allowed to dig to the bottom for favourites, you took from the top or went without. No one questioned this golden rule. Gwen and Harry called each other 'dear'. Harry, as the head of the house, came first and was served first, then came the children in order: John, Tony and Barbara, and Gwen always put herself last. My forthright views were dismissed with a friendly sniff from Gwen – 'Joyce is on her soapbox again!' – and she held to but one, simple moral judgement: right was right, and wrong was no man's right. She was happy and even-tempered. I never heard her shout or raise her voice. Flustered, maybe, and indignant, yes, but for the space that two more people took up in that tiny two-up and two-down, not one grouse or grumble did she ever utter. I shall always be grateful to those two people for the love they extended to Patty and me.

At five-thirty each evening, Gwen took Patty to meet Harry from work. He was a railwayman and worked on the station right by the side of the house. Patty got a special hug and a kiss from Uncle Harry, who was a firm favourite. When he was locked away in his shed she knew he was making her something special which was a secret and he wasn't to be disturbed. He made all the children's toys: a toy duck that bobbed up and down when she pulled it along, a wooden clown that jumped over a bar when you squeezed the sides together, a wooden cot for her dolly with blankets that Auntie Gwen had made, and now he was making her a small trolley. A new tooth, first steps, and first words were a celebration for the whole family. Sometimes I felt a pang of sadness that my own mother missed all this, but I took heart from the fact that these simple but precious things were valued in this family and I felt proud and important because of it.

Whilst Gwen looked after Patty, I went to work at Magna Products at Warmley, a big engineering firm with huge wartime contracts. Because of the shortage of men, women were coming into the foundries and works. There were women conductors on the buses, taking over until the men came home again – though, at the end of the war, they were not quite so keen to let go of their new-found independence. The end of this war brought many unheard-of and undreamed-of changes.

I was introduced to a great monster called a milling machine. A press of a button set the whole thing in motion and a huge saw cut slots in round chunks of metal. A trickle of milky-white liquid played onto the saw and it was part of my job to ensure this lubricating fluid was always kept running, otherwise the saw would buckle with the heat of the revolutions –and it was a very expensive machine. Anyway, I became proficient at handling this machine and so they gave me two to run. As one machine stopped, the other was set in motion. From time to time, a white-coated inspector came round with a micrometer to make sure the slots were exactly the right size. This was extremely important, as they had to be milled to a thousandth of an inch. Apart from the boredom of merely walking up and down to stop and start these great things, I had very little else to do, although I was thrilled and proud to learn that it was my two milling machines that helped to make the bonus for the whole shop. With the extra money in my pay packet, I was able to save more and have money to give to Gwen for my keep and give Patty pretty dresses.

One morning, on day shift and just about to clock on, I saw my father in the queue ahead of me, and called out to him. His face lit up when he saw me; he was so pleased that he walked with me all the way to the foundry and insisted on introducing me to his foreman and the rest of the men already there. He said that because of the war they could not get the young lads to make the cores for the moulds, but now they had taken on women for the work. He looked down at the floor before admitting that they were far better at it than any of the men, with far fewer 'wasters'. I noticed that he was careful not to use factory slang, which was 'shitters'. I smiled now when I remembered how my mother always told him off when he used the word at home.

'How is everything?' I blurted out suddenly, for I was anxious to know how Dad came to be working at Magna Products, since the last time I saw him he was so full of going into business with Mum. Again he looked uncomfortable. He shuffled his feet and cleared his throat. My directness always disconcerted him and having to be disloyal made him feel uneasy.

'Not enough for both of us to do in the shop,' he said gruffly. 'And your mother is a better business head than I shall ever be. This is what I am better at.' He spread his hands expansively around at the factory. 'She is happy at what she is doing back there.'

His head jerked backwards, indicating some obscure location that he hoped I wouldn't probe into, but this hesitancy only made me more determined, so that my next question made him even more flustered than before.

'Where is this shop of yours, then?'

'At Ashley Hill.' His answer was evasive and came much too quickly, but I was not about to be put off now.

'Whereabouts in Ashley Hill?'

'About halfway up the hill,' he said reluctantly.

Like some revelation, it became obvious to me that there must be some other reason for Dad's disinclination to disclose their present whereabouts. I met my father's eyes in an attempt to compel him to be honest with me so that we could get back on the same footing I had enjoyed with him as a little girl, but he shifted his gaze to the floor and refused to look at me. In that instant, I knew for certain that he was remembering incidents which had caused him so much pain, and which, because he could not or would not blame my mother, he was shifting the guilt onto me.

'Dad,' I said and moved towards him, wanting to plead that this alienation was more than I could bear, and talking might ease our pain, even if it didn't solve anything.

'No, don't say anything.' His voice was dull and flat and he stared into space. 'I blame you, Joyce, for what happened. You were there and knew what was going on. You should have told me.'

Well, it was out now; he knew about Patrick and blamed me. It was another load of guilt to carry on my back, and it never occurred to me to defend myself against his accusations. I was glad at that moment to hear the works bell, a summons for commencement of the day's common tasks. Dad still stood there motionless with his hands thrust deep in his pockets, and with a look of torment on his face. I knew I would never penetrate that formidable wall of resistance, and I walked away and left him standing there.

I sighed and pushed the button of the great milling machine and heard it whirr into activity.

It was spring again, and I had slept long into the morning. Night shift at Magna Products always drained me and I never quite got used to sleeping during the day. The incessant chattering of the birds outside my window and the warm May sunshine now filling the room disturbed me so that I stretched lazily and lay there wide awake. From my bed in the tiny front room I could see trees in blossom all the way up the valley. From time to time I heard Patty pulling the wooden truck that Harry had made for her, scraping past the window as she followed Gwen about the garden or helped her collect eggs from the henhouse.

I yawned and proceeded to dress. Life was peaceful here in the valley, and the past eighteen months had passed happily and quickly. I came down into the kitchen just as Gwen was making a pot of tea, and then sat by the window, keeping an eye on Patty, still busily pulling her trolley along, her face red with the exertion of piling stones into it, and trying to extricate the wheel from where it had lodged round the canvas-chair leg.

'God bless her,' Gwen said. 'She ain't a ha'p'orth of trouble.' And she went out immediately to help Patty with the truck.

I followed Gwen into the yard, still sipping my tea, and sat in the canvas chair. Harry, who had been digging in the garden, was shouting something to Gwen, and pointing excitedly up the valley. I saw Gwen shading her eyes against the sun and looking in the direction to where Harry was still pointing. Suddenly she exclaimed:

'My God! It's our Bert.'

Then, scooping Patty up in her arms, she too pointed to a figure striding down the valley. 'It's your daddy, my love. It's your daddy coming home to see you.'

Dazed now, I got up and went to stand by her side. Then he was standing there before me, this tall, tanned serviceman, his eyes in that bronzed, smiling face seeming more startlingly blue than ever. A lock of wayward hair over his brow was bleached a corn yellow. I went forward to greet him, and stood in the circle of his arms whilst Gwen and

Harry clucked excitedly round us, and Patty hid behind Gwen's skirt, not very certain yet about this stranger. Finally we all moved towards the house, with everybody trying to talk at once, until Gwen in her practical way marched in front, saying she would put the kettle on.

It was about an hour later, when John had washed and changed, that he motioned me to come outside. We began to walk up the valley and towards St Anne's Woods.

'You've changed,' he said at last, after we had walked along in silence for a while. 'I can't say how, but you have changed.'

'You mean, two years and a baby later,' I replied.

He didn't answer right away, but I knew he was remembering the house at Mill Lane when he was packing to go to Gibraltar, and his last goodbye to me before Patty was born.

'Don't make it too hard for me,' he pleaded. 'You know that when a posting comes through, on active service I have to go. It doesn't mean I don't miss you.'

I didn't answer. I knew it would always be me that had to understand. I would always have to be ready to care for him, and to make things easy for him, and to be strong enough for the two of us.

He pulled me to him once more. 'I'm home on leave for a whole fortnight. Let's make the most of it.' And he bent his head to kiss me. It was then that I remembered I was due to go to work on the night shift that very night.

I could tell by the way Gwen gave a genteel little sniff when I returned to the house that she was not at all in favour of the idea. 'Go to work,' she said, 'when our Bert has come all the way from Gib just to spend his leave with you?' And her voice held a note of incredulity.

Harry winked at John and said, 'No celebration for you tonight, my son. She doesn't have a headache, but she does have to go to work.'

'The war effort can't stop just because servicemen come home on leave,' I retorted, and felt I had scored a point. But the weight of opinion was against me, and I phoned the works to say I wouldn't be in that night. It was obvious that John wouldn't be able to stay with me at the cottage, so we arranged to go together to his mother's at Repton Road. Patty was used to waving me bye-bye when I went to work, and was happy to give us a send-off from the safety of Uncle Harry's arms. I knew she would be well looked after for the week I was away, and she waved to us all the way up the valley until we turned the corner and were out of sight.

My mother-in-law greeted us with warm enthusiasm, overjoyed to see her 'darling Bertie' home safe and sound once more and to know she would have the pleasure of his company for a whole week. She pressed her hands together and thanked the good Lord for returning her dear boy to the bosom of his family.

Later, when we were drinking tea from the best china tea service, which had been hastily taken from the sideboard, she suddenly remembered that she must make up the big double bed in the front bedroom. As she passed me on her way up the stairs, she nudged my arm and whispered, 'My Bertie was conceived in that double bed.'

I slopped some tea into my saucer for she made me jump,

215

not from the news but from the sudden jogging of my arm. When she returned from making the bed, she had on her outdoor things. 'Come and have a little drink on me, kiddos,' she said, looking at us both. 'A nice glass of stout makes me sleep and this calls for a celebration.'

Outside, she linked her arm through John's and put him in the middle so we could share him. She walked very tall and straight and was proud to be on the arm of her uniformed son.

The lounge was quiet and held an air of respectable decorum, not at all like the noisy bars at Grimsby, with their crowds of servicemen and the beer-swilled tabletops. Somehow, although I could not have explained why, I missed the free and easy atmosphere. Not even in the public bar was there any sound of laughter, or singing, or a piano-player – perhaps that would come later.

I sat in a corner and watched John's animated conversations with the older men. I guessed they were the fathers of schoolfriends and old neighbours. Several women came up to speak to Minnie, their gaze going swiftly to the bar when she indicated her son standing there. For the better part of the night, the men propped up the bar and the women stayed in the seats, and they made no attempt to join us. Sitting in the corner, with a glass of cold shandy more lemonade than beer, I was bored. The drink did nothing for me except fill me up with gas and chill my stomach. I yearned for one of those delicious egg-flips, but it never occurred to me to go to the bar and ask for one, or ask Minnie to get me one. I began to yawn.

Minnie was on her second stout when I was startled to

hear her comment as though she read my thoughts, 'Have a decent drinkie on me.'

I watched her go to the bar and wondered if she was clairvoyant enough to know what I would like, but she returned with a new drink for me called port and lemon. Things brightened up considerably after that, and as she lifted her glass to say, 'Cheers kid,' she gave a little giggle as her nose went into the froth at the top of her third milk stout. It was sometime later, when the barman was clearing the table of glasses, that she decided to burst into song. She reached out and grabbed his arm and began to serenade him. Whilst he gave an embarrassed little laugh and tried to disengage his arm, she gave a rendering that would have done music hall star Florrie Ford full justice. When she came to the end of the song, in a fit of devilry and making my voice as common as possible, I joined in, 'You're my heart's delight, I love you, Nellie Dean. Sweet Nellie Dean.'

John hastily left the bar and hurried over to help Minnie into her coat and usher us both through the door. When we got back to the house, Minnie was begging me not to make her laugh any more or she would wet her knickers. We both sat on the bottom step and laughed hysterically. Without a word, John swept passed us and went upstairs. I knew he was embarrassed at being shown up in company, but Minnie and I didn't care.

One day at the end of the week he came down to breakfast to discover he was out of fags. To run out of the weed was a dire calamity, second to none, and he stared at the empty packet with a dark face. I pushed a cup of tea in front of him and waited for the outburst. 'How can I drink tea, woman, without a fag?'

His mother came into the room at that precise moment, wearing a faded dressing gown and shuffling along in a pair of slippers several sizes too big. 'Out of ciggies, dear boy?' she cooed. She immediately went to the dresser, where three jugs of varying sizes hung from brass hooks along the shelf. From the middle jug she extracted a fresh packet of cigarettes and beamed with pleasure when her beloved Bertie threw his arms around her neck and kissed her. The black cloud vanished and the sun came out. When his gaze travelled over to me it conveyed the clear message that, just as his mother spoiled him, so he expected me to do the same. And I wondered why mothers spoiled their sons so.

A few days later a temporary posting to Ilfracombe came through for John, and I saw him off at Temple Meads. It seemed I was always waving goodbye, and he seemed always to be a slightly shadowy figure, only popping up from time to time, not staying long enough for either of us to get to know the other properly. Impulsively, he leaned out of the compartment window and said, 'If I can get digs, perhaps you and the nipper could come and join me. I'll write and let you know.'

A few weeks later I received his letter saying he had found lodgings if I still fancied joining him. He said they had not been easy to find, because the damn Yanks were everywhere, chucking their money around like confetti, waggling nylons and chocolates in front of the girls, who fell for them hook, line and sinker. 'Overpaid, oversexed and over here' was how he described them.

A family group – Gran and Gran'fer (*centre*), with brother Dennis behind them
Inset: Joyce, as a child, sitting in front of her Mum and Dad

Joyce's Mum
and Dad

Joyce's Mum
on her bike

Joyce in her
precious coat

Bertie,
at eighteen

Joyce, with her Raleigh bicycle, in the countryside near Fry's factory in Somerville

Joyce and her brother Dennis in 1942

Bertie and Joyce on their wedding day in 1939

Bertie with Joyce
and Pat on his only
leave in 1941

Joyce in Grimsby, 1940

Pat, Jacky and
Julie at the prefab

Darrell as
a toddler

Joyce at eighty

The weather was perfect, so I let my heart rule my head. I threw some things for Patty and me in a suitcase and made ready to leave. I was also ever so slightly inquisitive to see all those damned Yanks.

Ilfracombe

*I*t was true that the Yanks were everywhere. After John met us and escorted us into the main street, a jeep full of uni-formed airmen shrieked to a halt in front of a hotel and they all tumbled out, noisy and brash. My guess was that this little seaside town had never seen anything quite like it before. John watched them with disgust. Still piloting me by the arm, he hurried us past the hotel and on towards the top end of the street. Outside a café there were more Americans, sitting at little round tables with bright-coloured umbrellas, sipping cool drinks, and looking very tanned and good-looking.

'If you so much as encourage one of them . . . ' John was hissing in my ear.

'I will contrive to resist a mad and wild urge to hurl myself at every Yank I meet,' I hissed back at him, and wondered why he had brought me here, if they were going to bother him that much.

The guest house that he brought me to had an attic. I might have known it would be ours. To get up to this tiny room, you had to pull down a ladder. Patty thought this was a wonderful game, but I had my doubts. I saw the disadvantage of having to manoeuvre it in the middle of the night in order to get to the bathroom, which was on the next landing down. I hoped the bed was not next to a wall. It would be just my luck to have to climb over both of them when duty called.

I breathed a sigh of relief when I saw the bed set squarely in the middle of the room, although there was only just enough space to walk around it. There was just one other piece of furniture, a chest of drawers. A rough piece of wood with hooks attached served as a kind of wardrobe on which to hang clothes, and around the room was an assortment of tapestry texts. One proclaimed Behold I stand at the gate and knock. Feed my lambs, begged another. Over the head of the bed was a king-sized masterpiece: I am the unseen guest in every household, which I thought was a bit intimidating.

I tested the bed by lying full-length on it and bouncing up and down. I distrusted all beds after the lumpy sack in Mill Lane. To my delight, I found myself on a feather mattress. This was a bonus indeed. When we prepared for bed that night, I put Patty in the middle of us and ignored the pained expression on John's face. I told him that he had omitted to feed his flock or answer the door, and we could not make love because the unseen guest might be watching from the top of the bedpost. He failed to see the joke.

I was awakened by a woman's voice singing the latest hit song whilst brushing down the stairs: 'You must remember this, a kiss is just a kiss.' I lay for a long time listening to her sweet voice until she must have completed the stairs, and I heard the low tones of a conversation further downstairs. I yawned and began to dress to go in search of breakfast. When at first I did not see John I thought he had gone to the base, but to my surprise he was on the landing, ready to help Patty down, and over breakfast he offered to show us around Ilfracombe. He had a day off and we might as well make the most of it. The following Saturday would be my twenty-sixth birthday and our fourth wedding anniversary.

Even so, it took me a little by surprise when we stopped at a gem shop and John asked if there was anything in the window that took my fancy. When I began to show an interest in a tray of silver rings, he invited me into the shop and asked the assistant to show me some. I was particularly interested in a black onyx ring that fitted the little finger of my right hand. It felt and looked just right, and I was delighted when John passed the money over the counter to pay for it.

To get to the beach, we had to go through a quaint little tunnel. Patty was not impressed with the rather boisterous waves that broke onto the shore with the incoming tide. When the waves receded, they took with them tons of pebbles and sand, and made a great sucking, swishing sound. Those same waves pounded the formation of rocks along the shoreline and sent spray high in the air. Only when the tide was on the ebb and left behind safe little rock pools and warm inlets would it be safe to take her to that part of the beach to play.

We came away from the beach and made our way to a

green-velvet stretch of land called Hillsborough. We had bought Patty a small pink celluloid windmill on a stick. When you held it high above your head, the wind would send the tiny propellers flapping furiously around with a mad whirring sound. She ran along with it, laughing as she went.

At the top of the knoll, we could look right over onto another part of the beach, which, from where we were standing, looked like a series of tiny coves and inlets all along the coastline. The strong sun made the sand a deep golden colour, and with the brilliant blue sky this perfect setting was enticing. From where we stood looking down, it seemed possible that one small jump would bring us onto the inviting shoreline. I allowed my gaze to wander away, up to the line of scrub at the top of the beach. Rolls of barbed wire reached all along the clifftop, sticking out like a sore thumb and a stark reminder that in wartime nothing was as it seemed. I shuddered slightly and turned away, walking back down the hill again. I was getting hungry and John promised us tea. He knew a café that sold a smashing plate of fish and chips.

Joe's Café was in the High Street. You couldn't miss it, as it had his name in big black letters painted over the door. Joe did everything himself, there was no assistant. Before the war, Ilfracombe slumbered in an easy-going pace that seemed never to have altered, but the arrival of the Americans brought a buzz to the place. Whilst he worked, Joe kept up an informative stream of conversation. With his sleeves rolled up and a big white apron tied around his waist, he told us that the small hotel over the road was his, and that before the war he and his wife could depend only on the summer visitors. That was why he had opened up the café as another source of income. All this changed with the arrival of the air-force base and the coming of the Americans, who had commandeered both of the hotels in the main street. His wife ran the hotel now. He helped her all he could during the day, but enjoyed the work in the café, and that too was always busy. His wife was desperately looking for a bit more help.

'Just the job for you,' he said, looking directly at me. 'That's if you're interested.'

Walking back to the guest house, I mentioned to John that I would think about that offer. I began to enthuse about the nursery just around the corner for Patty, but stopped when I saw the look on his face.

'I want you to promise me that you will go home when my posting comes through. Promise me now,' he said. He stopped and took hold of my shoulders, as if to stress the point.

'What's so wrong with wanting to take a job in a hotel? It beats a dusty, stinking machine shop any day. And if it's the damn Yanks you're so afraid of, I could have just as much suspicion about you with all the damn girls in uniform.'

We walked back to the guest house in an angry silence. When we got there, he turned and left us without another word. I looked down at the tiny ring on the little finger of my right hand. Wearing a ring on that finger was a sign of independence. My independence and John's stubborn streak always seemed to meet head-on. Somehow, I could find no way to defuse the situation, and he could find no way to cope with a strong, independent-minded woman. I resolved that I would go to see Joe's wife to see what the job entailed. Before drifting off to sleep, I felt sad that the day that had started out so well had ended so badly. John's birth sign was Cancer the crab, a water sign, and mine was Leo the lion, a fire sign. I concluded that his water was always putting out my fire.

Joe's wife was plump and efficient and very well dressed. She smiled at us when I explained that her husband had mentioned she might need help, and opened the glass door wide and invited us inside. She led the way into a large bright kitchen and beckoned us to sit down at a big wooden table. She gave Patty a big glass of orange juice and poured two cups of tea from a large pot.

'I'm Doreen Cummins,' she said. 'You can call me Dora, everybody else does.' She put a piece of cake in front of Patty then leaned forward briskly. 'I need some help with the breakfast in the morning, and of course there will be the washing-up and the dining hall to be tidied, beds to be made each day and the laundry checked on Fridays.' She paused to look at Patty. 'There is a nursery round the corner. You could be away from here by early afternoon every day and I would give you two pounds a week, plus your breakfast and bed as well if you've nowhere to stay. How does that suit you?'

I blinked. Gosh! The money was a king's ransom with the breakfast and a bedroom on top. A nod was all that was needed to clinch the deal. And I could start on Monday, if that was all right with me. All was right with my world at that moment. It was only when Dora had seen us to the door and, still smiling, waved goodbye to us, that I remembered John. What if he refused to let me do it?

My heart gave a sudden lurch when, as we reached the café, I saw a familiar figure seated outside. All trace of his anger had vanished, and when he saw us he got up quickly to help me into a chair and order drinks for us. It was only when we were walking back to the digs that I blurted out that I had taken the job. It was out now. I screwed up my eyes and waited for the explosion. When nothing happened, I opened my eyes to look at him and to my surprise he remained calm. Presently he said, ever so quietly, 'I guessed you would.'

I rushed on regardless. I had to tell him about the bedroom, which was twin-bedded and had a toilet and bathroom just next door. Dora said he could stay any time he had a day off and I was sure he would love her. I stole a sideways glance. He wasn't mad, I could see that. Quite amiable, in fact. When eventually he did break the silence it was to tell me that the following weekend he would be off, and as it was my birthday and our anniversary he would come to the hotel and stay. Saturday he had a surprise in store for me so he wanted me to be ready to make as early a start as possible. Then he kissed me and was gone.

I paid the bill at the guest house and moved into the hotel on Sunday, ready to take up my duties the following morning, early. I buttered piles of rolls and toast, put them on plates and sent them along a smooth white countertop, along with mountains of sausages and beans. Bacon and eggs were served three times a week and always on Sundays. I sloshed coffee and tea into mugs set over a wire tray to take the spillage, and tackled the piles and piles of dirty crocks, never stopping until the last one had been dried and put away. Dora and I then sat down with a well-earned cuppa before going upstairs to tackle the bedrooms. On Fridays, the dirty washing was sent down a chute to be collected in bins and sent to the laundry. On Tuesdays, the clean bedding was checked and put away in the linen cupboard. The work was hard but enjoyable, and Dora was full of energy. We got on well together and she was a firm favourite with the Americans.

As promised, John arrived at the hotel on Friday night, and was introduced to Dora and Joe. Joe and John were soon talking about the high-speed launches of the RAF, and the Air Sea Rescue Service, and Dora thought my husband 'a grand fella'. She shooed me off at twelve-thirty the next day when she realised John wanted to take us out.

A blazing sun beating down on a white main street made a shimmering heat haze which dazzled and hurt our eyes and drained us of all energy as we walked along. I was glad when we turned towards Hillsborough and the belt of grass that was more restful to our eyes. The faint smell of driftwood mingled with seaweed and flotsam on the shoreline as we reached the top of the knoll, and the tiny cove below us seemed more inviting than ever. It was only when I became aware that we were dropping down towards one of those white-dotted coves that I began to look anxiously at John. We were actually walking along by the barbed-wire fencing.

A huge board with bold red letters warned us that this was GOVERNMENT PROPERTY, PRIVATE, KEEP OUT.

'Do you really mean to ignore all this?' I said, stopping to look at the warning notice.

John had Patty perched high on his shoulders. The silence all around us was broken only by the slight breeze off the sea, which turned the sails of her little coloured windmill. He didn't answer, but went on striding ahead. I followed, feeling slightly apprehensive. He stopped a bit further on and then I could see where an opening had been cut in the barbed wire, just wide enough to squeeze through. John and Patty went through but still I hesitated.

'Come on,' John was calling. 'The lads found this way in, make the most of it while you can.'

Throwing all caution to the winds, I raced after the both of them down to the water's edge. Patty caught our excitement and began to jump up and down. We took off our clothes and waded into the water until it reached our waists. It was a safe beach, flat and firm to our feet, and I was glad that it did not shelve deeply. We lifted Patty up and over the gentle waves as they washed in, leaving a band of white frothy foam on the edge of the sand. John took a header into the sea and began to swim in a clumsy breast-stroke, then took an accidental mouthful of water and spat and spluttered like a small whale. It made me laugh.

We ran in and out of the water like small children and lay on the hot sand with the sun drying us. John took my hand and we waded out to where the water almost covered my shoulders. I could not swim, but he held my hands in those beautiful hands of his, and encouraged me to bob up and down to get used to the water and not be afraid of it. It was a perfect day, with the continental blue of the sky and the hot sun beating down.

We had been asleep for some time when I felt John stir and when I opened my eyes he was dressing. My first thought was that he must get back to the base, and then I remembered that it was only Saturday and he had the whole weekend. He didn't say anything, but I thought I detected something that felt like a sense of urgency in this unexpected move. I called to Patty, who came obediently, and I dressed her. We walked back up the beach to where the rolled barbed wire with that defiant cut in it became our exit now. Passing the big notice with the bold red letters, making the word DANGER stand out, my gaze caught and held on the word. Just for a second, in my imagination, I saw the red letters blur over and run down the board, and the paint seemed to hang from the bottom of the letters to resemble red, red blood.

The War Department would not fence off that stretch of beach for nothing. I felt myself hold my breath. We had been foolish to take such a risk, but I could not dare voice the dreadful thought that was in my mind, that the beach was probably mined. John did not release the hold he had on Patty. In fact, he did not put her down to walk until the path had been skirted, and we were once more on top of the knoll and reached the velvet green of the grass.

I had been at the hotel for about five weeks and was beginning to settle in. John came often and stayed. I still could not fathom why he had accepted the situation so calmly, but concluded that I would leave well alone. He was liked and accepted by Joe and Dora. Much more to my surprise, he even stopped to talk to the damn Yanks. That made me scratch my head in wonder, but I did not comment.

All through September and well into October, the beautiful weather continued. The trees retained their autumnal glory and no cold wind removed their leaves. Only one thing marred the ordered routine of my life. For some weeks I had been feeling listless and irritable. I watched the men at breakfast consuming mountains of food and swilling down great gulps of coffee with a growing feeling of disgust. It was enough to make you sick, I thought.

I brushed aside the thrill of fear my words brought up. No, that couldn't be true. I had been working so hard all through the heat, and that was the reason I felt this way. A week later it was confirmed when suddenly, in the middle of sliding a great tray of bacon along the counter, I had to dash to the toilet and be sick. I leaned by the sink, splashing my face with cold water. No mistaking that sign. Oh no, I thought. Oh no.

John's posting finally came through. On Saturday I was going to have a farewell drink with him at the local pub. The awful irony of life. He was going away whilst I . . . I began to cry. I wouldn't even be able to stay here and work and save for a home of our own. The dream of my cottage was fading, along with the desperate knowledge that Gwen wouldn't be able to house me and Patty and another baby. Miserably I sat opposite John in the pub on that Saturday night.

He leaned over to ask, 'Are you all right, sweetheart? You're very quiet.'

'No, I am not all right. I'm pregnant. On the eve of you disappearing once more into the sunset, I am about to be grounded.'

He sat there quietly finishing his beer. Then, getting up with the same deliberate movements, he walked slowly to the bar to order another. I could have screamed. He sat for a long time just looking at me, his expression conveying nothing.

'You will go home now.'

The words, spoken so quietly, came like a blow. There was no commiseration in their tone, no sympathy. Just a cold statement.

'Damn you,' I muttered almost inaudibly. 'Damn you.'

There was no fire in that sad little response. I was defeated.

Repton Road

I settled back into life with Minnie at Repton Road. Her second husband, Fred, John's father, had died in 1942, a year after Patty was born. John was overseas when the news reached him. Fred had never been a robust man, and after their marriage had stayed around long enough to produce a son and then gone back to his mother. None of his family had approved of Minnie pursuing Fred because of the many years' difference in their ages, and by way of defending herself she would defiantly exclaim, 'Well, we just clicked and that was that.'

Now she was impoverished and had found it necessary to let a couple of her rooms just to keep body and soul together. The two tenants she took in were as different as chalk and cheese and they hated each other. Emmy was a meek and mild little soul and scuttled to her room as soon as she heard Gert's brash and common voice. She had the added advantage of being able to lock her middle-room door and disappear into the scullery through the french doors, and she buried herself in her room like a little quiet dormouse. She only emerged to pay a tradesman, or to get her evening paper as it slid under the front door before Gert got there first to have a sly look-through. It was a nightly ritual, with both of them ready and waiting to outwit the other.

Gertie was as rough as Emmy was gentle, and worked at Thrissels, the rope factory in Brislington. The stories she told about the daily doings at the factory were extremely lurid. At the end of each tale she would laugh in such a way that it sounded like hitting a high note and prolonging it. Emmy said she was both stupid and as common as muck. But she was very good-natured, and surprisingly enough she and Minnie, whom she called 'Ma', got on very well together. On Fridays, they went to the pub together, Minnie walking stiff and upright, nodding like royalty to all who passed, and Gertie, with her loud voice and almost imbecilic laugh, by her side.

'Taking Ma for a drop of how's-yer-father,' she informed acquaintances who passed them. 'She likes her glass of stout. Right, Ma?'

Towards the end of May, we had an air raid. I was in bed and muttering curses because I did not want to push the large lump under my nightie down the stairs, and sit, cramped and uncomfortable, in the cupboard. Gertie's voice rose to a shriek as the air-raid sirens wailed and the first two bombs fell rather too close for comfort. Minnie called out that she couldn't find her teeth or her knickers.

'Never mind yer nashers, Ma, just make sure you put yer bloomers on!'

By this time, we had all assembled under the stairs and were either crouching or sitting on the mattresses that covered the floor. More bombs fell on the city that night, each one close enough to make the doors and windows rattle and the whole house shake. The dull thuds made us close our eyes and hold our breath. We heard the raider turn and head for home and a long silence followed before the all-clear sounded.

We didn't know it then, but that was the last load of bombs to fall on Bristol. The end of the war was in sight. Gertie laughed when she saw Minnie with her hands clasped together, and said to me:

'If one of they whizz-bangs had come through the roof tonight, Ma would a bin glad she 'ad 'er bloomers on!'

By now I was eight months pregnant and flagging in spirits. I was never one of those women who bloom in pregnancy and I was never in love with it. I was relieved when Gwen offered to have Patty during my confinement and she went to stay at the cottage. I howled with fatigue and at Patty's tearful face. She was too young to understand what it was all about.

At least the news on the wireless was good. Montgomery had halted Rommel at El Alamein, and had pushed him back over the Libyan desert. The Russians were chasing the Germans back from eastern Europe, and here on the home front our troops were massing for a landing in France. On the eve of this great event, at about seven-thirty in the evening of 5 June 1944, I called for the ambulance to get me to the hospital for the birth of my second child.

Frenchay Manor was still standing in 1944. The Americans had acquired several acres of this prime site to build a hospital for their troops. It was a very up-to-date hospital, the design of which England had never seen before, with wards leading off great long corridors.

The manor itself was now a maternity ward, and it was to this once-beautiful house that the ambulance clanged its way on that night so many years ago. I remember so well my surprise to find, as I was helped into the brightly lit delivery room, that American and English staff were working together there.

If I had any fears that my second delivery would be a repetition of the first, they were swept away as soon as I encountered the trio of a doctor and two nurses who smilingly came forward to greet me and immediately put me at my ease. As the stages of labour progressed, I was helped and encouraged with soft and supportive words. And the utter relief that at all times there was a hand to hold and cling to was the biggest help of all.

I gave birth to Jacqueline at two-thirty on the morning of 6 June. She was a compact, sixteen-inch, eight-and-a-half-pound little bundle and the easiest birth of all my four babies. I gave birth to her in a sitting position, propped up against the doctor's chest, which I found easier in every way. Apart from anything else, being able to see what was going on around you was more rewarding than gazing dejectedly at the ceiling and bright lights.

However, in my particular case the reason was a slightly

complicated one. Because of a retroversion, or slightly tilted womb, it was necessary for the doctor to press down gently on my stomach to encourage the baby's safe passage through the birth canal. So the simple explanation was that this was the best way to deal with the situation.

I called the baby Jacqueline because it was my father's favourite name, and partly out of a sense of gratitude to the doctor, who told me that he had a daughter whose name was Jacky. Even he commented on the colour of her eyes, which he said would be a cornflower blue, just like her dad's. When I was wheeled back to the ward, I breathed a sigh of relief that it had all been over in so short a time and with comparative ease. I had been dreading it. I went to sleep almost at once.

In the morning, we were awakened by Sister walking briskly into the ward and exclaiming, 'Isn't it wonderful, mothers, our troops have just landed in Normandy!'

Only one thing marred the serenity of my twelve-day stay at Frenchay. One baby disturbed the normal quiet of the nursery and howled for long periods, sometimes well into the night. We all speculated whose baby it might be, with half of us dismissing the possibility that it could be ours. Then, when the day dawned bright and clear for my departure, they brought a transformed little Jacky to me and placed her in my arms. She looked so sweet and angelic in the dainty things I'd packed for her, and I stood gazing down at her; she was exquisite.

'Maybe we shall get some peace at night in the nursery now,' the nurse said.

I saw my American doctor briefly before I left. He used my Christian name and wished me well. The interview was professional and lasted long enough to explain about the retroversion syndrome. It was neither serious nor uncommon. So long as my medical practitioner was in possession of all the facts, in the event of a subsequent birth the same procedure could be followed. 'However,' and here he paused to consider his next words, 'sometimes, not always, any future birth could get harder, especially as the woman gets older. The ideal family quota for you, my dear, might be the two you now have. Although I must add that this is a matter for you and your husband to decide and not me. Advice is all I am able to give.'

I felt embarrassed. I wanted to tell him that two babies were more than enough for me, and what could I do to prevent another pregnancy? But I felt myself blushing. I could not talk about these things, not even to a doctor. In the taxi going home, though, I had time to reflect on my reticence to discuss something that was becoming very urgent to me. I resolved that I was going to tell John, at the very first opportunity, that two babies and no home was enough for me to be going on with. It seemed ridiculous that the subject of sex was such a delicate one that I shrank from talking about it to a doctor or even John. It was an issue that had to be broached, but I was at a complete loss how to resolve it.

Jacky was as changeable as her birth sign, Gemini the twins. Her lusty yell could disturb the whole neighbourhood and at times nothing would appease her, no matter what we tried. I could cuddle and walk about with her for hours, but nothing worked. And at other times she would lie, angelic and contented, in her cot, quietly playing with her fingers, which held a kind of fascination for her.

It came as a bit of a shock when, six weeks after Jacky's birth, I got a letter from John to say he was back in England and stationed at Pembroke Dock, where he'd been stationed before the war. They would not be there for long as they were expecting another posting quite soon. They were entitled to some leave and in order that he might see his new daughter he thought it might be a good idea if he arranged some digs. I could travel down to Pembrokeshire and spend a precious fourteen days with him. He could take me around and show me some lovely places, and it would be a holiday to share together.

Instead of being elated, I was beset with fears and apprehension. Sooner than expected, I would have to tell him what the doctor had advised and ask that we talk about limiting our family. Very much aware of that stubborn streak of his, I knew it would not be easy. Yet it had to be spoken about, it was so important to me.

I told Minnie that her beloved Bertie was home and in Pembrokeshire, and about his invitation to join him for a holiday. She was puzzled that I was not very enthusiastic about the reunion or the holiday. If I had told her the real reason, that my not wanting to go was because I was scared of coming home with another bun in the oven, she would merely have stated, 'That's life, kid. Tell him to get off at Crewe.'

Pembrokeshire

I knew I was going to love Pembrokeshire the moment I stepped from the train onto the quaint little station and saw the white-painted seat with the bank of flowers behind it. There was a delightful smell like musk roses in the air, and it looked as though nothing had ever changed, or was likely to change. I sat with my two children in the warm August sunshine, waiting for John and drinking in the peace and serenity of that magic place, for the past seemed to be all around me.

The train barely made a noise as it slid lazily out of the station and out of sight. It was Patty who first saw her father and ran to meet him. I watched the pair of them as he bent to kiss her, and then she was holding his hand and skipping back towards us. When he came up to us, I noticed he was just as tanned as he had been when he returned from the Rock, and his wavy hair was just as boyish. He asked about the journey whilst gazing intently at his second daughter, then, placing her easily in the crook of his arm, he picked up my suitcase with the other. So our little party made its way out of the station and along the quiet country road towards the town, and then past row upon row of terraced houses with no front gardens.

At last John stopped in front of a Methodist chapel. The sandstone façade stood out boldly, and the blazing sun on that hot August day turned the warm stone to an even rosier glow. On a wide paved courtyard in front of the church was a noticeboard proclaiming in bold black lettering the name of the clergyman who would be leading the service the following Sunday. Adjoining this was another large poster with details of the choir practice for the male voices the following Thursday in the schoolroom. For all those attending, the keys could be obtained from Mr and Mrs Evans at the caretaker's house adjoining.

The house was demurely screened by a row of laurel bushes and a black, spiked iron gate which had to be lifted up in the middle to allow us to walk through; it squeaked badly. John left it, hanging almost pathetically off its hinges, as we proceeded up a path to a side entrance with three steps and a porch with two imposing pillars on the wide top step. John found a bell-push, which he pulled in and out several times. Standing on the path and listening to that strident peal, I noticed that three tall cypress trees hid the garden. I peered through the foliage and was surprised to discover that only a small wall separated the garden from the neat row of graves on the other side of the churchyard.

The door was opened by a well-built woman in her sixties, with a black shawl around her shoulders and a neat bun at the nape of her neck. She beamed at us from the doorway, and it was evident from John's answering smile that the pair of them were already well acquainted. She welcomed us in that lovely, musical Welsh lilt.

'Well now, my lovelies, here we are then. Tired, now, you must be, coming all the way from Bristol and those dear babies so good and quiet. Come in, come along in now. I'll run and put the kettle on; you'd like some tea now, I shouldn't wonder.'

She led the way through the hall and into a bright little kitchen at the far end of the house. The window gave a full view of the garden and the side of the chapel.

As we sat there drinking tea, with John and Mrs Evans talking easily to one another, it was explained to me that John was no stranger to this household and had walked out with their daughter Christina some few years earlier when he had been sent to Pembroke to do his training. It was strange, sitting there listening about a friendship that had unfolded in a part of his life that I knew nothing about. Mrs Evans met John's questions about Christina's whereabouts with a kind of guarded vagueness. She was over Haverfordwest way, happily married now with two boys.

Mrs Evans refilled John's cup and as she pushed the tea towards him she looked directly at me. 'Well now, that's all in the past. And you with a lovely little family of your own.' Then, as if she guessed my embarrassment, she changed the conversation abruptly. 'Tell me, my lovely. Are you chapel?'

I nodded and almost choked on a biscuit to answer. 'Methodist.'

Her eyes lit up with pleasure and she went on to tell me that Reverend Eli Thomas was ever so nice, and how she and Mr Evans went three times on a Sunday. At this point Mr Evans himself appeared and, as soon as he saw John, strode towards him with his two arms outstretched in welcome, grasping both of John's in his own as they shook hands.

At last, Mr Evans turned to me. 'We had this young man of yours staying with us when he was just a whipper-snapper,' he laughed. 'I had to keep my eye on him, I can tell you. But I dare say you can keep him in order now, eh?' The older man thumped John playfully on the back.

And Mrs Evans brought more tea in the big brown teapot and filled up the cups again. 'I dare say you can find your way around the house and show your wife the bedroom. You don't need me to show you round, do you? I've no doubt you know every nook and cranny, eh?' She gave him a playful prod, then addressed me once more.

'Tomorrow is the Sabbath and there is one rule we always abide by on the Lord's Day. There is to be no washing put on the line. Six days shalt thou labour and do all thy work but on the seventh thou shalt rest and praise the Lord.'

I was about to ask her how I could prevent my baby using nappies on a Sunday, and realised that my limited stock of terry towels was now sadly reduced to just two, but decided to hold my counsel. I would investigate the possibilities later.

The following morning we all slept late. When I came down into the kitchen, Mrs Evans was busy brushing down her husband's coat whilst he brushed the felt hat smooth with his arm. He eased the stiffness of his white collar with a couple of circular neck movements, inserting his two thumbs in the space between his tie knot and his Adam's apple. My bet was that both tie and collar would be removed in those intervening respites at dinner time and tea-time.

Mrs Evans adjusted her big, wide-brimmed hat and thrust a big gold hatpin through it and the bun at the back of her head. Then she pulled on long cotton gloves, picked up her large handbag and placed the handles over her arm. When she reached the door she picked up two hymnbooks waiting on the sideboard. She gave one to her husband then, with a final wave to me, they disappeared through the hall and out through the front door.

I looked at the bucket full of soaking napkins under the sink and began to tackle them. I tutted with annoyance about not being able to dry them on the line because in the summer breeze they would have been dry in an hour. As I was squeezing and wringing them, I wondered how she would know if they were on the damn line or not? I could have them dry and get them in long before she was home for lunch. Singing a little song to myself, I picked up the bowl with the washed terry squares and nipped quickly down the yard.

From the open window of the chapel next door came the strains of a hymn. I began pegging the napkins on the line, kicking the bowl along with my foot until the whole line of them flapped like small triumphant flags in the breeze. I picked up the bowl feeling slightly guilty, like a small thief having pinched some sweeties from the jar. I had only to pop on the kettle for a well-earned cuppa, but it never had time to come to the boil. It never occurred to me that I could be seen and every action examined by the whole congregation. Into the kitchen marched Mrs Evans, her mouth in a tight line of disapproval and her head moving in the agitated jerks of righteous indignation.

'There's nasty you are, and after me telling you there was to be no washing on the line on a Sunday. 'Tis wicked of you to be so defiant of God's laws. There's me sitting there with you in full view and everybody flabbergasted watching you. I don't know how I shall lift my head up or explain to Reverend.'

Here she stopped for breath, but pointed down the garden to the offending terry squares brazenly flying high. I had no choice but to slink back down the path and retrieve the damp washing. Only when I had placed the bowl on the scullery table did she glare at me, as if daring me in peril of my life to repeat this mortal Sabbath sin. Then with her head held high she disappeared through the door. I made the cup of tea and sat down rather weakly after this outburst.

I felt slightly guilty, not about the washing on the line, but because I had caused her such trouble as to make her upset. She had been very good to all of us, after all. I wondered if it had been her honest belief that fire and brimstone might follow my ungodly action. Or was it because, as custodians of the Church, their livelihood had been put in jeopardy by a foolish action on my part? I resolved to apologise as soon as the opportunity arose.

When John and Patty came down for breakfast, I enthused about the weather and John said we would go to Bosherton Lily Fields, a local beauty spot about five or six miles away. If we hurried, we could catch a bus that came along the street at eleven. There was another that returned at four. We hurried around to get ready. With two small children, there always seemed so much to do and take with us that we had to rush in order to catch the bus.

But, once aboard, I sat there relieved and relaxed. It was just wonderful to sit and watch the green and magical countryside speed by. There were ruined castles that set my mind racing to the medieval days of knights in armour and the ladies of the court. The past was just a veil away and the story in the stones as real and as alive as ever.

Only a few other people alighted with us at our destination, right by the side of an old church. In the silence of that perfect summer day, the years had done nothing to change it. I would not have been surprised to hear the sound of horses' hooves on the highway, or see the medieval rider dismount, tether his horse, remove his headgear and walk reverently through the oak nail-studded door. I felt that I too had stood outside that ancient door before. Walking around the quiet graveyard that contained black tombs in a surround of rusty black iron spikes, I felt all of it was strangely familiar.

I wanted to stay there, caught in that strange dream-like trance. All was silent save for the bees diving into the honey-sweet nectar of clover growing by the time-yellowed stone resting place, the inscription of who lay buried there long since erased. I was brought abruptly back to the present when John said we must get a move on if we wanted to get everything in by four o'clock, and I followed him and Patty out of the church and along the road, vowing that I would come back again one day to that sacred place.

Further on, we left the road and entered a wooded valley. We had to make our way cautiously because the ground began to slope downward. I handed Jacky over to John; she was beginning to weigh heavily in my arms and I was glad to be relieved of my burden. She was wide awake, her brilliant blue eyes were clear and shining and she smiled up at me. Jacky was truly exquisite and I stopped on the muddy track to reach for her finger and talk to her. Then we made our way carefully along the track, going slowly so that we could help Patty over rough ground, and finally got to the bottom of the wood.

There we stood transfixed at the sight of two lakes, covered with creamy white and pink water lilies. A brick causeway, broken in places, ran between them and extended to the far side. The dark woods on three sides formed a secluded and shrouded valley. The lakes shimmered and the lilies swayed lazily as bright emerald-green and iridescent-blue dragonflies darted across its surface. In this lake it was said that King Arthur saw the hand holding his sword Excalibur rise and hold it aloft thrice. Here on that magical afternoon, if the whole of King Arthur's court had appeared, I discounted nothing. For Merlin with one wave had brought it all to life for me.

When I set out on the causeway to follow John, I stopped

halfway to gaze into the lake, half wishing and half believing that the hand holding Excalibur could break the water and rise just for me. Only those who have ever ventured to this lovely spot can appreciate its beauty and serenity, and I was caught and held in its spell of magic. Believe that you have this thing, and you have it.

For all those brave souls who finally made it to the other side, there was a tea shop run by two sisters who specialised in delicious home-made scones filled with jam and cream, with welcome pots of tea and wafer-thin slices of bread and butter. You went in through a green-painted door and there was a black latch on the door which, when you pressed down hard on it, made a bell tinkle. I don't know if the tea shop is still there, but the lily fields are there and the ancient church by the side of the woods. A newer and safer causeway has now been built. No one who visits could ever dispute its magical atmosphere. I went back with Patty forty years later and it seemed I had never gone away.

Later the following day when I came face to face with Mrs Evans I could sense that she was still peeved about the washing, but I launched into my apology with such humble contrition that the stony look on her face softened. Leaning over, she touched the back of my hand as though imploring me not to go on.

'Well now, my lovely, we won't say another word about it, but as long as you remain under my roof, the Lord's Day must be observed.'

Her smile was warm and genuine and I was glad I had

made my peace with her. That afternoon she took me and the girls for a walk and showed us the barracks where the boys in the RAF came to be trained. That was before the war, and before John had transferred to Air Sea Rescue.

'Smart those young boys were, marching out of the barracks and all through the town. Proud we were, too, standing there watching them. Specially that young man of yours. Proud of him when our Christina first brought him to our house.'

I looked at Mrs Evans, for it seemed her voice was conveying some faraway time that held a vague regret. I hoped she might reveal more, but the next moment she was back in the present again. 'There now, life plays some strange tricks. You have a good man as the father of your two babies, look you.'

Her voice trailed off a little and it seemed she was back again to some time in the past. Her head was turned away from me but I thought I caught the words, 'Our Christina was the loser, her and the boy.'

It was Wednesday before John was able to arrange another treat and we set off for Tenby, another seaside resort and another bus ride away. If there is any place I would like to live and die in, it is Tenby. So pretty, with its harbour and sandy beach and little houses and cottages tumbling down the hill towards the sea. Like all the rest of that part of Wales, it weaved its magic everywhere. Houses, shops, streets, and hotels all slumbered peacefully in an endless idyll.

And at Saundersfoot we spent one more perfect day, where Patty and her father ran in and out of the water all day and the water finally covered and destroyed the sandcastle he made for her at the water's edge. It had been a perfect holiday.

A posting came through for John the next day for Port Said in Egypt. I was thinking about Ceylon as I packed our battered old suitcase, and how I had once longed to go there. I said as much to Mrs Evans.

'Five years ago I was going to Ceylon with John.'

'Five years ago, lovely, he might have been my son-in-law. All things turn out for the best for somebody now, look you.'

Then she pulled me to her ample bosom and hugged me. She came to the gate and lifted the sagging piece of iron up by its middle and shifted it to one side so that we could pass through. She only laughed and said that one day Mr Evans would get round to fixing it, and she waved us out of sight.

We waited on the station for the train to take us home. The scent of musk roses came to me again, and a bee buzzed lazily around. Then the train came in and John helped me into a carriage before he kissed Patty and told her to be a good girl. Then he hugged me and said he hoped I'd enjoyed the holiday. I nodded, but could not tell him how I felt, about the magic and the fantasy. If he had laughed, those images would have been blown away and destroyed. So I kept those thoughts to myself, locked away inside my head. They are things that are kept secret, things that make you remain yourself.

'Goodbye, John,' I said and kissed him once more. 'Goodbye, Pembrokeshire, goodbye, Wales,' I whispered to myself. For, after so much beauty, how could anyone willingly go home?

The War Ends

The year that Patty started school, the war ended. It had lasted six long weary years, and for those of us who had been young at the time it was a big slice out of our lives. When it was finally all over, there was singing and dancing in the streets. Victory bells rang out and people laughed and cried at the same time and hugged each other for joy. We had street parties for the children, and although both of mine were too young to know what it was all about they caught the excitement of the moment, and with balloons and streamers joined in the fun. I helped to make sponges and jellies and paper hats, along with other neighbours.

News filtered through that the war had ended because a special kind of bomb had been dropped on Hiroshima. Nobody questioned why it had come to an abrupt halt. Like thousands of others, we were relieved and happy that hostilities had ceased and that normal life could be resumed once more. Much later, we saw and heard the full horror of this weapon that had been used and we were appalled. Impossible to think, then, that nuclear weapons would become the ultimate deterrent. Impossible also to believe that when the final page of history was being written, we discovered that Germany was busy perfecting this deadly weapon of destruction and it could have been us, not Hiroshima, that was the target.

The men from the forces came slowly back. They were welcomed home with gaily coloured bunting that was stretched across the road from house to house. The parties started again, but this time in the houses rather than the street. Every one of the neighbours contributed to the meal, and people filed in and out to drink the health of the man who had returned and to receive a hug. John was not demobbed with that first contingent of men; the spring and summer of that year would pass into late autumn before he was released. Besides, John was a regular, and I was under the impression he would want to stay in the services and make it a career.

One Saturday afternoon, I took the girls shopping with me in Sandy Park. I needed some things for the weekend and especially some bread. I stopped by the cake shop and pulled the pushchair by the side of the window, and told Patty to keep an eye on her sister while I went inside. Jacky pointed and said she wanted 'a grewsbree in a pot'.

'What?' I said, mystified.

'A grewsbree in a pot!' Her voice rose in frustration, then she perversely covered her face in both hands.

I tried to keep calm. 'What on earth is a grewsbree in a pot?' I asked Patty, who was skipping about on one foot, but she didn't know. Jacky began to strain at the harness that held her, arching her back and jerking. In desperation, I undid her harness and pulled her into the shop. In another moment I knew she would burst into tears, and I felt hot and angry. The assistant looked curiously at Jacky and the other customers in the shop tried in vain to help. Was it an iced bun she wanted, or perhaps the jam doughnut? The small crowd gathered round, trying to coax her into telling them what she wanted. All she did was shake her head vigorously from side to side and slip prostrate and heartbroken to the floor. Then the green-coated assistant reached forward to take a solitary cake, forlornly left on the shining glass window display.

With a triumphant cry, she addressed my infant. 'This is what you want, isn't it, dear? Your nana buys you one of these each week when she comes in for her bread.'

The pastry was in the shape of a small tart filled with gooseberries with a small blob of cream on the top. A grewsbree in a pot. The mystery was solved. Jacky sat up obediently, and took the gooseberry tart. The tears still glistened in those clear blue eyes. The women in the shop all murmured, 'Oh, bless her little heart.'

I wheeled Jacky, happily nibbling at the cake and oblivious to the fact that crumbs were falling down the front of her clean coat, out into the street once more. I felt as if I had been unjust and unkind, for more patience and diplomacy may have averted the scene. We seemed always to reach a point where the sparks would fly between us, yet I always felt guilty when she was reduced to this helpless state of angry frustration. I was still trying to fathom out my inadequacies when I glanced down and realised that I hadn't offered a cake to Patty. She was still skipping along happily by my side. She wasn't bothered.

Minnie was in a twitter of excitement when we arrived back at the house, holding a telegram for me. It was just one short line to say that John was arriving home the next day on the ten-thirty train; could I meet him at Temple Meads?

'Your daddy is coming home, my darling,' Nan Storey was saying to Jacky, bending down and rubbing her chubby little knees. 'Tomorrow you are going to the station to see your daddy come home on a chuff-chuff.'

Jacky shook her head obstinately and said stubbornly, 'No, swings.'

I groaned inwardly. Not another battle of wills, please God. The rest of the evening was a mad rush to find clothes for the girls and get them clean for the morning. It would mean an early rise if I had to get to the station by ten-thirty. I had recently bought them matching blue skirts and tops with animal motifs on the blouses. Patty was ready first. At five she was independent and could dress herself. Jacky was having a tussle over the top that I needed to stretch to go over her head. The seconds and minutes were ticking past and I had no time to play games so I gave the top an impatient jerk down over her head and pushed her arms through the sleeves.

Jacky screamed that the top was itchy and began to arch

253

her back in preparation for another tantrum. I shouted to Patty to go and stand by the door to be all ready for when I had finished the tussle with Jacky. I did not want to face a new flood of tears, so I yanked off the offending top and allowed her to wear a blouse from a pile of grubby, unwashed things. I buttoned up her shoes and pushed her down over the stairs and along the passage to the gate, there to be confronted with Patty talking to her father in the friendliest terms. His kitbag had been placed on the wall and he was deep in conversation with his eldest daughter.

'Chuff chuff,' said Jacky imperiously, tugging at my hand to pull me past John and his rather startled gaze. This was some homecoming. Patty looked up at her father, endeavouring to clarify the situation by gravely explaining, 'She's been promised a walk to the trains and the swings, and if she doesn't go she'll only play up.'

We all stood there, with Jacky threatening to throw herself onto the pavement if her demands were not met. It was John who saved the day.

'Tell you what,' he said. 'I'll dump the kitbag, and we'll all go to the park with Jacky on the swings. It will give us an appetite for our dinner.'

When he came out of the house a few minutes later, we walked slowly along the road. I was at a loss to know what to say. He looked at me and we both looked at Jacky. His only comment was, 'Well I never. Well I never did.'

John found it difficult to settle. In our cramped surroundings, the one tiny bedroom and lack of space and privacy stifled him. He was used to the great outdoor life with male companions and he had been away from a real home life for six years. He was irritable. I did not improve matters by choosing this rather fraught time to insist that we talk about some form of family planning. This news, delivered one morning at the breakfast table, was met with quiet but hostile pomposity.

'My dear,' he said, reaching for the cornflakes. 'I am not the giver of life or death, and whether you have one child or fifty makes not the slightest difference to me. If you don't want any more children, then you must do something about it, not me.'

Once again I felt angry and resentful. I shrank from going into a chemist's shop to ask for any contraceptive aid, even if I knew what to ask for. Men had a secret system of nods and winks, they could emerge cheerfully from the chemist's or barber's whistling, but no self-respecting woman could think of such a thing. Modesty decreed that a man knew all about these things and women should not. And I did not know where to go, or who to turn to for advice.

Very, very slowly, rubble was being cleared and a new building programme was under way. The Council acquired land in semi-rural areas on the outskirts of the city, and big estates began to be developed. Builders were asked to submit tenders for cheap rented dwellings, and soon developers' names like Laing, or Willerby, or Stone, began to appear on huge hoardings. A Housing Committee was set up to deal with the tens of thousands of applicants who rushed to add their names to the formidable list of names already there.

A prefab was my heart's desire. These little homes consisted of pre-fabricated pieces, mass-produced in sections, loaded onto lorries, and taken to the site where they could be assembled almost overnight. They were delightful little chalet-type dwellings, made of some kind of asbestos. Although it was thought that they were only temporary, made to last just ten years, they did enable many thousands of people to be rehoused quickly, and they were firm favourites because of their compactness and ultra-modern design. Most of these prefabs were surrounded by a decent-sized garden, a feature that appealed to me. Over the little porch, I could picture roses and honeysuckle. I wanted one of those prefabs more than anything else in the world.

We all made trips to the Housing Committee, foolishly thinking that by harassing them we would get a house all that much quicker. We were allocated points, according to circumstances, and those who could wangle a few extra points by stating special hardship got in there first. Some people even went to see their local councillors to further their cause. Caring local representatives, who knew just how desperate people were to be rehoused, did a lot of hard work at that time.

With all this rehousing going on, there was a tremendous demand for furniture. We'd had to make do and mend all through the war, but rationing did not stop with the coming of peace, for raw materials were still in short supply. The new furniture coming into the shops was 'Utility', and had to conform to the government's guidelines on manufacture. The Utility bedroom, kitchen and dining suites were good solid stuff, with not much style, but they were durable and came in three choices of wood finish, pine, oak or mahogany. Shops did a roaring trade. Most young people ordered their suites and started paying for them long before a house of their own was even remotely possible.

My neighbour Jean Brodie came rushing over one Monday morning, brandishing a letter from the Housing to tell her that she had been allocated a prefab at Shirehampton. Her luck in getting one was due to having two children of the same sex, for the prefabs had but two bedrooms. Any increase in her family would mean that she would have to apply for a three-bedroomed house and endure a longer wait.

'You'll get one with your two girls,' she said excitedly. 'I told my Fred that all *his* energy would have to go on workin' 'ard to buy a few bits and bobs for the new 'ouse, cos we ain't got nothin'.' She nudged me and said with a wink, 'Tell your old man to tie a knot in it!'

Here was my chance to extract any secret knowledge she had to impart. 'Getting off at Crewe' had already been tried without much success; it made us both irritable, and it was unreliable. In the next few minutes I gathered from her that she used a product called Rendalls. These were small, round pessaries of a soap-like substance. To quote Jean's delightfully quaint description, 'Shove 'em up as far as they'll go and wait till they fizz!'

She rushed back over the road to get a couple that were left in the box for me to try. She omitted to tell me that the effervescent period was limited, or maybe time had rendered their effectiveness to nil. Whatever the reason, they did not work for me and, a few weeks later, I found myself once again experiencing the joys of early pregnancy by being revoltingly sick and irritable.

My dream of a prefab was shattered. I went to see Jean in her new home and wept, even while enthusing about the way she had already transformed it and planted grass in the front for a lawn. A young sapling by her gate would soon spread its foliage over the path, attractive and inviting. It wasn't fair. I wanted a home like this, and once more I was being denied it.

Jean commiserated. 'Take a load of Beecham's Pills. Have a mustard bath. Drink loads of gin. Move all the furniture. Mangle a wet blanket.'

I tried it all and nothing worked. Then Jean offered a ray of hope. She said that if I went to the doctor and convinced him that having another baby would prove detrimental to my health, mentally or physically, he might just agree to terminate the pregnancy. 'Squeeze a few tears out,' she advised.

The tears were genuine enough and I shed them unashamedly. Then I became aware that the doctor was scribbling something on paper and never once lifted his eyes to look directly at me. Eventually, completely unmoved by my sad saga, he coolly remarked that he was unable to help me, but that he would refer me to a gynaecologist who, in his opinion, I ought to see.

Filled with doubt but still hoping, a couple of weeks later I walked into the clinical purity of the consulting room of the great woman, who surveyed me quizzically, like some rare germ under a microscope. It was obvious that her views coincided exactly with those of her male counterpart.

'Mrs Storey,' she said at last. 'What you are asking me to do amounts to murder.' Her eyes did not rise from the papers on her desk. 'As far as I am concerned, you are going to have a baby, and that is precisely what you will go home to do. Should any foolish action of yours bring about an abortion, may I point out that you are liable for prosecution? I shall write to your doctor and your husband to make sure that they, too, are in possession of the facts.'

There were not many choices for us in those days, and choice means freedom. The winds of change did not blow early enough for me, and I am glad that time dealt more kindly with my three girls. That same woman who sent me away feeling desperate smilingly invited my own daughter into her waiting room to arrange a termination as a matter of course twenty-odd years later.

This was a period when men were trying to adjust to rebuilding severed relationships and establishing their place in a strange, changed world. John found himself a job with a construction works making bus engines, but found a nine-to-five job boring and restrictive. He changed his job and became a conductor on the buses. He still hated the early-morning shifts and the unsociable hours, and I found it difficult to keep the children quiet when he was trying to sleep.

I decided to write to our councillor for an appointment and I was writing the letter, sitting at the window, when I saw my brother Dennis come in at the gate. I rapped at the glass to attract his attention, and he looked up at me and waved. I was four months pregnant. I went rushing down the stairs to let him in, tearing off my pinny and throwing it on the hallstand as I went.

Den stood there on the doorstep looking brown and happy and I threw my arms around his neck and drew him into the hall. Arm-in-arm, we went through into the kitchen for me to put the kettle on – I wanted to know everything that had happened to him since the last time we had met.

All the time I'd been in Grimsby, my mother had only written three times, and she had never visited me. Den, on the other hand, had written regularly, so I knew that he had met his wife-to-be, Audrey, when he'd been based in Staffordshire. Audrey worked in the NAAFI, and she and Dennis were married in her home town of Burton-on-Trent. My parents had gone up for the wedding. Den told me that he and Audrey were now living with Frank and Ada in Birchall's Green Avenue, and added that the real reason for his visit was to find out how many points I had towards a house.

I gathered from his conversation that things were not easy living with Ada and Frank, especially now that Audrey was pregnant. Ada found fault with everything Audrey did. I brought in some cups and saucers on a tray and a big pot of tea. I pulled up a couple of chairs, and went in search of milk and the biscuit barrel. I poured out the tea, then, without looking, went to sit down on the chair that I had just pulled out for myself. To my surprise, it wasn't there and I fell heavily back on the bar of the brass fender round the grate. I experienced a sharp pain, but it was soon gone, and Dennis was helping me to my feet, looking concerned and contrite, saying that he had pushed the chair away because it was in direct line with the door. He wanted to give me enough space when I came in with the milk and biscuits, and was surprised that I hadn't seen what he had done. He was very upset, and kept asking me if I was sure I hadn't hurt myself.

'Come on, tell me the rest of your news. Of course I'm all right.'

As he had no children, he hoped Audrey's pregnancy might make a difference to their chances of getting a house. He was surprised we were not already rehoused, and it came as a shock to realise that I had been married for eight years yet we and thousands like us had never had a house of our own.

Den began to talk about the war and his bomber raids over Germany. As I sat there and listened to him, I was amazed that he had chosen such a dangerous job as rear-gunner in this war. He was such a gentle person. I remembered him as a child, the anything-for-a-quiet-life brother who had elected to stay locked in that front room to be as far away as possible from the bickering that went on in the rest of the house. Why, of all things, had he chosen Bomber Command?

'Well,' he said, 'one day in the spring of 1942, I was visiting a friend in Canterbury, and there was a massive air raid. We took shelter under the stairs for a couple of hours while

Canterbury was pounded. Afterwards, as I took in the scene, a great wave of anger and frustration crept over me. Here was a lovely, historic city which up till then had survived intact – it just made me so mad.'

Here he spread his hands in a helpless gesture. 'So the first thing I decided to do when I returned to my unit was to ask for a transfer to Bomber Command, where a new head had just been appointed – "Bomber Harris", we called him – who felt that intensive, massive bombing of Germany could win the war.'

He stirred his tea and stared into the distance, alone with his own thoughts. Without being told, I knew what he was thinking about: all those thousands of young men who would never come back.

'At the end of the war, I managed to get a flight over Germany, you know. I saw for myself the devastation of industry and the cities of the Ruhr, and I saw the awful mess that had been made of Cologne and Essen. I wondered what the German people felt towards Hitler, who had sown the seeds of their destruction.'

'Tell me about your Distinguished Flying Medal.' I was full of curiosity, and knew he would never mention it himself.

'Oh, it wasn't just me, you know . . .' He was embarrassed. 'I just spotted an enemy fighter and we took evasive action and . . . Look, it was a team effort, all of us in it together and nothing especially heroic. Something I shall never forget, though, was being decorated by the King. It was a very great honour and a moment I shall treasure all my life. I felt so proud.'

He smiled and took another sip of his tea. Looking at him, I felt I was seeing him for the first time in my life, and I, too, felt proud. Proud to have such a man for my brother.

Miscarriage

I had been to the park with Jacky. Afterwards I collected Patty from school and was pushing the pram through the front door when I felt hot and very dizzy. I sat on the bottom step of the stairs, shooing both girls up to the bedroom and telling them to play until I could come up to get them their tea. Presently the faintness passed and I tried unsuccessfully to wedge the now folded-up pushchair into the tiny space behind the glass door. Something seemed to be blocking the way and with annoyance I jabbed the thing impatiently, scraping the hood along the wall so hard that I dislodged one of the protective corner bits and it fell to the floor with a tiny metallic click. As I bent to feel for it, there was a loud singing in my head and another wave of sickness swept over me. I just had time to rush outside to the loo when a great blackness came over me and I knew nothing more.

When I came round a few seconds later, I was sitting with my back propped up against the wooden post of the door. I felt cold and very ill. I rose unsteadily to my feet. My head swam and I thought I would faint again. I crawled on my hands and knees to the stairs. The top seemed so far away and there was nobody about. Gertie was not yet home from work and Minnie was at Gwen's. John was on the late shift. When I finally made it to the big double bed, I lay there for a long while with my face into the pillow, fighting the black waves of sick faintness that swept over me.

From a long way off I heard Gertie call out from the bottom of the stairs, 'Anyone alive in this joint?'

Both the children rushed down the stairs to greet her. I didn't care that she would be stuffing them with cakes and sweets. I lay face-downward for a long time. Deep inside, I felt a tiny 'pop', like the bursting of a pea pod, and something wet and sticky around the top of my legs. Then pain like I had never experienced before took my breath away, and enveloped me so that relief came only with blackness and I floated away. Muffled voices came and went.

'Be you all right?'

Somebody groaned, 'Oh my God!'

I was dancing again on Pagan Hill. Pagan Hill was a favourite walk where two young nurses brought us on sunny afternoons, way back in Painswick when I was a small child. They often told us stories of how the witches danced in the magic ring on Hallowe'en on Pagan Hill, calling on Diana, their queen, to come at midnight and grant them a wish. The nurses had been amused when I took off my shoes to run barefoot on the grass to dance. The stories the nurses told didn't scare me, not even when they recited poems about calling on Diana.

'Will she really, really come if I call on her on Hallowe'en?'

'The magic is in the believing,' they said.

I was going to ask Diana to send my mother to see me. But no one had come that night in Painswick. Perhaps I had not believed hard enough.

Now I was dancing again on Pagan Hill. The grass was emerald green and I was light as air. The sky was bright with stars and I heard a bell ring. I felt a rush of wind and heard a sound like the wheels of a train clacking on the lines as it passed through a tunnel, but there were lights that suspended, and hurt my eyes. As I rushed past them, I saw Diana's face float close to mine. She wore her lovely dark hair piled high on top of her head with a white crown holding it in place. She should let it fall loose around her shoulders just like a mantle, black and shining in the wind. She bent over me and took hold of my hand. She was very beautiful.

I tried to say, 'I knew you would come,' but she was fading away and a loud male voice shouted, 'Make way for the suicide case.'

'Can you hear me, Mrs Storey? Try opening your eyes.'

I struggled desperately to open my eyes. I wanted to see Diana again, but where she had been was a nurse standing by my side. On the bibbed front of her pristine white starched apron was a brilliant scarlet stain. I was lying on a red sheet, the same colour as the crimson slashes on the white uniform, except the sheet was wet and shiny, and the colour was blood. There was blood everywhere. There was something else on that crimson sheet. Something so small, so perfect in its compactness, that I felt a sense of utter loss and pity and began to sob uncontrollably. With grim faces, they cleaned me up and removed that miniature, lifeless form that filled me with such sorrow and anguish.

The following morning, I was awakened by the sounds of an all too familiar routine as beds and lockers were pulled aside, the ward was cleaned and flowers that had been taken out of the ward the night before were brought back. When all was ready, Matron, in her starched white headdress, came into the ward ready for the daily round. She turned her head to smile at the great man who, with a retinue of students, came through the door at that precise moment.

I lay there passively, watching the small procession as it moved along the ward. Apart from a brief 'Good morning' or 'How are we today?' any discussion about the patient's condition was delivered solely to the students, who hung around in a small circle at the bottom of the bed, out of earshot of the patient herself. They seemed to hold the view that what you didn't know about, you couldn't worry about.

It wouldn't matter in my case, I thought grimly. Everybody knows about me.

Only that morning, I had heard the woman in the bed opposite whisper loudly to her neighbour, 'I've been waiting five years for a baby, and she gets rid of hers.'

When the small party reached my bed, I opened my eyes to receive the customary greeting, even stretching my face into a semblance of a smile. After all, being polite cost nothing. But both Matron and doctor kept their eyes averted. No greeting for me and, feeling more like a leper than ever, I slid back against the pillows and endeavoured to keep as far down in the bed as possible and out of sight. I felt a slight indentation at the bottom of the bed and surmised that someone was sitting there.

I kept my eyes closed tight and heard a man's voice commanding sternly, 'Mrs Storey, have you any idea how this could have happened?'

I chose not to answer. His voice was loud enough for the whole ward to have every ear inclined and every muscle tensed to hear this interrogation and to await the outcome. Through the grapevine of the medical staff, from the gynaecologist to the trainee nurse, would have gone the saga of my previous visit and request for a termination. Oh wicked, wicked woman, in the eyes of the Church and of God, what terrible mortal sin had I committed? Sackcloth and ashes and the wearing of them for the rest of my life would never atone. Once more the question was repeated, and once more I could not speak one word in my own defence. In sheer desperation, I covered my head with the bedcovers. I felt the weight on the end of my bed suddenly lift and a lighter weight thrown onto it. I guessed that it was my case-history folder that had been thrown with anger on my bed.

This convinced me that they had washed their hands of me. In defiance and frustration, I moved my foot under the covers and dislodged the folder with its sheaf of white papers and sent it crashing to the floor. The doctor and his entourage continued on their way. They gave not a hint that anything was amiss or that they had even seen what happened. And when the final patient had been greeted and examined, Matron rustled to the end of the ward and disappeared with the doctor through the great swing doors.

At seven o'clock that night, the first visitors began to arrive. I watched them coming in, all bearing gifts. Lockers were opened to house goodies, flowers were held aloft for other patients to admire. Chairs scraped next to beds, hands were held, and intimate low-toned whispers came to me as I lay there waiting for John. Tearful and sad, I waited to be reassured and consoled. More than anything I wanted a shoulder to cry on. I watched the door, for it seemed John was a long time putting in an appearance. When he did at last come, there was no welcoming smile on his face, and when he bent to kiss me I saw that his eyes were wet with tears. I thought he wept out of concern for me and I hastened to reassure him that I was all right.

But when he spoke, his voice was gruff with emotion so that when his words sank in they were like a body blow. 'I have just been informed that the child you aborted last night was a boy. You have murdered my son.'

I was drowning again and I hurt.

For the whole of the three days I was there, nobody spoke to me and my misery was complete. I was frozen inside, and I prayed that I might never feel anything ever again, neither love nor hate.

They dismissed me on the third day. Before I went, I had to see the almoner, who told me that I would be charged ten pounds for my short stay at Bristol General Hospital. I could pay it all at once or, in the case of extreme financial hardship, in three monthly instalments. I chose the latter, knowing it would be equally difficult to pay out of our meagre income. She then said that she could arrange a taxi to take me home, but I brushed that suggestion aside. I had no money for a taxi. Without looking up from the ledger in which she was writing, she informed me that I could wait for the ambulance, but as they were busy in the mornings it might be late afternoon before one was available to take me home. On the spur of the moment, I made the rash decision that I would walk home, something I had reason to regret long before I got even halfway there.

I walked down the steps of the hospital and out into the street. After the warmth of the ward, the keen October wind felt cold. I made my way along York Road towards Bath Bridge, stopping several times because of my weakened condition. Walking along the Netham and on towards Newbridge Road, I stood for a long time watching the river and remembering when, as children, we were taken up to Bees' Tea Gardens every Whitsuntide in a barge. The old barge on the other side of the river was solitary and empty now. Its dirty black hulk periodically bumped the side of the bank when the fast-flowing river tugged at the rope moorings. As I stood there, deep in thoughts of the past, the sad little poem we once learned at school came into my mind.

> Willows whiten, aspens quiver –
> Little wavelets dusk and shiver –
> In an island in the river
> Going down to Camelot

I shivered. I was glad I was on the last lap of my journey now. The short-cut along Whitby Road and past the Co-op Dairy would bring me into Sandy Park and Repton Road. All I could think of now was that big double bed and a long, long sleep. There was no one at home and, when I had wearily climbed the stairs, I found our room full of children's muddles and the bed unmade. I took off my coat and threw it on a chair that was already half submerged in clothes and books. Not caring very much, and longing for a cup of tea, I debated whether I would descend all those steps again to the kitchen just to fill the blasted kettle. In the end, I decided against it. It was just too much of an effort. I felt irritable and weepy, so I got into the unmade bed and was asleep in no time at all.

When I opened my eyes, the two girls were clambering all over me and snuggling down, one on each side. 'Mummy's home,' they kept repeating.

'Why didn't you let me know you were coming home today? I would have come to fetch you.' John was bending over the small gas ring when he asked me the question. I watched him strike a match and saw the ring of blue flame flare up, then it was covered by the kettle and the thought of the welcome cuppa made me feel good. I settled back against the pillows with the children and watched him performing these small domestic tasks.

The wind was whipping up outside and making the windows rattle. After a while I got irritated by the sound. I looked around this pathetic little shambles of a room that we all shared, both as living room and bedroom. A well-known cliché came back to me: 'Start off with nowt, always have nowt.'

'For God's sake, put a bloody wedge in that window,' I yelled at John. I was surprised at the anger that welled up from so deep inside of me. He looked up, startled at my outburst, but got up and obediently wedged the window and pulled the curtains. After a while, the small glow from the fire, along with the rise and fall of the children's breathing, softened the room and I fell asleep again long before John came to bed.

The following morning I was awakened by John shaking my shoulder. I was surprised to find that he had already taken Patty to school. Jacky was demanding that she be taken to the swings. The unlit fire, the unmade bed and the pile of unwashed crocks all added to the general squalor of the room. I listened to John's voice, not fully comprehending at first what he was trying to say. The good-natured banter of the night before was gone and in its place a note that indicated his patience was wearing thin.

'Will there be any dinner for me tonight when I come in?'

I thought dully, What does he mean? Wasn't there always a dinner on the table for him, whatever time he came in? I blinked and continued to stare back at him. He mistook the silence and the stare for insolence and continued angrily, 'Look, I can't take any more time off work. You are home now and have all day to rest if you want to. I will take a few bob from your housekeeping to buy my dinner at the canteen; that way you will only need to see to the kids and yourself.'

I watched him take the money from my purse and then heard his footsteps clattering down the stairs. The front door slammed so hard that the knocker at the top of the door gave an extra angry little rat-a-tat. I surveyed the room with dislike and distaste, from the grey embers in the grate to Jacky, who was by now squatting on the floor and in a very bad temper because we were not going to the swings.

'Shut up!' I yelled at her through clenched teeth. She was so surprised that just for a second she sat there with her mouth wide open, then with renewed vigour she let rip again. I sat and watched her. As far as I was concerned she could sit and howl all day. Getting up to restore the room to some sort of order would be more than enough for me to cope with.

'Who's being murdered up there?' Gertie's good-natured and strident voice came from the bottom of the stairs.

'None of your business!' I shouted back, and then sat bolt upright in bed. What was the matter with me, wanting to strike out at everyone in sight? Some little demon leaped out from inside of me on the slightest provocation.

Gertie opened the door very gingerly, because Jacky's bottom was right behind it. She took in the situation and in her rough way tried to resolve it.

'Come on my babby,' she said coaxingly to Jacky. 'Come on down the shops with Gertie.'

'Swings!' Jacky said defiantly, but got up to take Gertie's hand and follow her down the stairs.

273

'All right then,' Gertie replied, placating her and looking apologetically towards me. 'It'll give 'ee a bit of a rest,' she nodded and beamed. 'Shan't be much more 'n half an hour.'

Again I closed my eyes, but now the untidiness of the room got on my nerves. Besides, I was so thirsty I felt I could drink a gallon of tea. I rolled out of bed and began to dress. When I went to the recess to pull the curtains, I spotted the half-finished letter that I had been writing to our councillor on the morning when Den had visited. It was still in the pad, but as someone had put a cup of tea on the page there was now a brown stain obliterating the words. I sat down at the table and tore it all up.

I lit the fire and tidied the room, made a pot of tea and again sat in the window, sipping the brew and reflecting savagely on my beleaguered environment.

'Somebody ought to see the way we have to live.' I said the words aloud because I felt so desperate. And then once again it was anger that made me pick up the pen and write to the Council for an interview. Nobody had come as yet to assess us, or given us any points, and in that moment I was determined to keep fighting until we got a home of our own. I walked to the post office and fixed the stamp. When I finally slipped it through the pillar-box, I heard it flop to the bottom. That's when I looked up to the sky. 'I've done my bit, now you do yours!'

A few days later I wrote another letter to our local councillor. I was going to leave no stone unturned this time. It was a week later that a man from the Housing came out to see me, and Minnie had been primed to say that she couldn't stand the noise the children made and wanted her bedroom back, otherwise she would have to give us notice to quit. The man from the Housing thought this was a disgraceful thing for a mother to do, and couldn't bring himself to believe that she'd actually put her own flesh and blood out on the street.

However, although we were quite high on the list for points, he could not say how early we would be housed. Incredible as it seemed, there were a great many families living in worse circumstances than us. For instance, some lived with leaking roofs and damp walls, and in some cases bugs and infestations to contend with.

Everybody must fight for what they believe in their own way. So, when I received a reply from our local councillor granting us an interview the following Monday evening, I pushed John out through the front door even before he'd had a chance to have a cup of tea. He grumbled all the way, but I told him he could have dinner and supper all in one when we got home.

The two men chatted for an hour about Air Sea Rescue. I stifled a yawn as the conversation turned to gardening, and John was asked if this was a favourite hobby of his. John was wise enough to expand on this subject and declare that the loss of a garden was his one regret now that he was back in Civvy Street. He said that if he was lucky enough to get a council house, he hoped it would be on a corner plot so that he would have extra garden to work. Councillor Brown leaned confidentially across at John and said earnestly, 'Yes, my son, work the garden. It will pay off dividends.'

On the way home, I asked John if what he had told Councillor Brown was true. 'Do you really like gardening?'

'God, no,' he replied quickly. 'A plot bigger than a postage stamp would kill me.'

A House of Our Own

The miracle finally happened. One day I came down the stairs to find a long white official letter from the Housing Committee there on the mat.

I opened the letter and read that we had been allocated a house at 123 Ullswater Road, Southmead, at a rental of sixteen shillings a week, paid fortnightly in advance. A house! A house of our own! I promptly burst into tears.

'Absolutely ridiculous,' John exploded when I told him later that day. 'How in the world will I be able to afford that kind of money in advance?'

At that precise moment, I knew exactly how Jacky felt in one of her paddies. I felt like sitting on the floor and letting out a howl of rage and frustration myself. Gertie poked her head round the scullery door, where she was frying her supper on the stove.

'Bain't you goin' then?' she demanded.

'Yes we are! Even if I have to go out to work to help pay for the damned thing,' I shouted at John.

John's face was grim. 'You'll not do that,' he said. 'No wife of mine will go out to work. Your place is in the home, looking after me and my children.'

I decided that a king-sized sulk might bring quicker results, and flounced upstairs in a temper.

The following day I was staring miserably out of the window when I was surprised to hear John say, 'Get your coat on and we'll go and have a look at this house. I'm not promising anything, mind, but there's no harm in having a look.'

So it happened that, on a very grey and miserable day with a fine misty drizzle falling, we all went to visit the house in Ullswater Road. The estate was vast and the streets were wide, and only on one side of the street had the houses been completed. On the other side of the street, what was once a field was now a hive of building activity. A giant bulldozer was busy gouging out chunks of earth in preparation for the foundations of yet another pair of houses. A concrete mixer kept up a steady whirr of grey mixture, and all along the road piles of sand, cement, bricks and roof tiles lay in great neat heaps. Sounds of hammering came from inside the half-finished houses.

The site manager took the keys to our house from a great row of them hanging along one side of the hut, and pointed across the muddy road to a completed block of four houses with an alleyway between. Most of the other houses were semi-detached and I experienced a tiny pang of disappointment. I would have preferred one of a pair. They seemed to me to be superior, a little less lumped together. Still, anything was better than the one room we were living in, and I followed John and the children over the rough boards that had been laid from the road up to the front door.

On this wet day there seemed to be clods of yellow clay everywhere, but once inside the house, surveying the spacious rooms and the cupboards, the greyness of the day was left behind, and I became excited and enthusiastic. John had brought a pad and pencil and was making small steps across the lounge in an attempt to estimate the square yards of lino we would need. I noted and admired the large bay window and asked him to measure the length for curtain material. This information also went onto the pad. Next came an inspection of the grate, which had a back boiler to give us hot water. It also had an iron shutter which, when pulled down, acted as a drawing device to raise the temperature and send the warmth through air vents let into the walls of all the other rooms. I thought this was an ingenious idea, but John scowled and said that this ingenious little gadget would probably eat up a ton of coal in no time flat. I tried to remain silent after that, as my future happiness depended on whether we could afford this brand-new council house.

I wandered upstairs to look at the bedrooms and to stand at the door and imagine all of them carpeted and furnished in different colour schemes. Then I came to the bathroom, the ultimate luxury. Never in my whole life had I lived in a house with a bathroom. At South Road and Repton Road, the tin bath was housed on the wall in the back yard and hung on a six-inch nail, usually opposite the privy door, also outside. No more having to drag it down every week and boil up saucepans of hot water to have a bath. I closed my eyes in sheer ecstasy. Just thinking about it brought a feeling of pride at the thought of owning a bathroom.

There was more. There was a toilet upstairs next to the bathroom and another one in the garden along with a coal-house and tool shed. No more chamber pots under the bed and the drudgery of having to toil up and down stairs with slop pails to empty the wretched things. I made my way downstairs once more and into the kitchen. I opened drawers and cupboards, making little squeals of delight at the discovery of all the up-to-date fittings. Please God, I prayed. Please let it be possible for us to move into this house. And I vowed I would even go out to work, despite what John said about married women working.

When we had all gathered once more in the lounge, I waited for his verdict. He was still making notes on that pad of his. His face had not relaxed at all and still wore the troubled look of a man about to start a life sentence. It wasn't the joyous occasion I had imagined – two people deliriously happy about the first home they were going to move into.

'Well,' he said at last. 'If your heart is set on it, I can just about manage it. Mind you,' and here his voice grew very stern, 'I can only promise you the bread and not the butter. As it is, I shall have to do all the overtime on God's earth to manage this little lot.'

'I'll get a job to help out,' I began.

But he cut me short. 'Over my dead body,' he said. And the dark scowl returned to his face.

I knew we had not a stick of furniture of our own to bring with us, and I wondered at that moment how we really would be able to manage, but we held the key, and we were going to accept the house. The rest could take care of itself.

On a very cold day in February 1948, we finally moved into the house in Ullswater Road in Southmead. John had applied to the Soldiers, Sailors and Airmen's Association for some money to help with furniture and removal expenses. They had generously awarded us thirty pounds and a voucher to obtain some surplus government blankets and beds. We bought twenty square yards of brown jasp lino – a very dingy solid brown floor covering which was used in offices and warehouses – which was going cheap because it was being discontinued. It covered the lounge except for the bay. The damned stuff would not wear out and I grew sick of the sight of it long before it showed any signs of wear. The rest of the house remained bare boards.

A friend of John's who was demobbed at about the same time was enterprising enough to set himself up in the upholstery business in the basement of his parents' house. His first attempt was a hideous green hessian three-piece suite, which was not only big and ugly, but one of the armchairs did not sit straight on account of the frame being warped and twisted. One night in the pub, this monstrosity was offered to John as a gift, an offer that John was not in a position to refuse. In fact, neither of us could refuse such generosity, especially when he himself packed it in his van and delivered it to us the same day as we moved in, together with a bottle of British sherry to toast the success and fortune of our new home. We sat in the bare bay window and drank out of cups. As yet I had no wine glasses, and indeed it would be years before I got any.

I dyed some single sheets bright yellow for curtains, and we strung them up on wires that sagged dismally in the middle. I never did get to like our unlovely suite, but I must give it full marks for the best plaything the girls ever had. The arms of the settee became horses that must have galloped halfway round the globe, and the armchairs, put back to back and draped with an old sheet or blanket, made a wonderful tent. They printed the words PRIVATE, KEEP OUT on a piece of cardboard. From the giggles and contortions that went on under that blanket, it was evident that a good time was being had by the pair of them.

One more item of furniture graced our lounge, taking pride of place in the far corner of the room next to the fireplace. Cash had been extracted, from the thirty pounds that the services association had allocated us, for a writing bureau. John insisted it was essential for all his private papers, and he kept it locked at all times. I admit to having tried a few hundred keys in my attempts to open it, but I was doomed to failure and throughout our marriage the door remained locked.

There were two wide doors, painted a battleship grey like all the rest of the paintwork in the house, dividing the lounge from the small dinette. We furnished this with a white-topped table and four chairs. There was no money for a sideboard or dresser. A plain net curtain at the window simply enhanced the starkness of the room. I scrubbed the tabletop the way of the grain religiously every week, and polished the black bitumen floor to a high degree of brilliance with lavender polish.

The girls had two iron hospital beds and there was an abundance of army surplus blankets. Two lockers and a wardrobe graced their room. They had been quite generous to us at the government stores, and when we had more cash, we meant to go again. I had very recklessly gone into debt over our bedroom and bought a Utility full-sized double bed and dressing table. I chose a warm shade of mahogany, and got a telling off from John, who said I was far too extravagant for going twenty pounds into debt.

There were no frills, no pictures on the walls, no books or bookcases to hold them, no cushions for the chairs. But it was home, and everything else would come in time.

And there was one other extravagance, which nobody grumbled about and was enjoyed by all in that cold winter. I had the foresight to order a whole ton of coal, and paid the coal man plus a tip when he delivered it straight into our brand-new coalhouse. I counted the bags as he passed by the window and along the alleyway. I was thinking how wonderful it was that he was not coming through the hall.

The boiler gave us lashings of hot water, and the warm-air vents kept the chill off the dinette. Best of all, the bare boards upstairs were always warm to walk on. Cold lino and freezing rooms became a bad dream of the past. However, just as

John had predicted, the fire simply gobbled up the coal. If you wanted a warm house, it demanded to be fed. Sometimes the coal man came and dropped in a couple of bags of coal, and because I was stony broke I pretended I wasn't in. The coal bill grew alarmingly, but still I couldn't pay. Although I knew that the day of reckoning would surely come, and I would have to face John's wrath, what was coming was mercifully concealed.

John found out about the coal bill when someone from the coal merchant called round to ask about the unpaid debt. John said he knew nothing about any unpaid bill, and the caller was invited into the house for an explanation. He was a middle-aged man, and was obviously very aware of the explosive situation he had created. His tone was apologetic and conciliatory. He explained that his firm would accept two shillings a week off the arrears and still continue to deliver two hundredweight of coal. They did not want to be responsible for any hardship in a household with young children. He made out a debit card for the amount due and very leniently said he would accept five shillings off the arrears now.

Silent and white-faced, John handed over the five bob and courteously showed the man to the door. When he returned he just as quietly told me that I was no longer to be trusted with money, and from now on the rent and other bills would be paid by him. All the cash I would ever handle would be for housekeeping. Furthermore, I was not only extravagant, I was secretive too. Well, it was evident that the small amount of housekeeping he left me was far from adequate, but when I protested, he pulled out the linings of his pockets to prove to me that he couldn't give me what he didn't have. It was clear to me at any rate that I would have to find a part-time job.

Next door was a four-bedroomed house occupied by a family of six lads whose ages ranged from eighteen down to a boy of six. We never did see any sign of their father, but Mrs Cook, their mother, was well in evidence. She was a big, blousy woman who ruled the roost, kept the boys in order and whose word was law. They played football in the alley-way and drove me crazy. When the ball was kicked onto the garden, they trampled all over it, and our gate was continually left open when, without so much as a by-your-leave, they walked in to retrieve their ball. No amount of yelling had the slightest effect, they merely scooped up the ball and, with a cheeky grin, kicked it back down the alley. I swore I would confiscate the damn thing the very next time they kicked it over to my garden. Finally, in desperation, I did just that, and carried the ball triumphantly into my kitchen.

Round came Mrs Cook a few minutes later, and with arms akimbo demanded the return of the ball.

'The kids have to play somewhere,' she said belligerently. 'Your old man wants to give 'ee a couple of lads, then you might be a bit more tolerant towards 'em.'

'I believe in quality, not quantity,' I said icily, and almost shoved the ball in her face. Matters were not improved when, every time John came home, he actually joined in the game with them. Obviously, this made him 'a rattling good sport' and me 'a miserable old bag'.

Meanwhile, at every opportunity, Jacky used to slip out the back way and through the alley to cross the road to the site manager's hut, where she was a firm favourite. Here she was spoiled with cups of tea and biscuits and cakes. I saw the danger behind every pile of sand and bricks but, despite all my scolding, that was where she could nearly always be found.

When Patty arrived home from school one afternoon, it was already getting towards dusk. I called for her to go and collect Jacky and come for tea. Half an hour later, Patty returned on her own: Jacky was nowhere to be found and the site manager had not seen her since three o'clock. I experienced a ring of fear. Telling Patty to have her tea and remain in the house until I came back, I ran over the road to look for Jacky. The piles of bricks and roof tiles seemed dark and forbidding now that there was no sign of activity around to give them meaning. When I called her name, the brooding silence mocked me. Where could I begin to look? Perhaps she was in some other child's house. I could try knocking on doors. I looked up the deserted street with dismay.

Please, God, show me where she is, I prayed, then began to laugh hysterically. Why do we call on an unseen force, one that we don't even believe in, as a kind of last resort? I shivered, and realised I had come out without a coat. And I would need a torch. How stupid to have come out without either. I suddenly thought of the pond at the edge of the estate. I closed my eyes. Jacky would not venture that far, she had been warned never to go there. I tried not to think of the pond.

When I got back to the house, Mrs Cook was leaning on the gate and watching out for me. As I approached, she spoke to me with real concern in her voice.

'Our Charlie's round your house with your big un. She come crying round our house sayin' she was frit, and that your little un's lost. I've sent our Sidney out on his bike to have a scout round the block. If I was you, I'd let my eldest come round with you and have a look in they 'alf-finished 'ouses up top. Kids da sometimes like playin' in um.'

I looked at her. Surely she couldn't think Jacky was still out playing? When long evening shadows fell, what child would dream of lingering? Darkness sent children scurrying homewards to warm fires and security. However, her concern did make me feel less cut off and helpless. There was another person with me now and I was able to breathe more easily. She broke off to shout at Frank, her eldest boy. Her voice was strident and authoritative. Frank was suddenly by her side.

'Go with missus and search they 'ouses up top. If they'm locked, get our Sidney to ride to the site manager's 'ouse along there in Southmead Road. He da know where he lives.'

Mrs Cook called after us to make sure we had a torch, and Frank held it aloft for her to see. As I ran along by his side she called, 'Don't 'ee worry about your big un, we'll 'ave 'er in alongside we.'

All the houses on the other side of the street were empty and locked. I almost sobbed with relief when I heard Sidney arrive. He jumped off his bike and leaned it against the side of the house. He jangled the keys in front of me and helped me to my feet. All three of us went systematically through the houses, shining the torch and calling for Jacky. There was one last house to search, and as the key was inserted in the lock I was the first one through the door and into the kitchen. The torch circled the room and picked out the form of a small child crouched in a corner but not saying a word. Her eyes were wide with terror so that I rushed forward and held her in my arms.

She shivered with cold and shock, and I tried not to think of the hours she had been there, or how scared she must have been when the foreman locked the door, unaware that she was playing in the house. Frank took off his coat for me to wrap her trembling little body. Every so often, little dry sobs shook her small frame. 'I called you, Mummy,' she said at last. 'I called and called you and you didn't come.'

I was crying with her now, and the two lads turned away. 'I'll always be here when you call, Jacky.' And I held her closer. 'I must have heard you, because here I am.'

The two lads helped me to my feet and together we walked back down the street. Mrs Cook gave a grunt of satisfaction and disappeared with Frank and Sidney inside the house. Frank brought Patty round ten minutes later. I gave Jacky a hot drink and tucked her up in bed.

Several days later, the lads were playing football in the alley again, and the ball was once more kicked onto the garden. I gave a sigh and waited for the sound of boots outside the window. To my surprise, there was a knock on the front door instead. When I opened the door, Charlie stood there, smiling timidly.

'Please, missus. Sorry but the ball's gone on your garden. Can I get it back, please?'

I was so taken aback that I stared at him until he began to shuffle his feet uncomfortably. Then I laughed. 'Of course you can.'

I felt that I was making progress.

Ullswater Road, Southmead

The houses were completed and the pavements laid. The site manager's hut was dismantled and the board with Laing's name on it long gone. Trees began to appear in front gardens and at weekends men could be seen digging energetically, preparing that heavy, uncultivated soil for fruit and vegetables and flowers. A few streets away a doctor's surgery opened up and, much to everyone's surprise, the doctor was a woman. A storm of protest greeted this new arrival. Comments at the local newsagent's or post office ranged from 'Fancy! We got a lady doctor in Dunmail Road!' to ''Tain't right 'aving to drop yer trousers in front of a woman!'

Despite all the prejudice, she stayed, along with all the other changes going on around us. The landslide victory of the Labour Party at the end of the war ushered in the Welfare State in a new world for all the poor, but especially for women. For the first time, women visited the doctor on their own account. Before, it was all they could afford to get the kids there in emergencies, and it was common to see women almost limping with the pain of untreated ulcers, bad veins and worse. Minor ailments would drag on and on, dosed up with home remedies or ineffective commercial preparations. Now we had free hospital and dental treatment, free glasses and the Family Allowance (for the second child).

A few weeks later, Woolworth's were advertising for counter hands and Mrs Cook kindly offered to look after Jacky so that I could earn a few extra quid a week. It was only a part-time job, just a few minutes' walk away, and I was home again by two in the afternoon. I was working for a whole week before John found out and was predictably angry. John was not an aggressive man. He just held to an old-fashioned idea that a married woman's place was in the home where she could look after the family and be protected. It must have worried him to discover that he had married someone with such strong views. But he capitulated after a week and I now had my housekeeping plus a few bob of my own.

I lost the job at Woolworth's a month before our first Christmas at Ullswater Road. Jacky developed chickenpox and needed attention. Day and night, I sat with her, painting her spots and trying to prevent her scratching them and leaving a permanent scar. It was a bit of a blow, because those few extra pounds would have made all the difference to our first festive season, in buying modest little gifts for the girls. However, I knew that the needs of my girls came first, and we would just make the best of it, as we always had. At least they were kept happy, gluing long strings of paper chains, which were hung up from each corner and held in the middle by a large paper bell. We even had a small tree. Silver strings of tinsel hung from the branches, and we had a fairy on the top cut out of painted cardboard, with more tinsel for her dress and wings. The girls also made paper lanterns decorated with crayoned patterns and hung around the room.

We had four unexpected visitors that Christmas. Strange to say, if it had not been for their arrival and the goodies they brought, our Christmas would have been lean indeed. We were woken early on Christmas morning by the two girls, who had discovered the stockings at the bottom of the bed and now came into our room proudly displaying the crayons and colouring books and chocolate selection boxes that Father Christmas had left for them.

Just after lunch came a rat-a-tat-tat at the front door, and both girls ran to open it and admit Dennis and Audrey with their little daughter Anita and my mum and dad. They came bearing gifts for all of us, together with sherry, Christmas cake made by my mother, and a large trifle, which Audrey declared was liberally laced with sherry, with real cream on top. Den put the presents round the tree whilst Audrey tied gold chocolate coins to the branches.

John allowed himself to be dressed up in an old red dressing gown and a copious beard made from cotton wool as Father Christmas. All this was done very secretly out in the hallway whilst Audrey urged the girls to be very quiet and then they would hear Santa arriving on his sleigh. Presently, we heard the sound of sleigh bells ringing and then we all began to sing 'Jingle Bells'. The girls' eyes were as big and round as saucers, and they sat as quiet as mice when this big man in red advanced to the small tree and then began to distribute presents all round. My mother had given them baby dolls, which she had dressed herself.

That Christmas Day was as near perfection as I could ever wish for. Dennis brought sherry and we drank each other's health and to the success of both our new houses, for Den and Audrey had just been allocated a new house at Fortfield Road in Hengrove. And we ate the sausage rolls and mince pies that Audrey had made and which proved her to be a wonderful cook.

It was a wonderful day. I was sorry when they left and bundled into Dad's little car and drove off. Mum and Dad were now running the West End Café down in Bruton in Somerset, and we were given an invitation to come and spend a holiday there as soon as the weather was nice enough. Dad said we were to let him know, and he would come and fetch us all in the car. After they left, I had a warm feeling that things were definitely getting better. I had made a friend of my new sister-in-law, who insisted that we keep in touch with each other, and Mum and Dad had helped to make the day so special. I began to hum a song to myself: 'When you come to the end of a perfect day and you sit alone with your thoughts – the bells ring out in a carol gay, for the joy that the day has brought.'

Now we had free dental treatment for the children, we were informed that visits to the clinic at Southmead Hospital were essential, and they became routine. That morning, I looked out at the weather and wished that our journey was not necessary – it was cold, with a bitter wind blowing, and it was a fair step to the clinic. When we got there, the hall was packed with parents and children, sitting on benches. Lots of the children were already scared and beginning to cry before they were even called. Apprehension and fear travelled quickly round the room.

I assured Patty that I wouldn't let anyone take her teeth out unless she herself agreed to it. She looked at me disbelievingly, but I think we both felt better after that and she began to chat to the little girl sitting next to her. This was my cue to start talking to the elderly woman with her. It needed only a sympathetic listener and soon her story came tumbling out. She was the child's grandmother, and had come all the way from Leicester to look after Trudy, because her daughter had tragically died of cancer. She wished the prefab was bigger, it only had two bedrooms and she had to share with Trudy. If it were possible to get a bigger house, on an exchange basis, she would gladly come down to Bristol permanently to look after her son-in-law and his little daughter.

I sat staring at her, completely tongue-tied. Here was my heaven-sent opportunity to get my prefab, but the chance was so unexpected, coming like a bolt from the blue, that I stuttered for words. I heard the nurse calling Patty's name and said, all in a rush, 'I've got a house we can't afford. I should love a prefab. I've always wanted one. Look out for me when we've finished with the dentist, and I'll give you our address. Won't do any harm to come and have a look, will it?'

At the door to the consulting room, a nurse tried to disentangle the hold on our hands, saying to Patty, 'You're a big girl now, you don't need your mum with you, do you?'

But I was determined to stand by the promise I had made to her and said firmly, 'I need to be with her. I need to know the results of the examination.'

Very reluctantly, she allowed me to go in, where a male dentist with a shock of red hair drew up a chair for me to sit on. He began checking Patty's teeth, calling out numbers to his assistant nurse. When he had finished he said to me, somewhat curtly, 'Your daughter has two tipped teeth that need to be extracted. If you will kindly leave the room, we can get on with the job.'

John had often told me of the wonderful job they did at saving the teeth of servicemen by doing fillings rather than pulling them out. Extractions were very much a last resort.

'Can't you fill the teeth?' I asked, and watched a shade of impatience settle on his face. Patty sat looking from one to the other. I fought her cause that day.

Finally he gave up the fight. It was obvious that I wasn't going to give in and now he just wanted to get rid of us. 'Make an appointment for a further visit,' he said testily. 'And I'll see what can be done.'

Out in the corridor we saw Trudy and her grandmother waiting their turn. I sat down by the side of them, wrote out my address and gave it to her. I explained the way she could best get there. All this while Trudy was screwing up her handkerchief and I could see she was a bundle of nerves. I could also see that all the teeth in the front of her mouth were black. No amount of bullying on Gran's part would save them. I smiled at Trudy and then looked at Gran – 'Hope to see you soon, then' – and waved them both good-bye.

About a week later she kept her word and came to see us. She was delighted with the house and said she would bring her son-in-law to see it and to meet my husband. John did not put up any resistance to the move. The prefab would be much cheaper to run and relieve the constant worry of the endless bills and trying to maintain the upkeep of the larger house. We were invited back to the prefab in St Lucia Crescent and saw the warmth and comfort that this small dwelling could give. I had so much to thank these people for: they even left the carpets and the curtains for us, a three-piece suite and a red-topped enamel table in the kitchen. Both men went to the Council House on College Green to ask permission to exchange, and on a very sunny day in April 1950 we moved into the prefab.

The Prefab

I loved my prefab. Anyone who ever lived in one loved them. Built in pre-fabricated sections, they could be erected quickly and easily. They were the short-term answer to the homelessness caused by wartime bombing and the forces all returning home after the war. These little square bungalows had a central solid-fuel fire which provided warmth and hot water, two bedrooms, a bathroom, a sitting room and a modern, fully fitted kitchen complete with built-in cooker, sink and fridge. It was labour-saving luxury and I considered myself fortunate to be living in one of them. We were a proper family now.

The two girls attended the little church school on Horfield Common, and I took my turn with the other mothers to take and fetch them – walking across the common, past the drill hall and Manor Farm, where in those days the fields still stretched all the way down to the back of the Beehive Inn.

On Sundays and precious days off we all went for long walks down through the fields of Manor Farm to Westbury Village, and on through the quiet countryside to Blaise Castle Estate, or along the road to cross the ford at Henbury to arrive at the front entrance of Blaise. In the early fifties it was quite safe for us to walk together in the road because motor traffic was rare. Children still played safely in the street and we had no worries when later the girls got bicycles and went off for picnics on their own. And we never locked our back door.

In those far-off days of the summer of 1950, I even found time to take a blanket and spread it beneath the high magnolia tree that grew at the end of our neighbour's garden and gave us shade. The end of her garden touched our front lawn and we were separated by a wire fence. From this corner vantage point I could see our front gate and the short path to the road beyond. I usually had two whole glorious hours before the girls returned from school, bursting through the gate like two small hurricanes, demanding drinks and asking what there was for tea.

I settled back with my hands clasped behind my head and closed my eyes. It was very pleasant lying there and listening to the drone of the bees. Sometimes an ant would explore the contours of my face and I would brush it away. Then I heard the gate click and glimpsed two young men walking towards me. Their eyes were bright and their faces gleamed. They both seemed handsome in a wholesome, well-fed sort of way. Both had close-cropped crew cuts and what little hair they had shone in the bright afternoon sunlight. As they approached they extended their hands to greet me and I heard the Midwest drawl of American accents.

'We're surely pleased to meet you, ma'am. Elder Drew and Elder Smith from the Church of Jesus Christ of Latter Day Saints at your service, ma'am.' And they both grinned broadly.

I could only stare. They seemed like an apparition. As I made no reply, Elder Smith rushed on, 'We surely would like to stay awhile to discuss the Bible with you, and talk about the Book of Mormon and the message of salvation for us all.'

The war had left me with a gaping hole where my religious beliefs were concerned. I had been brought up to believe in God; I went to Sunday school and Chapel as we all did in those days, unquestioningly. Looking directly into the fresh, smiling faces of these two young men, I replied firmly and quietly, 'I'm sorry, but I have no wish to discuss religion with you now, or at any other time, for that matter.'

If I had expected persistence, it did not come, and their farewell handshakes were just as warm and genuine as their greeting. They retraced their steps to the gate and closed it carefully behind them. Then Elder Drew leaned over the gate to call to me, 'We're having a social evening this Saturday at half past seven. We'd be happy to welcome you and your fine family if you'd like to join us.'

I lay for a long while, allowing my thoughts to run on. There were beginning to be so many things to be optimistic about. In the first government after the war it was not Churchill with his fat cigar that the people voted for, but – just as my father had so long predicted – it was Labour who romped home. A landslide victory. We danced in the streets, laughed and cried alternately. This was our dream come true. Our Utopia. Our Shangri-la.

And despite the hardship and the years of austerity, the Labour government did usher in the Welfare State, which would look after you from the cradle to the grave; and the bad old days were gone for ever, we thought. We had a health service that was the envy of the world. They got rid of the dreaded means test. And there was universal secondary education for all. So at the beginning of the fifties it felt as if things were going to get better and better . . .

The following Saturday I was taking the girls for a walk on Horfield Common. John was now working as a postman with the GPO and, faced with an evening on my own, whilst he was on a late shift, I suddenly remembered the invitation to the social evening and mentioned it to the girls. It was met by a kind of mild enthusiasm, just enough to send us off searching for Zion Hall.

We caught the bus to Old Market and walked through to West Street, where we finally found the hall, tucked behind Trinity Church. It was an old, dilapidated building with a corrugated-iron roof. But if our first sight of the place was disappointing, the welcome when we stepped inside more than made up for it. I recognised the handsome American missionaries immediately, and Elder Drew came forward to escort us into the hall and put us in the care of other members of the church, who called each other 'brother' and 'sister'.

The place was gaily festooned with huge bunches of balloons and flower garlands, beneath which trestle tables groaned with tempting things to eat. The girls were whisked away by other children anxious for them to join in games, and I was soon made to feel completely at home. It felt like a kind of extended family, where I could join the easy conversation and enjoy the stimulation of a friendly crowd. That evening came to an end all too quickly, but not before I had made the promise to come again soon.

I think it was the social side of the Church that called to me, the friendliness and companionship they offered. And so I became involved, though not committed, and it took a long time to finally realise that their way was not for me, and to understand that, whilst we are all travellers along the same road, in the end I had to find my own faith in my own way.

So for a while I joined in and began to thoroughly enjoy myself. When it was suggested that we stage a production of *Snow White* to raise money for the repair of the roof, I offered my services as prompter. Sitting on top of the piano, I rehearsed the kids until they were word-perfect. As the opening night drew nearer we all prayed for fine weather, for the iron roof of our ancient building leaked like a sieve. And the pattering of raindrops had often drowned our adult singing, so what would it do for the children's reedy voices?

Luck was with us and gave us a fine, clear night. I peeped through the old faded stage curtains and saw the hall filling up fast. Behind the scenes, fond parents were putting the last-minute touches to the children's costumes, tucking and pinning and making slight adjustments. The line of grown-up brothers and sisters rustled song sheets and formed a line behind the stage. Their main task was to add a little volume to the songs and choruses of our young cast, and to provide frightening screams and growls at appropriate moments during the show.

'Everybody on stage!' came the voice of our director. The great moment had arrived. I delivered the prologue with all the dramatic gusto I could muster . . .

> ''Twas many, many years ago,
> When softly fell the silver snow,
> A queen sat sewing in her room,
> All safely sheltered from the gloom,
> And to the mirror on the wall
> She asked, "Who is the fairest queen of all?"'

All went well until the final act, when the wicked queen rode out into the teeth of the storm and disaster struck. Brother Lewtas was an electrical engineer. He had devised a couple of super special effects for the thunder-and-lightning sequence which involved vigorously shaking a thin sheet of metal to produce an excellent imitation of thunder whilst simultaneously rapidly switching the house lights on and off. Together with the hideous cackling of the wicked queen, it warranted an Oscar.

Alas! Old buildings have old wiring. Brother Lewtas fused every light in the house and the hall was plunged into darkness. It soon became apparent that they were not going to come on again either, and very reluctantly we had to abandon the show and go home. With the aid of a few miserable candles rustled up from somewhere, the seven little dwarfs were hustled through the hall and out into the darkness, still in their costumes and carrying their fake lanterns. Hi-ho, hi-ho. I collected my own two little dwarfs and went home as well.

It was obvious that Zion Hall would not do; it was old, it was damp, and the roof leaked. And it was too small for our growing membership. But when we moved, we left many happy memories of the young church in that shabby corrugated-iron hut.

We moved into a large, gracious building on Cheltenham Road, large enough for all our activities within the Church, as well as having living accommodation for our two new missionaries, Brother and Sister Gale from Salt Lake City. I joined the women's section, which met on Thursday evenings and was called Relief Society. I enjoyed the fresh ideas and the lively social life; there was something of interest going on all the time. The Church really did become part of your everyday life and was not just kept for Sundays like the Church of England.

We even tried to follow the strict dietary guidelines of the Church by forsaking tea, coffee, alcohol and tobacco. The friendly missionaries were particularly keen to gather John, as head of the household, into the faith and often called at our little prefab for an impromptu discussion and prayer session. It was particularly important that the whole family should join the Church so that we could all worship together in peace and perfect harmony. But all too often the missionaries would call just when John and I had settled down for the evening to listen to a radio programme, mugs of tea by our sides, both of us puffing away on our welcome fags. The gentle tap at the door would be answered by one of the girls, who brought the somewhat disconcerting news that elders from the Church had arrived.

There was hardly time to crush out our fags and remove the offending mugs of tea before they would be ushered in to begin the meeting with a prayer. Both of them would look slightly pained, and rather pious – bathed as they were in a haze of tobacco smoke – as we put our hands together, bowed our heads and closed our eyes in prayer.

As for me, I always felt so embarrassed that I had nothing to offer them by way of refreshment; it was tea or tap water in our house. But they assured me not to worry and said that, if we could obey the precepts of the Lord and forsake tea, they would bring us an approved drink called Instant Postum for us to try the following week. They talked to us gently about the evils of tobacco and the demon drink and after an hour or so of this John meekly agreed that he would give it up to keep the word of the Lord and for the sake of his health. Elder Smith held out his hand for the offending fags and John simply gave them to him.

We honestly did try, but it was so hard to break the habits of a lifetime, and those few days we went without our two luxuries did seem like an awfully long time. And Instant Postum proved to be no substitute for a decent cuppa, either. At our meetings on Sundays we praised the Lord heartily and took it in turns to stand up and bear testimony to the fact that this was the true church of Jesus Christ and to our pride in being Latter Day Saints. And dear Sister Jenkins, who must have been ninety, would get to her feet to exhort us to 'Smile. Smile. Smile a smile and after a while, there'll be a whole mile of smiles. So smile!'

Sister Perry, who played the piano and often fell into a poetic reverie, must have had intuitive feelings that our thoughts were straying from the straight and narrow path, for she told us a little anecdote about the good man who had been a perfect Christian all his life, and who stood at the gates of heaven waiting to enter the glorious kingdom. But Saint Peter sadly shook his head; the man couldn't come in.

'Why oh why?' begged the man. 'I've led a blameless life.'

St Peter said nothing, but merely pointed to the teapot in the man's hand – it was enough to send him down below.

In spite of warnings like these we did indeed slip back into the old ways. The Church, in any case, did not especially appeal to John, who felt he should not be deprived of the few comforts that life offered him. Truth to tell, without his mug of tea and his fags he was unbearable to live with anyway. And when he discovered that one of the teachings of the Church involved baptised members donating a tenth part of their income for its upkeep, he was even less impressed.

Meanwhile I continued to enjoy my evenings in the Relief Society, and it was here one Thursday that I had an unexpected invitation for a holiday in Devon. One of the sisters had married and was leaving Bristol to go and live in a village near Newton Abbot in Devon. They had bought a cottage in Kingsteighton they intended to use as a guest house, for Sister Abby had several awards for her catering skills. She gave a little speech on the last afternoon before she left for her new home, and assured us all of her love for us and for the Church. If any one of us ever felt the need for a holiday in her home there would be a true Latter Day Saints' welcome and special rates.

Sister Stanbury was sitting next to me and whispered, 'Fancy a holiday?'

Sister Stanbury was a widow, so she could make her own independent decisions. The war had swept away a lot of the old Victorian concepts about the different roles of men and women but that still didn't mean I could just say yes, and go off on holiday on my own. But John was surprisingly amicable about the holiday and admitted it would do me and the girls a lot of good to get away. He even promised me some extra money towards our fares. I was elated. I had not had a real holiday since long before the war.

I couldn't wait to tell Mary Stanbury. And together we organised bring-and-buy sales and children's hand-me-downs to secure holiday clothes for ourselves and our girls. Mary had been left a widow with three young girls of her own to bring up so she had an eagle eye for any bargains going.

We slowly collected all that we would need and managed to put by a few shillings each week and talked of nothing else but the coming holiday for months.

At last came the Saturday morning when we met in Anchor Road for the coach to Teignmouth – surrounded by suitcases and bulging bags, so many things bought simply because you never knew what you might need and anything might come in handy. So there we all were, five excited girls with their two, scarcely less excited, mothers on a warm summer's morning, bound for adventure in faraway Devon on the exotic English Riviera! It felt like the destination of a lifetime.

The cottage was thatched, whitewashed and unashamedly quaint. It was surrounded by a low whitewashed wall, and heady-scented jasmine grew all around the porch. Inside, in the tiny front parlour the low ceiling was heavy with blackened beams. Old plates hung on the walls and horse brasses on the old beams, and when the late sun dipped through the latticed windows they shone like burnished gold.

We slept under the sloping roof, in tiny single beds that had been cut down to fit in the available space. We almost kissed the floor. The five girls were in the tiny L-shaped annexe to our room, which allowed them turning space but little more. The floorboards were stained a dark shiny black and everything smelled of lavender beeswax polish.

On the bathroom door there was a framed Mabel Lucy Atwell print that showed a row of round-faced cherubic children announcing, 'Ours is a nice house, ours is!' At night it was dark and quiet, save for the murmuring of a stream by the side of the house. In the morning the screaming of the gulls as they came up the River Teign, following the fish, wakened us. As we lay in bed we smelled bacon frying for our breakfast, so we rushed to sample the culinary delights of Sister Abby's cooking. Her talents had not been overestimated and our empty plates, scraped clean at both breakfast and evening meal, bore ample testimony to that.

Buses and trains were cheap and frequent. We went into Teignmouth and caught the train that ran right along the water's edge to Dawlish. It cost us threepence. Mary and I giggled together like schoolgirls over the saucy postcards in the shops. And we ran in and out of the water, laughing and splashing each other and generally behaving like a couple of kids ourselves. I felt so relaxed and happy; it was wonderful. I began to acquire an attractive and healthy tan.

Sometimes Mary and I just lazed on the beach at Teignmouth and let the girls go off on their own on the train. Things were so much safer then for kids on their own. One day we caught the bus into Newton Abbot for market day. Sometimes we took long walks along the river. Every day, we arrived home in time for supper, ravenously hungry, always expecting a feast and never disappointed. Sister Abby cooked us roasts, a steak-and-kidney pie, stews and casseroles and chops. Some different and wonderful dish surprised us every day. Her pastries were light and airy. We gobbled apple pie and cream, and fruit fools and sponges and crumbles. And she enchanted the children one evening with a jelly set in multi-coloured stripes and refused to tell them the magic secret of its making.

The golden days passed by on wings and it was Thursday before we knew it. At breakfast I suggested a coach trip. This was not very well received: the girls wanted to go to the beach again, not sit in a stuffy coach. Mary then came up with the idea that she would take the girls into Teignmouth, where they could shop for souvenirs and gifts to take home, and I could have the whole day to myself to do as I pleased.

'Go and commune with nature!' she laughed.

I caught a coach just leaving for a tour of Dartmoor, including Widdecombe-in-the-Moor and the famous tors – those giant granite outcrops that are scattered across the moors. I sat in the front seat and settled back to enjoy the ride and the lush green of the passing countryside. It was a warm day with a breeze that nudged big frothy white clouds along and sometimes hid the sun from view. The weather was increasingly hot and humid; thunderstorms had been forecast for later.

I got off the coach with the rest of the passengers to walk over the grass as far as Haytor Rocks. Some of the more adventurous began to climb to the top. I followed, surprised a little by the steep climb but enjoying the sensation of gaining ground and with every step getting nearer to the summit. Standing there, on the top of that great granite rock formation against the backdrop of the purple, lowering sky, I suddenly remembered the muck heap of a mountain that I used to love to climb as a child. It was just a pile of earth at the end of the lane, but to me as a three-year-old it represented the real challenge of life – the struggle to get to the top and the glorious view into the doctor's garden when I finally managed to get there.

Now I listened to the rising wind blowing through the short stems of tough grass on the tor, with its eternal rhythmic sound, and it seemed I understood the law of survival and the need for a kind of discipline in the primitive urge of being. I also recognised my own rebellious nature and my desperate need for some kind of freedom. There was a similarity in that mountain I'd climbed as a child and this heady clambering on Haytor Rocks – the desire to stand apart, to be free.

I took a deep breath and threw my arms wide to a vista of unsurpassed wild beauty and knew I would always need to return to the imagery and magic of the landscape I had experienced and captured that day. There was something elemental and as yet imperfectly understood within me that needed expression.

We came home to Bristol brimming with health and vitality. With eyes shining and the words tumbling from our lips we rushed through the gate, eager to tell of our great adventures and to give and receive the affection and cuddles of the welcome back.

At first, in the confusion of our exuberant entry, I failed to notice the quiet, almost stilted welcome. Whilst the girls scattered coats and parcels everywhere and fell upon cases to search for sticks of rock and presents they had brought home, I followed John into the kitchen to sip the cup of tea he had prepared and to tell him of the wonderful week we had spent in Devon. Later, when the girls were in bed, I slipped happily into bed beside John. He was lying with his arms clasped behind his head, staring up at the ceiling. Only then did I become aware that he was ominously quiet. Some intuitive fear prevented me from asking what was wrong and I waited for him to break the long emptiness of silence. I knew it portended something, but what? When he spoke, he did not look at me, and his eyes remained staring up at the ceiling. His words came quietly and simply.

'I want a boy,' he said. 'You have your two girls, but I have no son.'

If the request seemed reasonable enough, the timing certainly was not. The glory of the holiday, with all its memories, seemed to vanish in a giant wave that sent showers of cold spray high in the air and then left nothing. I blinked hard and thought about the effect of that simple statement and what it would mean to me. For a start, I had been down that road three times already – the two girls completed our family and I certainly didn't want to repeat the experience of a miscarriage. We had moved into the prefab for financial reasons and another child would stretch our already slender finances to the limit – not to mention the fact that having a boy in addition to the two girls would mean us having to move. The final and most important reason of all – the one which began to make me feel angry – was that my precious yearnings for freedom would be curtailed once more.

I said tonelessly, 'I don't want another baby.' And then, with some heat, 'Don't you understand? I really do not want any more children!'

John turned away from me without another word. I had a sudden mental vision of the wind blowing ceaselessly, eternally and heartlessly through the grass at the base of the tor.

A Cycle Ride to Bruton

We all had bikes except Jacky. John had a heavy-framed black Raleigh roadster that he'd bought to get to work. I used my own second-hand bike for shopping and we bought Patty a new bike for her ninth birthday. We promised to look out for a second-hand fairy cycle for Jacky but somehow there never seemed enough money in the kitty. She ran behind her sister, begging to be allowed to have a ride on a bike that was anyway too big for her. A new bike for Jacky would make it possible for all of us to enjoy the delights of the countryside instead of using the bus and Shanks's pony.

It was one of those rare mornings when our compact kitchen was the scene of domestic bliss. As a disciplinarian I always insisted on some kind of civilised behaviour at the meal table, where even suppressed giggles were frowned upon. John was happily tackling the rare treat of eggs and bacon whilst I read aloud a letter I'd just received from my mother.

My mum and dad. They were always promising the girls that Dad would come from Bruton in Somerset and fetch them in his car (still the old black Austin 10 they'd bought before the war), and take them back to spend a holiday in that delightful country setting. The letter contained the disappointing news that due to pressure of work they would not be able to spare the time to come and fetch them at least for a week or two. The girls received the news with gloomy expressions and Jacky said that Cousin Anita had already been down to Nan's café for a whole week at Easter. Pop had taken her to a sawmill and she had been allowed to pick up some sawdust and put it into a bag to take home for her pet rabbit.

'Nita said there's a real stream in Nan's garden with real watercress growing in it that you can eat!' Jacky finished triumphantly.

The prospect of all these delights being denied was a major catastrophe as far as the girls were concerned, but of course there was nothing I could do to change their grandparents' decision.

So whilst the girls stared at their cornflakes in moody silence, John continued to munch thoughtfully on his toast. He kept a dead-straight face as he said mischievously, 'Of course we could ride to Bruton and surprise Nan and Pop.'

'How can we do that?' the girls demanded; but you could see they liked the idea already.

'We could ride down the hills on our flying bedsteads. We could picnic in the fields. We could even stop for a bottle of pop and a delicious sandwich of desert chicken.'

The bombshell dropped. He went on eating his toast and swigging his tea – just waiting for the effect of his words. I knew he was quietly amused at the pandemonium that followed, all my careful attempts at an orderly mealtime completely disrupted – cornflakes and sugar scattered in all directions as the girls leaped to their feet, shouting excitedly, 'Come on, Mummy, let's do it. Please say we can.'

Angry at John's deliberate undermining of my authority, I shooed both girls from the table and sent them outside to play. I saw their dark, conspiratorial faces glaring at me as they passed the window. John also got up and went outside. I began clearing up the mess. When I opened the door to give the cloth a vigorous shake I was amazed to see John inspecting the three bikes he had pulled from the shed. He was busy pumping up tyres and adjusting saddles. Every so often he pulled at the brakes and had obviously been busy with the oilcan on chains and mudguards, to make sure all was in running order.

'Bruton must be all of forty-odd miles away,' I said. 'How in the world do you expect Patty to keep up with us on her little bike – she's only nine?'

But John's enthusiasm could not be dashed. He carefully wheeled the bike to the shed and, taking an adjustable spanner to his own saddle, replied, 'We can give up at any stage of the journey and just come home. We can both give Patty a pull or a push whenever she tires. If we reach Bruton all well and good. If we don't, then at least the girls will have had a ride out in the country.'

'But what about Jacky?'

'That's just what I'm doing now. Jacky can ride on my saddle rack. I can rig up a basket for her to sit in.'

He grunted with the effort of turning the nut. And then he looked up directly at me. 'Come on, Joyce,' he wheedled. 'It's just a bit of fun. Think of it as a day out in the country.'

I didn't know how to climb down. But I wanted to keep control of this unruly mob of mine. 'I bet it'll rain,' I said.

'It'll be a lovely sunny day.' John proclaimed.

There was nothing that following Saturday morning to indicate that the weather would be anything other than just that – a perfect English summer's day. John rose early for once, without the aid of the alarm clock. His cheerful whistling from the kitchen was heard by the girls, who caught the mood of excitement and they were dressed in record time, even demanding to know if there was anything they could do to help.

It seemed I was outvoted; I would just have to make the best of it, despite my misgivings at this madcap adventure. I dutifully packed the corned-beef sandwiches (which John romantically named 'desert chicken', just to get the girls all excited), lemonade and a flask of tea. Plasters and soap and flannel went in my panniers as well. Best to be prepared.

In the cool of the early morning we skirted the town. Down Muller Road into Royate Hill and along Chalks Road. And so we negotiated Netham Hill and Newbridge Road, passing the board mills at St Anne's. And on up the hill, where Jacky was bribed with sweeties to get down and walk and join her sister pushing her bike up the hill. Out through Brislington to Whitchurch, where we bought fags, more sweets and a newspaper, and then into the open countryside at last. We'd left Bristol and all familiar places behind. It had taken us just three hours from the time we'd left home . . .

The lemonade bottle was passed around once more. Patty's little face was as red as a turkey cock's. I thought it might be the right time to ask if we had gone far enough – perhaps we could find a field, have our picnic, then cycle slowly back. The suggestion was met with cries of protest from the girls and a frown of disapproval from John. 'All right, all right,' I laughed, 'I only asked . . .'

But when I pulled my bike back onto the road to continue our journey, I tried to ignore the tiny twinge of muscle pain in the back of my leg, and began to wish that John had left the damn saddle at its original height. I was beginning to hurt in several unmentionable places.

The sun rose higher, the day grew hotter and our stops grew more frequent. We pulled and pushed Patty's little bike between us and the beads of perspiration stood out on John's forehead and dripped off the end of his nose. Patty's little feet went round and round like piston rods; John's breathing became more and more laboured. The only one who stayed cool and uncomplaining was Jacky, sitting up behind her father and enjoying every minute of the ride.

When we finally stopped for lunch I just fell off my bike and into the long cool grass of a welcoming field. The grumbles had stopped and I heard only murmurs of sheer relief. The packets of sandwiches were unwrapped and devoured greedily; the last of the lemonade was consumed; the Thermos-flask tea, milky and sweet, must have been as disgusting as ever, yet tasted like nectar. I drank two whole cups. Then I lay back amongst the buttercups, closed my eyes and promptly fell fast asleep.

I was woken by the sound of a couple of motorbikes whizzing past. I lay for a while listening to the powerful notes from their engines and thinking that the rest of the journey would be a piece of cake if our bikes could somehow miraculously be fitted up with motors. I looked around for the girls, half expecting them to be lying prostrate and exhausted. The long grass of the field hid them from view, but the sound of their laughter came to me as I caught glimpses of the tops of their heads as they ran about the meadow. They appeared to have recovered very quickly.

Still, I wondered about the advisability of continuing the journey. I thought it might be wise to retrace our steps in the direction of home and I voiced my concerns, this time seriously, to John. He consulted the map and reckoned that we must be just about halfway there. He also thought that the decision should be a democratic one. Racing towards us with their flushed faces, I could guess what the girls' answer would be. The climax of the whole adventure was to see their grandparents' surprised faces and to stay in that magical place with a sawmill and a real stream. And I found myself fervently hoping now that the dream would come true. I decided to throw myself completely into the adventure, to make it a success. We *would* get there, if it took us all day and all night.

Taking the lead, John jumped up and made for the stile, calling over his shoulder once he'd got a head-start, 'Last one out of the field is a sissy!'

On the road once more and heading for Temple Cloud and Stone Easton, John cycled out in front and we followed him in single file, down the long tree-lined hill. As we gained in momentum we took our feet from the pedals and felt the cool breeze blowing in our faces. The sun made lacy patterns on the road through the branches of the trees as we rushed past. 'Yippee!' John sang out and this was echoed by all of us in the exhilaration of the moment. When the speed slackened and we finally came to the flatter surface of the road I saw the flushed faces of the girls and felt a warm glow of pride and love. John possessed this Peter Pan-like quality that drew him to his children; he could be a child with them. There was no barrier to cross between him and them.

And so the long day went on. We stopped and bought more lemonade. And we promised the girls that if they were good we would find a pub with a garden where they would be treated to a packet of crisps. It was the final incentive. But it was still a very weary and subdued little family that filed into the garden of the pub at Evercreech and sat, quietly this time, on the wooden bench awaiting the promised bottle of pop and crisps. Shadows of evening began to throw purple pools of shade in secluded corners. The children's swing made little, almost ghostly, clanking noises as it moved in the slight evening breeze.

The last few miles were the real test of endurance and we were both unsparing in our words of encouragement. One last stop for breath on the run into Bruton as the evening began to darken gave us the truly unforgettable sight of an owl swooping down silently across the field in search of its prey. It was after sunset as we turned into Bruton's little High Street. We pulled up outside West End Café and began to ring our bicycle bells furiously. Dad was the first to open the door and came to the kerbside to investigate the racket. There he stood in his familiar pose, with hands in his pockets, his eyes lit up in recognition and wonder. As usual completely lost for words. I think we just couldn't believe ourselves that we had done it. The trip was a complete success.

Then my mother appeared, demanding to know what all the noise was about, and the incredulity registered on her face brought another burst of laughter from all of us. Dad stepped forward and lifted Jacky from the back of John's bike and carried her through to the big kitchen, where he rubbed the backs of her legs. All the way she had had to hold her legs away from the wheel, but had seldom complained and now her little legs ached. So the girls enjoyed the fuss their grandparents made of them, related all the adventures of the day, and went off to bed without a murmur, after Jacky had extracted a promise from Pop that he would take her to the sawmill so that like cousin Nita she too could have some sawdust in a bag. Never mind that we didn't as yet have the rabbit in a hutch to go with it.

It was much later when I gratefully climbed the stairs to bed. My mother called to say goodnight and when she came to stand by me her face seemed so hard and judgemental. She held a finger up and wagged it in front of me. 'I'm surprised at you, Joyce, making that girl of yours ride all that way on that little bike of hers. I can't think where you got the idea from. I would have thought you'd have had more sense.'

Our Family is Complete

John and I left the girls with Nan and Pop in Bruton, where they would stay for a couple of weeks, and cycled back to Bristol together. It was the first time we'd been alone since the early days of our marriage before the war, and at first we were awkward and almost shy with each other. When we got to the prefab it seemed strangely silent. But I began to enjoy the peace and the easy life without the children. I didn't have to be in for lunchtime or straight after school. I went to the hairdresser's, window-shopping, or over to see my best friend Vee without having to hurry home for the never-ending round of meals. One evening John and I even went out to the pictures together – a rare treat. That must have been the evening I felt so relaxed and happy. At any rate, I paid for it nine months later.

On 7 May 1951 Julie charged into the world like her proverbial birth sign: Taurus the bull. She was an eight-and-a-half-pound bundle, a small replica of her father, with the same brilliant blue eyes and fair hair and the same shaped hands and long limbs. When she was handed to him, John gazed at her a long time, unable to say a word, and I had no way of knowing if the tears in his eyes were for the beautiful little daughter so like himself, or the unbearable disappointment that she was not the son he had longed for.

Julie was six months old before the world seemed the right way up again. She brought a lot of love with her and was a delightfully easy baby. She was the apple of her father's eye.

Long before the first snowdrop hung its pearly blossom and peeped through the borders of the lawn, I knew I was pregnant yet again. I felt suicidal. I gritted my teeth and resisted the desire to tip John's dinner on his head. When he passed me he whistled cheerfully and said, 'It might be a boy this time.'

On a rain-lashed night towards the end of October 1952, a low wind howled around our little prefab. It crouched there like some animal, ready to spring into fury as the night unfolded. The hours passed, and the wind rose and shrieked and howled in a wild frenzy and the sixty-mile-an-hour gale tore through the night, leaving a trail of devastation in its wake. I was aware of the bustle of the midwife's uniform as she brushed past my bed to peer anxiously through the window into the darkness of the night.

All was not going well with my labour; the hours went by, the pains kept coming but this baby simply would not come, so the midwife waited for the doctor. The rain beat on the flat asbestos roof of the prefab with a sound like some frenzied ritual dance. There was a commotion in the hall, as though the door had been forced open by the wind, and several people were fighting to close it. The doctor came into the bedroom and towered over me. His hair was dishevelled and his shirtsleeves rolled to the elbow. The internal examination was quick, efficient and painful. 'Come along, Mrs Storey,' he said briskly. 'We can't have you giving up on us now.'

He shoved my knees into my chest and yelled at me to keep pushing. I suppressed a groan and wished the pains that kept on coming, coming relentlessly, would go away. I was hot and very tired and thirsty. It seemed I was walking along a hot dusty road. The sun beat down on my head and hurt my eyes. At the end of the road I could see a summer pool of clear water, which was fringed with trees that cast a delightful shade. Just a few more steps and I could take a long drink and fall into a sleep for ever, beneath the shady trees. But I couldn't make it, and I fell on my knees on the hard stony ground under the merciless sun. I heard a voice beside me say, 'You must get up and go on again.'

'I can't. I can't,' I said.

'Then I must go on without you,' the voice replied.

Then it seemed as if another Joyce materialised from that pathetic figure kneeling on the ground. I heard a faint cry like the mewing of a kitten and knew that with my last reserves of strength I had brought my baby into the world.

'You have a little boy,' I heard the doctor say.

I felt something like relief, but I was too weary to cry. As for the baby, he had suffered as much as I, and lay there dazed and gasping for breath in the little cot beside me. For

323

both of us it had been the struggle of a lifetime, and it was several days before the baby began to breathe properly without gasping, and we watched over him anxiously.

John called the boy Darrell Martin, after a friend from his RAF days. The doctor called him 'my little storm baby'. When he had been called out in the early hours of that dreadful night, his garage doors had caught the wind and blown back onto the headlights of his car and smashed them. So he had reason to remember that costly night.

In the days that followed I often looked longingly at the magnolia tree, especially in the springtime, when the pink and white flowers shed their petals over the lawn. I was no longer able to find time to relax and lie in its shade, to gaze at the sky and try to solve the riddles of the universe. Life now assumed a monotonous domestic pattern, an endless round of washing, cooking and cleaning which I believed would never end. The basket was always filled with rolled-up clothes waiting to be ironed, and the bath with washing waiting to be done, and the nappies just seemed to pile up.

I did not have a washing machine, and our method of dealing with the heavy cotton sheets was to drop them into the bath on a Friday night and leave them to soak. It was John's task to bend over, wash, rinse and wring them the following day, then peg them out on the line.

The small kitchen, which had once been ideal for us and the two girls, seemed to shrink in size with the advent of a high chair for Julie. I never quite found the right place for it – it either trapped the rest of the family in around the small table, preventing any exit whatsoever, or, if I placed it further away in the doorway between the lounge and kitchen, it caused a scene: Julie resented being so far away from the rest of us and usually protested by banging her spoon into her cereal bowl, scattering milk everywhere. For an encore, she would pick up her plate and pour the whole lot over her head.

Darrell was left in his pram in the lounge, a quiet, serious, peaceful little baby who slept and dreamed. My little prefab resembled a kindergarten and I often wished someone would come and look after me, or, better still, rescue me. I was so tired all the time.

One morning, after Patty and Jacky had left for school and I was left with the usual disarray of household chores to contemplate, I sighed heavily and began to clear up. Not even the cheerful tones of *Housewives' Choice* could cheer me, and I was up to my elbows in soapsuds tackling the washing when someone knocked at the back door. I went to open it and was somewhat taken aback when a good-looking young man enquired if he could do my washing for me.

'How did you know I was in the middle of it?' I stuttered. He threw his head back and laughed, assuring me that he didn't have a crystal ball, but that he was in the area demonstrating Hoover washing machines. If I would allow him to bring one in, he would have all my washing finished within the hour. I was surprised, and only too readily agreed. He returned minutes later with a compact twin-tub that he said would fit easily and neatly into any spare corner.

True to his word everything was washed, rinsed and pegged out blowing on the line within the hour, and we were enjoying a welcome cuppa. There was no way I could afford one of these miracle machines by paying cash, but he said I could pay a small deposit and he would arrange terms. He could not take my deposit though, nor allow me to sign the hire-purchase agreement – by law only my husband could fill in the form for the hire-purchase loan. He left the form, but wheeled the washing machine away. I felt a real pang, and thought a small treasure had gone from my life.

I took a lot of time and patience trying to convince John about the merits of a washing machine. He probably thought I had nothing else to do all day. Asking him to sign the hire-purchase form made him throw up his hands in horror at my audacity. He would never go into debt, the sure way to ruin. The only way to get something was to pay cash for it. I did not exactly give up the struggle. I merely threw three sheets into the bath that Friday instead of one. So one Friday night, a few weeks later, John finally capitulated and handed me the completed form, duly signed.

He said that instead of giving me a rise in my housekeeping allowance he would buy the washing machine for me, adding, 'Now that you have the machine, there's no reason to put the sheets in the bath any more.'

Coronation Day

*I*n 1952 we had a new queen. Although her father George VI had been popular, I never took much notice of the monarchy. When he died I heard the almost universal expressions of grief: 'Aah, he was a good king,' people said. But it didn't touch me much, this public outpouring of grief. To tell the truth I didn't care one way or the other – after all, what had they ever done for me?

Touching the forelock and bending the knee was definitely not my style, anyway. But that didn't mean that I wasn't going to join in the general celebrations planned for the coronation. Like a lot of working-class people we had scant respect for authority underneath our apparent obedience. Whilst we listened dutifully to the annual Christmas broadcast, and raised our glasses when a loyal toast was called for, we did it with a secret smirk. However, we were still determined to make the best of a rare day off work – any excuse for a party, that was our motto!

We looked forward to Coronation Day in June. My mum sold her business in Bruton and she and Dad returned to the house where she had been born in Sherborne Street, in the St George district of Bristol. All the family gathered there for the great day, 2 June 1953, and we watched the whole thing on television. It was the first time we'd seen television and Mum and Dad, like thousands of others, had bought a set especially for this – the biggest national celebration most of us would remember.

It was a typical June day – in other words it rained on and off. In London tens of thousands of people camped out on pavements all along the route of the procession, but nothing seemed to dampen their spirits. I thought they must be mad. The long parade of visiting royalty and foreign bigwigs seemed to go on interminably, all in their enclosed coaches and carriages. All, that is, except Queen Salote of Tonga (an enormous woman) who rode in her open coach with the rain pouring down on her. She just went along waving at the enthusiastic crowd, her broad black face wreathed in a beatific smile. We took to her immediately. My father said, 'Look at that, that's what I call real royalty. That beats all yer bloody archybishops with their bloody stuck-up airs!'

My mother told him off for swearing, like she always did: 'Less of yer language, Chas. There's kids listening.'

We had ham salad and fruit cake. On the sideboard stood a bottle of egg-flip, a bottle of British sherry and a bottle of British port. You'd almost think it was Christmas, because in those days no one drank except at weddings, funerals and Christmas, and foreign wines and beers were unknown. We had just discovered a drink they called 'Snowball', which was egg-flip topped up with fizzy lemonade. I loved it but, as usual, a couple of drinks soon had me feeling light-headed and drowsy.

It was probably the fact that we all had a few drinks that we were able to prevail upon my mother to read the tea leaves. Anything to do with magic or the occult was viewed with deep superstition and people did not do these things lightly, even if they only half believed in them. So although my mother would laugh and say, 'It's only rubbish!', when she read the leaves she did it seriously, and we listened carefully.

In those days, before we all used tea bags or even tea strainers, at the bottom of each cup you'd get the dregs of tea leaves. As part of the ritual of having your fortune told in this way, you would be expected to drink the tea right down to the dregs. Some people swished the last bit of liquid around and around and then stood the cup upside down to drain, leaving the tea leaves deposited evenly around the bottom and sides of the cup; others drank every last drop of tea and left the leaves in a little straight line, right to the rim.

This second method was considered more accurate in foretelling the future, but any liquid left, even a drop, was called 'tears' and indicated sorrow and perhaps grief. Naturally, then, people went to some lengths to avoid this predicament and often left their tea cups draining for some time before they brought them for reading. Then my mother would look into the depths of the cup and see tea leaves in the shape of figures, each one of which carried significance. A bird would token news; a horse or ship would mean a journey; a long, straight tea leaf always meant a stranger at the door; a parcel shape could mean the arrival of a new baby, and so on.

'Ooh, our Joyce has got a great big spider in her cup, and some tears,' my mother said, letting the minute drop of liquid fall onto the table. 'That means a big change in your life, and not for the better, neither,' she said, looking at me with dark suspicion. I expect she thought there was something going on I hadn't told her about. But if my life was about to change in any way, I had no inkling of it that particular June day.

After tea, we played all the usual family games, like spin-the-plate and stations. One of these almost ritual games was called pass-the-ring, where a ring was threaded on to a long piece of string which was then tied to form a circle. Everyone sat around, with whoever was 'it' in the middle, and tried to pass the ring from one to another without being caught. If whoever was 'it' caught you with the ring in your clenched hand, then it was your turn to stand in the middle and try to guess. As we passed the ring round and round stealthily from hand to hand, we used to sing, 'Oh we've got him in the middle, we've got him in the middle, we've got him in the middle, and so say all of us' (to the tune of 'For He's a Jolly Good Fellow').

It was considered very bad luck to remove your wedding ring in those days, so we usually used a brass curtain ring, but once I boldly removed my wedding ring for the game, and there was an almost audible, shocked intake of breath. Perhaps they thought a woman who would take off her wedding ring would do anything. In the evening we played cards. My mother loved cards and often played patience. Cards were another thing that a chapel-going community frowned upon – perhaps because they too were another form of fortune-telling, connected with witchcraft and the occult. However, on this evening we played snap, and Newmarket with the children. We always tried to conspire to let them win the jackpot, which was never more than a few pence (a ha'penny on the card, a ha'penny in the middle, then if the card came up you won the little pile of coins bet on it, and if you were 'out' first you won the little pile in the middle).

My father would always complain about the cards dealt him: 'I got another bad hand. I always get a bad hand. Look at my hand, Nell!'

And my mother would reply, 'I don't want to look at your hand. Come on, who's got the lowest red?'

Sometimes, if she were in a very good mood, my mother would tell fortunes with the cards. This was viewed as being a much more serious business than the tea leaves – almost as serious as having your palm read. I can't read the cards myself and know very little of their significance. All I know is that that day my mother read the cards for me and they also indicated a change in my life. This time, though, there were no tears to say whether the change would be bad or good. I cut and recut the cards for my mother while she muttered: 'Another high spade, another high club; hearth and home, hearth and home, and without a single red card.

Well, my girl, there's change all round, and with neither love nor money to go with it.'

I began to wonder just what life was going to throw at me.

Our New Home

A few days later my spirits sank to zero when a letter from the Council arrived, offering us a three-bedroom council house on the old estate at Horfield, on the other side of the Common. We had to give up the prefab now because our family was too large. I felt my heart would break.

It was late evening when I first viewed the new house. Two tall cypress trees, one on either side of the arched front door, cast long shadows down the path and blocked the light from the main sitting room. They made me feel slightly claustrophobic as I passed between them. A tall privet hedge, in desperate need of cutting back, covered two sides of the borders of the garden; the rest was lawn back and front, with not a flower to be seen anywhere. On the opposite side of the road, behind the houses, ran the main railway line to the north.

My heart gave a sickening little thump when I saw a

familiar and hated vision. Squatting behind the houses and overlooking the railway line from the corner of the bridge was a dark green gasometer. It took me back to the very early days of my marriage, and the rooms we had in Grimsby overlooking the gasometer. Hideous sight. Hideous smell. It felt like we'd taken one step forward and half a dozen backwards.

I remembered then my mother's prophetic reading of the cards for me on Coronation Day and wondered if this was the change she'd seen for me. Being catapulted from the safe and secure haven of labour-saving luxury in the little prefab to a pre-war house on a vast estate of identical red-brick, privet-hedged council houses was tantamount to being turned out of Eden.

No kitchen units, fridge or stove in the house I moved into. A glimpse into the kitchen and scullery on that first visit revealed ten square feet of primitive barrenness: dark-green-painted walls; a deep, chipped, dirty white sink supported on two concrete blocks; and a very unappetising greasy gas pipe, waiting to be connected, hanging halfway down the wall. This time around, there were no benefactors leaving behind carpets and curtains and even small items of furniture. I felt so dispirited and angry and in my anger I blamed our impoverished conditions entirely on John.

Standing there in the middle of the lawn, with our pathetic bits and pieces of furniture around us, I thought savagely about a lot of things. I now understood how my mother must have felt, with her first two babies just fifteen months apart, a husband on short time because of the slump, and dumped in a shared house with an extended family she had not chosen. 'Don't think your life will be any different to mine,' she had often reminded me. Now I saw that she had had no choice and neither had I. The awful inevitability of a woman's life pressed down on me. At least my husband was in a job, even if he did hate the unsociable hours of the shift system at the Post Office.

I began to pick up some of the lighter items to take indoors and to try once again to make a home. I thought grimly of the hard work and overtime John would have to do in order to maintain his growing family – the family he had wanted, not I.

My thoughts were dark and moody as I turned to close the gate. Outside was a wide busy road. I would need to keep my eyes wide open all the time if my two toddlers played here. I tried hard not to let my mind linger on the safe, magnolia-scented comfort of the lawn we had left behind; the golden days of my beloved prefab. I tried hard to fight back the tears of frustration and loss. They were very near.

Earlier that morning I had noticed a small girl of about Julie's age cross the road alone and stand by the hedge, watching all our proceedings with avid interest, one grubby thumb stuck into her perfect rosebud mouth. Her straight black hair framed a rosy-cheeked face, and her deep velvet-brown eyes were like pools of warm chocolate.

When she first made eye contact with my son, they each stood stock still in identical poses, thumbs in mouths, eyes glued in one long stare. I moved over the crumpled expanse of front lawn to close the gate, glad now that our shabby belongings were no longer under public scrutiny. The small child was still by the hedge, peeping through the wrought-iron gate railings. I smiled at the intensity of her stare and then, with a rush of maternal concern, took her hand and led her over the road to deposit her safely inside her own front garden. I stood waiting on the kerb at the side of the road for a lorry to rumble past me, all the while wondering at the parental unconcern for the safety of that small child, then skipped nimbly back across the road into my strange and unfamiliar new home.

Every day after that, the little girl would position herself outside the house, watching Julie and Darrell at play, listening to their whoops and shrieks with the same grave observance as before. With the memory of Jacky's previous adventure still fresh in my mind, I lost count of the number of times I reminded them both, 'Don't you dare go outside that gate.' I wondered if my concern bordered on the paranoid, except that the innocent but penetrating stare from the strange small child unnerved me more than a little.

Just when the little minx untied the gate I do not know, but once again it was the silence that alerted me and sent the alarm bells ringing in my head. There was no sign of either of my offspring, and beyond the open gate the wide busy road stretched and beckoned dangerously. I raced over the road and beat frenziedly on Mrs Martin's door. She opened it so quickly I almost fell over the threshold, garbling my anxious demands to know if she'd seen the children. My query was met with a loud, throaty chuckle that revealed a set of strong white teeth. The rest of her – bosom and belt – seemed to have collapsed into one shapeless mass that wobbled and shook like some grotesque unset jelly.

'They'm all out the back playin'. Your Darraw an your Julay,' she informed me. 'Our Mary likes your Darraw.'

She flattened herself against the hall wall to allow me to go through to the garden. She was still convulsed with laughter and wobbled up and down with each chortle. The house seemed to smell of stale cabbage water and the close, fetid smell of animals. I passed quickly through and into the unkempt garden, where there was still no sign of the children. A fence at the far end had several boards missing. As I drew nearer to this gap in the fence I could make out a big notice on the railway embankment beyond, warning people to keep out.

With my heart beating fast now, I scanned the grassy slope leading up to the tracks, searching desperately for the small, vulnerable figures of my children. Just at that moment, Mrs Martin squeezed her flabby bulk beside me and yelled so loudly she nearly shattered my eardrum, 'Mar-ray Mar-ray! Come yer!'

As if by some magic, three small heads appeared above the hidden slope of the incline. Puffing and panting and pulling an old raffia bag, they scrambled towards the hole in the fence. Their faces and clothes were black with coal dust and grime. Young Mary pushed the raffia bag through first. Mrs Martin examined the bag of shiny black nuggets of coal, smiled fondly at her daughter's efforts and explained, 'Just a bit of fire fuel, every little 'elps!'

Still panting with exertion, Mary pushed Darrell through the opening by placing two coal-black hands on the seat of his pants and shoving; Julie crawled through under her own steam and then Mary brought up the rear. When all three stood safely on the right side of the fence once more they looked like little chimney-sweeps. Despite the colour and the taste, Mary's thumb automatically popped into her mouth and she once again resumed her silent gaze at the world.

I found my voice and began indignantly to question how any parent could allow a small child to walk into such a dangerous situation along a busy railroad track. But I stopped short when I became aware that Mrs Martin was looking at me with a stare that indicated, only too clearly, there was something wrong with my brain rather than hers. There was only one thing to do. I took both my children by the hand, marched them back across the road and scrubbed them clean in the chipped scullery sink.

The next day I wheeled them in the twin pushchair to the local nursery school to have their names entered in case any vacancy arose. Then I trundled them round to the local health centre to register the whole family with a doctor. The grey-haired man who interviewed me and consented to our being on his list appeared sympathetic and understanding. I quite warmed to him and found myself relating some of the exploits my two energetic toddlers got up to. When I graphically described the coal-gathering expedition his head went back and he laughed uproariously. He finally agreed that the nursery school was the perfect answer, not only for Julie and Darrell but, he said soberly, 'for Mum's frayed and shattered nerves'. He scribbled off a letter recommending that both children be found a nursery place at the earliest possible moment and, signing it with a flourish, beamed at all of us and ushered us out of the surgery.

'That,' I thought as I walked home feeling uplifted, 'is what I call co-operation.' Within a week, the letter arrived to say the little ones could start nursery immediately. The following Monday morning, I deposited them both into the hands of cheerful, trained staff and when I looked around to wave goodbye they were both absorbed in playing with the toys and equipment.

That first day I couldn't wait to fetch them, and to find out how the day had gone for the youngest members of my family. They ran towards me when they caught sight of me standing by the school gates, both of them looking like little orphans of the storm. The bottom button on Darrell's jacket was fastened to the top buttonhole, his scarf dragged on the ground, and both socks were wrinkled down around his ankles. My first reaction was to ignore their excited chatter and make them look presentable. This involved arguing with Julie that she put her coat on instead of trailing it along the ground. So it was some time before I could settle them sufficiently in the twin pram, head for home and enquire about their first experiences of nursery school.

Julie was the interpreter for all of Darrell's baby babblings and she was eager to relate that her brother had played with a little boy called Jason on the slider in the playground, but that Jason had knocked Darrell off the slide and hit him.

'I hope you sloshed him back!' I said heatedly, feeling most indignant that my poor baby should have been subjected to such rough treatment on his very first day.

I walked around to the front of the pram so that I could decipher the baby talk, and knelt down close to him. 'Did you slosh him one?' I demanded.

Darrell shook his tousled head of tight brown curls and replied, 'A little voice whispered to me in my head, "He is your friend, give him another chance!"'

Julie, unable to restrain herself from completing the saga of the day, cut in loudly, 'Jason just hit him again, Mummy.'

'Well,' I said, 'what a naughty, rude and horrible little boy.' I felt that when I came face to face with this little horror I might even slosh him myself.

'He is my friend,' Darrell kept repeating defensively. 'He can have one more chance.'

I suddenly leaned over the pram to hug this gentle little boy of mine. How could I make sure he grew up to be non-aggressive, surrounded as he was by little roughnecks like Jason? I didn't know.

Instead I began to run with the pram, yelling, 'I'm a racing driver, brr-um brr-um.' Both infants rose to the challenge, taking an imaginary wheel each, and together we raced all along the street until we reached the house, laughing and quite out of breath.

It was my new next-door neighbour who gave me the idea that really made the next, and biggest, change in my life. She'd just got a part-time job as a home help with the Social

Services Department and was telling me all about it over a cup of tea one afternoon before I went to fetch my two youngest from nursery school.

'It's a bit o' help for pensioners or people just out of hospital, or in confinement, like,' she said helpfully. 'Sometimes I do a bit o' shoppin', fetch their bits and pieces, like. Sometimes,' she leaned closer and said in a confidential tone, 'all you 'as to do is sit there and talk to some lonely old soul what needs a bit of a chat, like.'

I was entranced. This sounded just the kind of job I could do. I'd be delighted to do a little light housework, or sit and chat to a lonely pensioner, and get paid for it. I saw myself as a kindly helper in time of need. The friend at your door when in trouble. Yes, the Lady with the Lamp (part-time, of course, to fit in with the nursery-school hours). I hurried down to see the supervisor the very next day.

I was elated to be accepted. I was sent the name and address of my very first client (as we were encouraged to call them), at an address in Horfield. When I called on her the following week, I noticed that the house was very dreary-looking and down-at-heel. Perhaps though, I thought, it just seemed more that way because the house next door was in the middle of a face-lift. I banged the heavy knocker. The door opened very suddenly and there stood a thin-featured woman of about seventy with bright beady eyes squinting at me.

'You the woman from the agency?' she demanded, and seemed very relieved when I assured her I was.

She beckoned me to follow her along the dark, dingy passageway. As I passed the stairwell I couldn't help noticing the wallpaper was peeling from the wall in long greasy yellow strips, and the dusty, dark-green lino covering the steps had worn-out patches revealing the dirty wooden boards beneath. Entering the kitchen was like stepping back in time. There was a black range and a massive iron kettle swinging over the hob; above the grate there was a green baize over-mantle secured with brass button tacks, and around the fire an ancient box fender that housed the paper and kindling needed to light the fire each morning.

The big wooden table was still laden with dirty crocks from breakfast, and possibly the meals from the day before; beyond that there was a deep single-pane sash window with a grubby broken cord hanging loose, with a grimy view of the path that led down to the back garden gate. My heart sank. It seemed ridiculous to ask this strange, thin-faced little bundle what she wanted me to do, but I really didn't know where to start. It was all so incredibly filthy that my two hours wouldn't even begin to make a dent in it. The house where I grew up in South Road had been built along similar lines, but, if we were poor, we were at least clean. My first instinct was to disinfect the entire house and scrub it till the old floorboards were white. My second instinct was to throw in the sponge and leave right now.

'I've got a nice drop of soda water left over from the washing in the boiler, and I wants 'ee to wash the bedroom and down over the stairs,' she said, all the while peering at my face enquiringly. 'Have 'ee brought a pinny with 'ee?' I nodded and followed her into the back kitchen, tying my pinny round me as I went.

As I suspected, the old boiler out in the scullery was the kind you lit a fire under to get your hot water, and next to it stood an old chipped china sink with a dripping brass tap. I filled a pail with the dirty grey water and she gave me a musty-smelling house flannel. The soda in the grime-ridden water would play havoc with my hands. I was fastidious about my hands; my only personal luxury was a tube of Lemskin to keep them soft, and I always kept my nails beautifully filed. I was beginning to have second thoughts about my new vocation.

I climbed the stairs and plonked the pail of water down in the front bedroom. The bare boards, which had once been stained dark brown and varnished, had worn into a pale, almost dusty buff colour, and the brass double bedstead filled most of the available space. Among the dust under the bed sat an old white china jerry. Above the bed was a photograph of a young man in army uniform, but it was the frame that caught and held my attention. With a start of recognition, I saw it was fashioned from dozens of playing cards – the ace of spades from many different packs.

I gave a horrified little shiver because I remembered how, as a young girl, the ace of spades was the most powerful fate card in the pack; we always thought of it as the death card. So as I studied the face of the young man framed in the square of black aces I had a strange, frightened feeling of something dark and sinister. Then I knelt on the bare boards and began to wash them over with the house flannel. As I worked, little black fleas jumped onto my legs. I cried out in some alarm and after that put the house flannel on the end of a broom. I hurried to finish and be gone as quickly as I could.

I brushed down the stairs, setting up clouds of dust, cleaned out the bucket and swilled the filthy cloth. I refused the cup of tea that the frail, thin-faced Mrs Higgins made for me. I told her I was already late and said if she would just sign my form I would be away and see her again on Thursday. She had been allocated four hours a week.

I itched when I got outside. I was beginning to think that one whole week in that house might very well be enough for me. I didn't feel quite so much like the Florence Nightingale figure I'd dreamed about, either.

On the following Thursday, Mrs Higgins was waiting for me with her pension book all signed. She indicated that I should fetch her pension, do her shopping and then return to tackle the housework, in particular the back kitchen and outside privy. It was very difficult trying to explain that I could either fetch her pension and her bit of shopping, or do the housework, but that in the two hours allotted it would be impossible to do both.

She began to get upset; her voice rose to a shriek, and her thin body trembled violently. 'I'll report you to the agency!' she threatened. In the end, I agreed that I would get her pension, do the shopping and, if there was any time over, I'd see what housework I could do. I gritted my teeth and walked to the post office, where a long line of pensioners formed to collect their money. There were about twenty minutes to spare when I returned from doing the errands, and I was expecting her to be ready with the bucket, filled with that grey awful-smelling water, ready for me to tackle the outside loo. She was sitting in the wooden armchair reading the paper when I walked in and laid her money and purchases on the table.

To my surprise she got up very suddenly and said pleasantly, 'I've got a little present for you.' She turned to the mantelshelf and took something in her hand. 'I have a little flutter now and then,' she explained. 'I've had a little win, so you have a bit of luck with me.' She put the coin in my hand and squeezed her wrinkled paw over mine to enclose it in a tight grasp. It was a shilling.

Of course we weren't allowed to accept any gifts as a condition of our employment. I should have got instant dismissal if it had been known, but she was adamant I should have it and I didn't know what else to do. She also insisted I drink the coffee she had poured for me, so I sat in a hard-seated, high-backed chair, wondering how I would ever find one hygienic spot around the cracked rim of that cup to drink from.

By way of conversation, I enquired if the photo of the young man in the army uniform above the bed had been her husband. She remained quiet for a while and then said yes, he had been.

'He's no longer alive?' I persisted.

She was staring at the cloth on the table and began fingering old cake crumbs into a minute heap. When she spoke again, her frail old voice seemed further away than ever. 'He had a little Jack Russell, my 'usband. That little dog, he was barkin' 'is 'ead off that day. 'E come down over the stairs barkin', back up the stairs barkin'. I wondered whatever was the matter with 'im, barkin' and yappin' away. Then I 'eard Stan, my 'usband crashin' down over the stairs, bangin' along the hall. And all the time that dog went on barkin'. And then I 'eard a crash. When I poked me 'ead round the door to find out what all the noise was about, Stan was lying there in a great pool of blood. Blood everywhere and the dog still barkin'.'

Mrs Higgins raised her eyes to look at me. I still held my untouched coffee. I was frozen.

''E'd took his open razor and slashed 'is throat from ear to ear.'

I leaned over and touched her gently on the hand, at the same time pushing my work form towards her for her to sign. The coffee was cold and she had not noticed it had not been touched. 'I'll see you on Tuesday,' I promised, and walked out of that dingy hallway and into the fresh spring air.

I'd been a home help for nearly two years when I went to work for Benny Barnet. By this time I think I'd learned the hard lesson that looking after other people's houses was never going to be easy and was rarely rewarding. I never thought about Florence Nightingale now, but I did enjoy having a little extra money to help with the household expenses.

Benny lived in a posh house in Westbury Park. A potted palm stood in the hallway, and behind it a thick green-velvet curtain was draped with a white, knotted cord. A little bent old man with a husky voice that wheezed every time he took a breath beckoned me to come in. I quickly discovered that he'd had cancer of the throat and this was an artificial voice-box that had been fitted.

He told me to start at the top of the house and work down. Everything I needed would be found in the broom cupboard. I went upstairs to start on the bedrooms and began hoovering the already immaculately clean carpets. I couldn't help noticing that the ebony hairbrushes on the dressing table had the initials B.B. embossed on them; so did the box which held his cufflinks, and even the pyjama case on the large double bed flourished two huge capital Bs on its blue satin cover. Above the drone of the vacuum I did not hear B.B. pad into the room until he was standing beside me. I turned off the machine when I saw he wanted to speak to me. He waved a hand towards the bed and said in that belching, husky voice, which was almost entirely without inflection, 'Such a big bed. No one to share it.'

He was so frail, old and bent. He reminded me of one of the seven dwarfs – I could easily have scooped him up. It gradually dawned on me that I was being propositioned to share the delights of that nice big double bed. I laughed it off, it was so preposterous, and went on with my house-work. But he was not to be so easily dissuaded. I could hardly move for B.B. As I dusted he was behind me, trying to touch me; as I hoovered down over the stairs I almost tripped over him as he reached to put an amorous arm around my waist. I was beginning to get thoroughly fed up with him. I actually smacked his hand at one point. As I said, the house was immaculate anyway, so I easily finished the whole lot by ten to eleven. I was ten minutes early (it would give me time to get to the butcher's to get something for our tea), but reckoned I might get my time sheet signed. I presented it to B.B., who glanced at the clock and then glared at me.

The husky, now far from friendly, voice belched, 'It's only a quarter to eleven.'

I tried to keep the irritation out of my voice. My job depended on tact, a bit of tender loving care and being polite. 'Well, what else would you like me to do?'

'DO?' he repeated, and the force of his anger made the mechanism in his throat whirr, reinforcing his indignation. 'You start all over again. That's what you do. Get the vacuum and do the bedrooms!'

'If you want a domestic servant, you ought to apply to the appropriate agency,' I said. 'A home help is merely a help in need, not a skivvy!'

That's when I found out he actually employed domestic help to come in every week. No wonder the house was so clean. Now he was spluttering and coughing and waving me away. That's what he did, he shooed me off the premises. Safely at the gate, I looked back. He was still standing at the window, shooing me away with his hands and poking out his tongue at me. I did the same back.

Before he could complain to Miss Epplestone I got in first and told her what I'd had to put up with. So he lost his home help for being such a pest. I also told Miss Epplestone that my Florence Nightingale days were over. I never did find a lonely old pensioner I could just sit and have a cup of tea with. But my time as a home help did give me something priceless – John's acceptance that I could go out to work, even if it was only part-time, to fit in with my wifely duties. Life had changed for ever now. I was beginning the long journey towards independence.

Our First Holiday

After years and years of filling in the coupon every week, John finally had a win on the football pools by forecasting three results. You had to choose three teams and accurately forecast the result of the game: draw, win or lose.

I remember vividly the occasion. We'd just come out of the pictures, where we'd been to the Saturday matinée. I was just starting one of the blinding migraines I often used to suffer from in those days (sometimes, almost blinded by the lights and the pain, I'd spend the whole day in bed until the sickness passed and there was only a black space where the pain had been). John was eager to buy the results paper – The Pink 'Un – on our way to the bus stop, and he checked his coupon as we waited for the bus to start. All he could talk about all the way home was the win and how much he thought it might be. 'Fifty or sixty quid at least, Joyce,' he kept enthusing. 'Maybe even more.'

The flashing lights across my field of vision were beginning to make me feel sick. I was desperate to get home and wanted only a darkened room and peace, where I could be ill undisturbed. If only I could take a couple of Beecham's Powders and just lie down somewhere. I couldn't share his enthusiasm that day, nor even comment on his plans for spending it.

The dividend was forty pounds, about three weeks' wages to us, and we bought our first car. It was a van really, and had been used to transport pig food. It ponged to high hell when we bought it, and we never did quite eradicate the smell, despite the times we scrubbed it out with disinfectant. The memories of that first vehicle remain evergreen. Long before the MoT test was introduced we ran on bald tyres, the radiator leaked, and we used chewing gum to plug the holes. Once the brakes failed coming down a hill, but John was such a good driver he brought the car safely to rest on a grassy verge at the bottom of the slope.

We put an old mattress in the back so the kids could sit comfortably, and it was our home on wheels in an emergency. We often headed south, making for Devon or, with fingers crossed (would we make it?), for my beloved Cornwall. Once, on the journey back from Devon, we broke down in Exeter. We had nowhere to stay, we were tired and hungry, and it was beginning to get dark. We stopped an elderly man in the street and asked if he knew of a hostel or very cheap bed-and-breakfast place. This kindly man took us home and he and his wife put all six of us up for the night, gave us breakfast the next day, and only charged a pound for the lot of us towards the cost of our stay. Bed and breakfast in those days cost about nine or ten shillings a night each, so you can see how generous that family was to us. And the next day they found us a mechanic who worked on the van to get it going again.

John never minded how many miles we covered in a day. Once behind the wheel of a car, he was as happy as a king. Everyone needs a sense of freedom, and that's where he found his. He had a knack of being able to be a child with the children and could jolly them along when signs of boredom began to show on a long journey. He invented all sorts of games – spot-the-car-colours; collecting-road-signs; I-spy – or he could get them singing all the old songs at the tops of their voices: 'Keep Right on to the End of the Road', 'Side By Side', 'You Are My Sunshine' and our family favourite, 'On Top of Old Smokey', which became Jacky's particular theme tune.

There were tangible signs that we'd never had it so good – some time in the late fifties we actually went away for a whole week's holiday. That was the memorable time we hired a chalet at Perranporth in Cornwall, long before the motorways made travelling easy. It used to take a whole day to do the trip and we finally arrived late at night, almost missing the camp because the entrance was right on a sharp bend. John got out of the car and went to the small office inside the camp to collect the chalet key. A young man got into a Land Rover and instructed John to follow him. The moon was bright and high in the sky. The scene was more like a framed picture of the Sahara desert, with every chalet hidden behind tall sand dunes. Old faithful bumped and jumped over the soft sandy road, with the engine labouring under the weight of everything we had packed into it. John's face was serious as he gripped the wheel, gritting his teeth. I crossed my fingers, hoping that the gods would be kind and the suspension would hold up just for this holiday, please.

The chalet was perfect. We opened the windows because the night was so warm and heard the gentle sound of thousands of grasshoppers in the grassy dunes and the Atlantic rollers breaking on the beach below us. All that week we had perfect weather, with day after day of blazing sunshine. We lazed on the beach, where the two youngest played happily with sand and water and Patty and Jacky showed off outrageously. We were a big, noisy, happy group, enjoying our first real holiday together.

One afternoon Darrell kicked a ball into some thick undergrowth and, searching for it, we found a path that led down to a secluded part of the beach. John instantly became the intrepid big-game hunter, hacking his way along the secret path. Dangers lay around every bend, and with every snap of a twig a lion stalked us or a crocodile lay in wait to snap at our legs. The kids thought it was great fun, even teenagers Patty and Jacky entered into the spirit of the game. Once through the jungle hazards, we lit a bonfire on the beach and made a quick change into Red Indians, dancing round the flames and making ear-splitting war cries.

As a sudden anti-climax to all the hilarity he himself had instigated, John declared he thought it might be a good idea to pack up and get on the road that very night, so as to miss the crowds of returning holidaymakers the following morning. The news was met with long faces, and silently we made our way back along the secret path. On the way to the chalet we passed a tiny plantation of Cornish palms growing in the soft loamy soil. I tripped and stumbled against a little baby one, knocking it out of its soft bed, leaving it lying pathetically on its side. The thought came to me that it might be nice to have it growing in my garden, so I heaved it up and staggered back with it to the chalet.

'Just what do you think you're going to do with that?' John demanded when I peered through the green leaves of a tree taller than I was myself.

'We can have it home and in the garden before anyone knows it's gone!' I said, laughing at the thought of the palm in the car with us.

John tied the palm tree to the roof of the car, grumbling because we were doing wrong but knowing that to argue with me at that point would have caused further delay. So, with everything packed in the van once more, we bumped and jerked our way through the sand dunes, handed the keys in at the little office and went onto the road to head for home.

After a while the headlights from other cars dazzled us, and twice John took a wrong turning. The gentle snoring and peaceful breathing coming from the rest of his sleeping family must have reminded him that driving through the night on such a long journey was not such a marvellous idea. With red, sore eyes, and yawning widely, he drew off the road into a lay-by and switched off the engine. Then he settled down in the front seat and was soon snoring loudly himself.

A light summer breeze gently rocked the van and sent the fronds of the palm tree tapping on the metal sides of the vehicle. As I nodded off to sleep I began to dream that a little man was running round the car, rapping on the windows in a vain attempt to get us all to wake up. It was hot inside the van and I thought I should rouse myself and open a window, but somehow I didn't have the energy. It seemed like I was coming out of a long dark space a long time later, when I became aware that both the doors of the van were now wide open and John was sitting on the ground outside with his head in his hands.

'I covered up the air vent when I tied the palm tree to the roof,' he explained. 'And I closed the windows as well. We could have all suffocated. We could have all been dead.' He stared unhappily up into the sky where the first pale-rose-pink streaks of dawn began to herald yet another warm and glorious day. 'It was only the scratching of the leaves on the side of the van that alerted me.'

'Saved our lives then,' I said and instantly wished I hadn't.

'Saved our lives!' he echoed with scorn. 'Crumps, Joyce, that damn thing damn near killed the lot of us!'

The memories of that holiday in Cornwall may have melted into the mists of time, but that battered and smelly old van, our first car, gave us some of the happiest times of our lives. Having a car allowed us to go out on expeditions to explore the surrounding countryside.

Old faithful came to a sudden and abrupt stop one afternoon when we were all heading for Mitchinhampton Common near Stroud, and refused point blank to start up again. We had to be towed home by the AA man, with Darrell and Julie going wild with the excitement of it all. It was the scrap heap for the poor van. John said the old girl reminded him of Black Bess's ride to York – she had gamely plodded on, giving of her best until her brave old heart had burst. At this dose of sentiment, both the little ones fell silent, for the story of Dick Turpin and the gallant Black Bess was a certain tear-jerker in our household.

Lady Luck had gone with us on every journey we'd taken in that old wreck. John deserved better, but it was several years before we could afford to buy another car.

Maybe, if it had not been for the winds of change blowing once again in our direction, we might have settled in Dovercourt Road for good. We certainly found a kernel of gold in the close-knit working-class community around us, and I made many friends. Even the smelly old gasometer seemed to slump more comfortably into its circular repository and become part of our surroundings, emitting its foul stench only on wet or windy days.

Just over the bridge, the new Lockleaze Estate rubbed shoulders with the old. Once farmland and meadow, it was now wide roads and new houses. On my way up to the post office I often made a detour along Landseer Avenue. All the roads around there were named after famous English painters – although, truth to tell, it was the first time in our lives we'd ever heard of such people as Chrome, Bonnington or Hogarth. The shopping area was romantically named Gainsborough Square, and outside the pub the sign that swung and creaked in the wind depicted Gainsborough's 'Blue Boy'.

One morning, as I walked along in the spring sunshine, the avenue was a delight with the misty-pink blossom of the newly planted Japanese cherry trees. The pastel pinks, greens and greys of the painted houses blended with the foliage and clustered blossom of these trees. I thought wistfully that this particular avenue would be a nice place for us and the children to live. Every so often along the avenue there were culs-de-sac, in front of which were large grassland play areas, which had also been planted by the Council with young saplings that looked as though they had been retained from the original meadow. It reminded me of the village greens of my own childhood.

My cousin, who lived on the estate, told me about two pensioners when I called on her later that morning. These two, already living in Landseer Avenue, wanted to exchange their three-bedroomed house for a pre-war house in the Dovercourt Road area. Luck? Fate? Haste? All three combined and sent me scurrying the few paces over the road to the address I'd been given. The first thing I noticed about the house was the Japanese cherry tree right outside; it was a good sign which immediately endeared the house to me. If I couldn't have a cottage with roses around the door, I could have a council house with a flowering cherry on the pavement. There was also a solid air of finality

357

about the place, which seemed to indicate that this would be my final home.

The move was effortless. The two dear old pensioners confessed that their main concern was to get back to a house with a cheaper rent and all their old familiar friends and neighbours nearby. Even more staggering, as we talked it became obvious that I was living in the very house in Dovercourt Road that they had vacated for their present one. With tears of gratitude in their eyes, they said they would be going home. I also learned then that Landseer had sculpted the lions in Trafalgar Square. It seemed a good omen that my star sign, Leo, was represented in my new home.

The first new comprehensive school was built near by, at Lockleaze. Julie and Darrell would benefit from the mixed-ability classes and the new methods of teaching. It was with a mixture of pride and hope for the future that I waved them goodbye on their first morning at this new school, wearing their new uniforms. My children, I hoped, would be working hard for 'O' and 'A' levels.

Mum and Dad paid us a visit to take a look at the new house. Mum made a tour of the large, airy but sparsely furnished rooms, sniffing delicately, whilst Dad stood staring at the unkempt garden with a jaundiced eye. No tenant had touched the garden since the house had been built in 1948. With hands deep in pockets, Dad could only mutter, 'Lot to do here, Johnny my cocker.' I offered to fetch the spade there and then so he could have a go if he felt inclined, but he only looked at his watch, cleared his throat and said that they ought to be thinking of being on their way home while it was still light.

Mum's final verdict on the new house was that I had some queer ideas about what was nice. 'It's a great barn of a place if you ask me,' she said. 'You'll never get this great lump of concrete warm in winter; you'll all freeze to death.'

Patty left school in 1957 and went to work for the Civil Service in central Bristol. We were glad that she had got a good position with a job for life. But it didn't suit her and within eighteen months she went to train as a nursery nurse out at Stoke Lodge. Then she dropped a bombshell – she wanted to leave home and share a flat with her friend, Dot. I saw the flat and was devastated. It was in an attic, up endless stairs. In the main room there were two beds and a gas fire with a greedy meter that gobbled up the coins. Around a corner, under the skylight window, a small sink and drainer plus a Baby Belling cooker was all that passed as a kitchen. There was a toilet on the next landing down. I never did discover whether there was a bath or shower.

I spent sleepless nights worrying over both Patty and her friend. Would they air their clothes properly or have enough to eat? I made cakes and pies and trudged up the dirty stairs to find out how they were doing in this dreary, godforsaken place. Most journeys were fruitless as all too often the pair of them were out, and, on the odd occasion they were in and I mentioned my concern, they fell laughing onto the beds and invited me to join them in eating cold baked beans from a tin.

Jacky was only sixteen when she was offered a job with

the Civil Service in Guildford. I agonised for days about letting her go all that way from home. But in the end it was her own decision, and she said she'd like to take the job. So my second daughter was leaving home too. I consoled myself with the knowledge that there was a welfare department I could contact which would ensure she was found suitable accommodation and that she would be well looked after. I couldn't help remembering how I'd left home at the tender age of fourteen to go into service myself. Reluctantly we drove Jacky to her new home in the Surrey countryside. It was John who kept reminding me that space and independence were precious to young people; that I must come to terms with the fact that my two eldest girls had already flown the nest.

'You still have the three of us to look after, remember,' he said severely, as if that made up for the loss of my two eldest daughters, and as if it was somehow rather strange for me to be so concerned about what was, after all, a most natural chain of events.

I decided it was time I went out and found myself a proper job to help pay the rent and get me some new clothes before I began to draw the old-age pension. I breathed a sigh of relief to discover that I was not too ancient, at forty-two, to be taken on as a trainee waitress at BAC, the big aircraft works at Filton, employing thousands and thousands of workers. I was to work in the directors' canteen.

It was a proper job. They taught me silver service and I really took to the work. The girls there were a great bunch to be with. Like all catering, waitressing is very hard work, but you are always compensated by the friendly chatter that goes on in the kitchen and servery. That first week I was appalled to see the lovely food that was left over after every lunchtime and which was just put out as waste. There were cutlets of fresh salmon, grilled chicken, fillet steak, Dover sole – stuff I'd never been able to afford to buy.

'What happens to all this food left over?' I asked, thinking that perhaps the chef used it in a delicious and imaginative recipe the following day.

'It's supposed to get chucked out,' said Vi, the mate I worked with. Then she lowered her voice and added, 'But we shares it out between us. You can't let it go to waste, can you?'

It was instant dismissal if you were caught taking stuff home. So, while it remained official policy that any leftovers went straight in the pig-bin, all that lovely grub actually found its way into our shopping baskets and got laid out on our own tea tables. I remember the day I put fresh salmon cutlets on the menu for my lot. Julie's reaction was that she'd rather have the tinned stuff she was used to, and Darrell said, 'Ugh, it tastes like slimy cotton wool!' Neither of them took to the hollandaise sauce either: 'It'll never replace salad cream,' they said, and both had a fit of the giggles.

But John had no complaints. He finished his meal with a broad grin on his face. And when I brought him home a nice fillet steak he couldn't help remarking that he fully approved of my new job.

John changed his job too, and went to work for a big city bank as a courier. He had always hated the unsociable hours and the shift work of the Post Office. He looked forward now to working nine to five, enjoying more restful nights and a congenial working atmosphere. He bought himself a smart mac, a dark suit and an expensive, rolled black umbrella. He'd always had pretensions of grandeur, but I must admit now he really did look the part. And I began to think about saving up for my red-velvet curtains.

In the early sixties the Council adopted a policy of selling off council houses to sitting tenants, and we were offered ours at a very favourable price. The idea of being able to turn our house, which was just the same as everybody else's, into something individual, seemed an exciting challenge and I urged John to take advantage of this offer.

Controversial discussions, for and against the scheme, became very heated at times. Some people argued that council houses had been built with public money and should not be sold off cheaply, whilst sitting tenants often expressed the view that 'I've bought this bloody house ten times over, the rent I've paid!'

The following day I foolishly confided to my workmate, Vi, that I had a burning desire to own my own house. She was filling the coffeepot at the time and the hot steam from the boiler may have accounted for her flushed and agitated face.

She retorted testily, 'If you buy your council house you won't be working-class any more. You'll have moved up into the middle-class bracket.'

I blinked. That seemed ridiculous to me. You didn't have to abandon all your socialist ideas just because you wanted the pride of owning your own place. I said rather naïvely, 'I thought everyone who worked for a wage was working-class.'

'Working-class people don't own their own houses, do they?' she demanded. 'You'll be voting Tory next!'

'Oh come on, Vi, I'm still the same person. Just because I want to have my own house, and live in a bit of luxury before I die.'

She turned on her heel and flounced off, flinging the words 'You're no better than a snob!' at me as she went. My mother's words came back to me: 'Don't get ideas above your station, my girl,' when I told her I wanted red-velvet curtains and wall-to-wall carpeting when I got married.

For a minute or two I stood there feeling confused and uncertain. Yes, I did want a fairer world and equal chances for all, but that surely didn't mean I had to live in poverty all my life myself? I really could see Vi's point of view, but I also wanted all those things that made life comfortable and bearable. I was fed up with bare boards and lino; I wanted all the luxuries of life. I really did.

I began to make butter pats for the bread rolls. With each little curl I scraped I became more and more determined, and more convinced than ever that one day I'd show 'em all.

The subject of the house was settled completely unexpectedly one Friday evening a couple of weeks later, when at the tea table John lowered the evening paper just long enough to announce casually, 'Oh by the way, I've bought the house!'

Those magic words filled me with so much joy and enthusiasm. I instantly began to plan possible improvements. My mind was so filled with the telly adverts about double glazing and central heating I did not see the obvious warning signs: a vicious jerk to straighten the paper John was holding; the sudden clenching of the fist that held it. My verbal flow did not diminish. I rushed wilfully on, where even angels feared to tread.

John's attitude seemed to imply that the arrangement of buying the house was far easier than dealing with me. The usual clichés followed in boring order. The gist of it was that we couldn't possibly afford to buy the house *and* make all the improvements to it.

He wagged a forefinger and said quietly, 'If you want all these things, Joyce, then you must pay for them. You know I can only supply the bread; you must provide the butter.' 'Tell you what, Joyce' – he was folding his paper and looking straight at me – 'If you want this new-fangled central heating installed, you pay for it and I'll make sure your name goes on the deeds of the house as soon as the completion papers come through.'

I looked up from the pile of dishes still in the sink, trying to read a measure of conviction into the words since his attitude had changed so suddenly. He was watching me intently, both his hands folded across his chest. Then, without waiting for an answer, he made an exit for the bathroom, whistling all the while. The world seemed the right way up again, and I even hummed a few bars of a song as I dried the plates and stacked them away.

I went to work now with renewed interest. I was determined that central heating would be my first priority, and there were several valid reasons for this decision. At the moment, when I came home at night, I had two fires to light: one in the lounge to keep us warm, the other for domestic hot water, independently fed from a Beeston boiler which squatted in the scullery. Sometimes when the wind was blowing it forced clouds of yellow, sulphurous fumes down the stack pipe, filling the kitchen with a poisonous smell that made me splutter and choke so that I had to stagger outside until either the smoke had cleared or the fire caught up. I longed more than ever for instant heat and hot water at the push of a button, just as the adverts on telly promised.

Like the wall-to-wall carpets and the red-velvet curtains, the dream of central heating came closer every Friday, when I skipped down the slope from the factory gates to the bank and deposited half my wages into a steadily growing savings account. There eventually came the day when I could actually pay a visit to the Gas Board and arrange for a team of workmen to call and discuss the type of work to be carried out. For the next few weeks I cheerfully put up with the inconvenience, the dust, and the gaping black hole in the kitchen where the old stack pipe and filthy old Beeston boiler had once been.

At last the work was completed and the new system switched on. It was strange at first to feel warmth but to have no fire in the grate. The foreman laughed when I told him this and convinced me that a nice little gas fire with coal-effect flicker fitted into the exposed grate would soon settle the problem. I felt proud that day, counting out the cash and paying for the biggest bill I had ever settled in my life. I was so sure that when John came home that night I would see the light of appreciation in his eyes.

The foreman picked up his tools and followed the workmen to the door. 'We've put you in a nice little system 'ere,' he said, and then pointed to the bay window. 'But you'm losin' all yer 'eat through they ol'-fashioned rusty steel winder frames. Double glazin' is what you wants next. No more draughts, nor paintin', and you'll save on yer 'eating bills an' all.'

I needed no further convincing; double glazing would be my next goal. But I was careful not to repeat the foreman's pearls of wisdom to John immediately. Timing and tact was the key. Anyway, now that I had kept my part of the bargain it was important to discover if John had kept his. I wondered why I felt so nervous about waiting for the right moment to ask. The direct approach would have suited me better. It irritated me no end when he walked into the house that night and seemed not to notice that anything was different.

Tea was over and the contents of the newspaper were scanned before I finally demanded, 'Well, what d'you think?'

Folding the paper, he spoke so quietly I barely caught the words: 'Very nice.' Then he got up from the table and walked to the window, where he stood staring into the garden.

I wanted to ask him about the deeds to the house: had they come through? And had he added my name to them as he had promised to do? It was now or never, and it all came out in a rush, which left me feeling breathless. Water gurgling around the new heating system was the only sound in the room as I waited for John to speak, to give me one sign of reassurance that the house was now partly mine, a joint venture, a partnership to be sealed with a smile and a hug.

No blow could have been dealt so casually or quietly. John delivered his announcement in a barely audible yet stonily decisive way: 'Your name will never go on the deeds to this house, Joyce. I pay the mortgage and it belongs to me. It will always be mine.'

Something seemed to explode in my chest – anger, disappointment and disgust at this betrayal – which left me speechless. I just stood there staring at him, unable to believe what I had just heard. He began to whistle in defiance and then he walked away from me, along the hall and upstairs to the bathroom. I heard him splashing about in the bath, still whistling, and knew it was his night out with the boys.

There was no milk the following morning for our tea, and I went to the gate to look for the milkman. I sensed something wrong as soon as I stepped into our little driveway. At first I thought it was the heaviness of my depression from the events of the previous day, but then I saw that my lovely little cherry tree had been vandalised, broken in half on its tender young stem. I bent down to pick up the limp greenery of a young bough, wanting to grieve for the loss of so much pleasure and beauty this tiny tree had given.

At the bottom of the road I glimpsed the milk van and heard the clink of milk bottles being delivered. Then I noticed that every single tree along the avenue had been snapped and broken. Some of the green foliage had blown into the road or was half lying in the gutter. None of these young saplings would ever blossom again. Probably a gang of beer-crazed louts had defiled them all last night on their way home from the pub. I wept. Broken blossoms, like my broken dreams, were scattered on the wind.

Vee Goes to Australia

A vacancy arose in the accounts department at the BAC and I foolishly allowed my workmates to persuade me that it was a doddle of a job that I could do standing on my head. So I applied for, and got, the job. It was true that I found no difficulty in doing the work, and the fresh office routine did seem good for my soul at first. My improved weekly pay packet was a good incentive too – there was something deeply satisfying about the early finish on a Friday, when I would rush out of the gates, across the busy main road, with just three minutes to spare before the bank closed. Just in time to push my deposit book over the counter and tuck away half as much again as I'd been able to as a waitress in the directors' canteen.

But as the months went by, I began to yawn my way through endless reams of paper and general requisition notes. In summer I blistered under the glare of glass windows that stretched the whole length of one side of the building. I sat squirming and sweating on a hard, cushionless office bench. In winter I froze under the single panes of glass and the demands from the fresh-air fiends on the other side of the office who clamoured to have the windows left open.

I missed the chatter of my former workmates and the clatter of the lunchtime rush. If waitressing was hard, at least the people I worked with were cheerful and very friendly. I began to hate working in a quiet atmosphere where you weren't expected to chatter. It was like damming up a river to me. So I learned, painfully, that as a person I worked better with people than with things.

In the midst of this personal revelation, Patty got married in a quiet ceremony at the local register office. My new son-in-law, Dave, had warm brown eyes and a disarming smile. Patty was very much in love with him and looked radiantly happy. It was a strange feeling, watching the pair of them standing there holding hands and repeating their marriage vows. Someone else loving her and taking care of her now. Me, her mother, shrinking into the background; the loosening of the bond that had existed through her childhood and teenage years left me with a sad and empty feeling, and to my surprise I felt jealous of him.

Later, sitting in the pub, sipping a drink, observing the other guests and listening to the happy chattering and congratulations of family and friends, I felt exposed and very much alone. I wished that John and I were closer. I so badly needed somebody by my side.

'Now you know why mothers cry at weddings,' was my friend Vee's comment when I next visited her, to babble an account of the wedding, my disillusionment with my new job, and John's betrayal. As always, she was a good listener and let me get it all out of my system. But she had her own news, too.

'Tea!' she announced suddenly, as though it were a cure-all for everything. Vee could drink tea by the bucketful, with neither milk nor sugar. Then she dropped her bombshell: 'I'm going to Australia,' she said, and waited for my reaction.

'Australia? For a holiday?'

'No,' she said teasingly, and her voice held the invitation for me to guess again. 'I'm going out there with my son Barry and his family. Barry thinks that there are better opportunities for him and his children in Australia. We've all had our papers from Australia House and our departure date is all set for next month.'

'Oh Vee, you can't.' I was rendered speechless as the enormity of what she had just said began to sink in. She and I had been friends since childhood. She was my first, my best, and sometimes my only friend. Hers was the shoulder I cried on in times of trouble; she was the one I confided in and laughed with and talked to. If she left for Australia, how could I bear it?

Seeing my downcast face, she laughed and hugged me and said, 'Come on, Joy, be happy for me. We'll write. We'll keep in touch.' So I tried to put a brave face on it and tried not to think of Australia and all those thousands of miles that would now separate us.

On the day she left I went with the rest of her family to see her off from Heathrow and we stood chatting awkwardly and once again promising to keep in touch. Then they boarded the plane and were gone from me. The drive home was quiet and subdued, each of us alone with our own thoughts. I never saw the passing countryside but was rapt in memories of our childhood together, Vee and I, when we used to sit together and play together after school. All those many, many years ago in the long summer of distant childhood, when we picked apples and plums in the orchard together.

I remembered how I used to go and sit with Vee in her father's den where he used to repair shoes at the bottom of their garden. Vee had her own special little wicker chair and the place had been fixed up very cosy, with cushions and rugs for us. And I remembered too how once her mother had held a table-tapping session to try to find the whereabouts of some money stolen when Vee's grandmother had died. I smiled now at the memory of that frightening childish experience all those years ago, and looked out of the window at the passing countryside. Every mile took Vee and me further and further away from each other and suddenly the loss of my friend seemed too much to bear and I felt the tears wet once more on my cheek. Through my blurred vision I looked at Anne, her daughter. The misery on her face matched my own. She would miss her mother. I would miss my friend.

In the months that followed I missed Vee dreadfully, not least because I needed her so badly during a time of terrible anxiety. I missed a period, and, despite all my desperate attempts to brush aside my fears, a heavy feeling of dread persisted throughout the following month. I thought grimly how it would be just my luck to fall for another baby at forty-four years of age and how it would have been nice to have experienced just one planned pregnancy, instead of a series of accidents.

At that age I just couldn't face another baby; the more I thought about even the possibility of it, the more the heavy feeling in my chest seemed to weigh me down. My marriage, like my mother's before me, just seemed to consist of babies coming along when you didn't want them. When I missed the second month I went to see the doctor. I still had that sinking feeling, as well as a touch of nausea. He just congratulated me and said he'd look forward to seeing me at the ante-natal clinic in a month's time.

In the weeks that followed I felt disinclined to get up and go to work. I felt dull and listless, like a great wall of concrete had descended on me. To make matters worse Patty bustled in one day, with bright and shining eyes, to let me know I was going to be a grandmother. I burst into tears, unable to explain how pleased I was for her because of the misery I felt for myself.

My depression deepened as the weeks went by and I kept my secret to myself. I certainly wasn't going to tell *him*. What sympathy or understanding could I expect? None. I confided to the doctor that I was experiencing some kind of depression and his look seemed to express incredulity that an expectant mother could be anything other than deliriously happy. However, he said he would put me on a course of anti-depressants and gave me a note to stay off work for a week.

For weeks I felt I was in hell. I seemed completely unable

to do anything except wallow in the total disaster that had become my life. I knew that everyday things had to be done, yet some deep inertia held me back from doing them. So household chores just piled up, washing-up was left in the sink and ironing was left undone.

What was worse, when I did manage to get as far as the butcher's or the grocer's, a complete blank often obscured my memory and I'd completely forget what I wanted to ask for. Sometimes it felt as if I'd been somehow transported to the butcher's up in the square – I'd have no idea how I'd got there. In a blind panic I'd turn and blunder out of the shop, completely oblivious to the stares of passers-by, and make a mad dash for home. Home was where I felt safe. Safe but sad. And sometimes in my wretchedness, halfway down the road to home I'd just sit in the gutter and weep uncontrollably. I felt like a small child very lost and very alone.

A woman who lived on the opposite side of the road looked out of her window one morning and saw me sitting in the gutter with my tears falling fast. She came over to help me but there was nothing I could tell her. How could I explain that heavy concrete wall I couldn't get out of, and the mental anguish that defied description?

'Come on, my lover,' she coaxed. 'Where d'you live? I'll take thee 'ome.' Incapable of protesting because of my deep sobs, I allowed her to take my arm and pilot me home and sit me in a chair. Then while the kettle came to the boil she sat with me, holding my hand and looking worried because of my deep distress. I found it impossible to explain that it wasn't any good her bringing me home, despite the fact that it was where I wanted to be. I still had to make that awful journey back up to the shops to get – what? I couldn't remember.

This pattern repeated itself several times, the futile journeys back and forth. Every time the same woman would come out, find me in deep distress and lead me home. 'You'm on the change, my lover,' she said. 'Don't worry yerself. We all bin through it. You'll be better soon, jest wait and see.'

John on the other hand was not supportive. He disliked coming home to find no cooked meal ready on the table for him. My tears and swings of moody silences or sudden bursts of temper scared and frightened him. He thought I was a madwoman who ought to be locked away. When he finally grasped I was pregnant he was convinced I was not right in the head. 'No other woman ever made such a fuss about having a baby,' he said with utter disgust in his voice.

At five and a half months I dragged myself to the antenatal clinic to find out if everything was as it should be. There was a look of puzzled consternation on the doctor's face as he gave me an internal examination. 'How far did you say you had gone?' he enquired, his fingers busy in a kind of frantic searching. 'When did you last see a period?'

No depression, however deep, could erode that fateful month now almost half a year away. 'I think we will have a pregnancy test,' he said quietly. 'I don't think you are pregnant at all.' He saw the despairing look on my face and wrote out a prescription for more anti-depressants and another note for time off work. He patted my hand and told me to pull myself together, adding that a lot of women thought they were pregnant when they were first on the change.

'Depression is a common factor as well. Now come along, Mrs Storey, we don't want to have to send you into a mental hospital, do we?' And he laughed cheerfully. He caught hold of my elbow and guided me towards the treatment room where they would do the pregnancy test.

I managed to stammer, 'How long before I know for sure?' I had a desperate desire to know immediately, so that life could continue without this terrible mental burden I felt I could no longer carry.

'Come and see me next week.' And again he laughed heartily. In my misery I wondered foolishly what on earth he found to be so bloody cheerful about.

Comprehension did not dawn, neither did my depression lift, even when I was informed, with the same level of amusement, that the results were negative. Inexplicably and perversely, there was now something else that saddened me: the part of my life that was tied up with my womanhood and my youth – the ability to have a baby.

The menopause threw me into this state of confusion and contradiction. I felt more than ever an insatiable desire to be comforted and cuddled, but when I turned to John as I lay by his side in bed at night, he read the wrong signals and thought I wanted sex. Then, when in a disappointed fury I lashed out at him, he became angry and perplexed, and with a sudden vicious twist he turned away from me, taking all the blankets with him and leaving me feeling very lonely and cold. So I slipped out of the bed and made for the spare room, John's voice echoing after me: 'You leave my bed, madam, I can divorce you!'

'If I thought for one moment that I would make another man half as unhappy as you keep telling me I have made you, then living on my own would be my choice. I might still be lonely but certainly not unhappy. Being married to you I am both!'

'You're a madwoman and you ought to be certified,' was his angry comment to that one.

Our marriage had always been stormy, but more than ever now our relationship became like a battleground. Sometimes, when I was busy at the sink washing up, John would take the tea-towel and flick the end towards my bare legs. Half the time I think he intended to miss, but when it caught me it would nick the skin, the pain would be sharp and it always left an ugly red mark. More than anything I hated such teasing because it made me feel powerless.

More often than not he'd play a silly teasing game like this when he was dressed and ready to go out with the boys – all the games were designed to annoy me, to let me know that he was the boss. They always made me angry. So there'd be a row before he went out and a quarrel on his return.

One night he just caught me in the wrong frame of mind. Instead of the usual irritated 'Stop it, John!' when he began his childish antics, I impulsively hurled the washing-up cloth at him as the tea-towel flicked the back of my legs. The suddenness of my response caught him fair and square with a dripping wet dishcloth in the face, and the water ran down over his brand-new tie and freshly laundered shirt.

He stared in disbelief at his ruined outfit. 'Ugh!' he yelled at me. 'You just can't take a joke, can you?'

But he never flicked the tea-towel at my bare legs again. It was some time later, several months in fact, and a year and a half since I first thought I was pregnant, when I was once more doing the shopping up in the square. I gazed idly into the window of the butcher's, looking at the display. As I stood there, my depression lifted – just like a cloud rolling away. That great heavy weight was taken from me and everything was all right again with my world.

There was no baby. There never would be now. The monthly curse was gone for ever. I suddenly fancied a nice piece of spring lamb with mint sauce and new potatoes. We would even have a rice pudding for afters. I sang all the way home.

My New Career

*I*t was a hot August day and I'd been shopping. I was tired, thirsty and irritable; the plastic carrier-bag handles bit into the palms of my hands like steel cords and my feet and legs ached. I staggered into the corner café and slid gratefully along the bench table near the window and kicked off my shoes. The cool feel of the cushioned lino squares under my feet was such bliss that I closed my eyes to relax a little. I ordered a pot of tea and noted from the menu that steak-and-kidney pie was the speciality of the day. Waiting for my lunch to arrive, I swiftly drank down two cups of tea and began to feel human again. Then I noticed a long queue of women outside and wondered vaguely what it was for. But the arrival of my lunch, with its delicious aroma tickling my taste buds, drove my curiosity entirely from my mind, and I tucked in.

Some time later I reluctantly scraped my plate clean, drank the last few dregs of lukewarm tea and prepared to go.

Gingerly feeling around under the table for my shoes, I discovered the left one gone under the bench. In order to grab it I had to disappear under the table. Halfway through this operation I felt a body slump into the empty bench beside me, and a deep male voice uttered, 'My God! Just look at all those women out there!'

I returned from the horizontal position to see a slightly built, middle-aged man addressing this remark to a smiling waitress standing by him, waiting patiently for him to place his order. It was obvious from her manner that she knew him personally, because she bent towards him to reply teasingly, 'You'd better phone that wife of yours to let her know you'll be late, on account of being tangled up with the ladies!'

She was still laughing as she walked away, leaving my table companion rubbing his chin in a nervous gesture. I followed his gaze to the line of women outside. The queue now stretched in front of the café and around the corner into the side street, completely blocking the café entrance. The man's next remark was directed at me and gave a clue to the reason for that long line of patiently waiting women:

'I never thought when we advertised for a manageress for our new War on Want shop that we'd encourage such an avalanche of females!' and he gave a hollow, humourless little laugh. He was clearly not a happy man.

I said, more in jest than in earnest, 'You'd better give me the job then, and all your troubles will be over.' I eased myself along the seat and stood up to smile a goodbye – I had my bus to catch; the queue of women and the vacancy were his problem, not mine.

But he was looking at me intently now and suddenly blurted out, 'What do you know about managing a charity shop?'

'Why, absolutely nothing – except a keen desire to learn something new and interesting, and to bring a lot of enthusiasm to something that's really worthwhile.' It wasn't until the words were out of my mouth that I realised that I meant everything I'd said.

I arranged my shopping so that equal weight was distributed on either side of me and turned to go. I was moving away from him when I felt his hand lightly touch the back of my coat. He'd come to an on-the-spot decision, and as I turned to face him he said, 'If you want the job, it's yours!'

I was stunned. We shook hands on the deal and after writing down my name and address he promised to confirm the position in due course. I would be required to go to the main branch in Weston-super-Mare for three weeks' training. I was suddenly completely elated – fate had thrown me into the charity business. I wondered what John would have to say about my impulsive action.

The new job carried with it responsibility and the need for management skills. With a smug sense of satisfaction I discovered I had a natural ability to manage a business, and each hour spent in the new premises for War on Want at Fishponds became a committed learning process. I spent hours cutting off bone and glass buttons from discarded garments and sewing them onto pieces of cardboard for resale. Dirndl skirts with four yards of unglazed cotton I painstakingly unstitched and sold for four shillings apiece. Fox furs graced the walls. And army greatcoats and black all-wool Crombie overcoats were all the rage one winter. I learned to recognise china marks so that when the antique dealers called in they didn't get away with too much of a bargain at the expense of starving people.

The zest and energy I threw into my new job were not necessarily shared by John. Collections were an essential part of the job, and as I could not drive John had to take me to pick up donations of clothes and bric-a-brac. His help was grudgingly given and he complained constantly about the cost of his petrol. Also, he would say bitterly, 'You become a different person when you enter that blasted shop!'

Quite right I did. At nearly fifty years of age I was my own woman at last. Motherhood had never been enough for me, and although I loved my kids and my new grand-sons dearly, there really had always been something indefinable missing from my life. Now I discovered that the exercise of power and responsibility gave me a confidence in myself I'd never known before. I was in charge in that shop in a way I'd never been in charge of my own home, and it showed, as John said, the moment I entered the shop. No wonder he resented it – it was the one thing he'd always feared. It reminded him more than ever of my own mother and perhaps of how she had dominated my father. He was determined, anyway, that it would never happen to him.

I had to admit, my energy and zest for the charity gift shop never wavered. I found a value in every pile of junk donated to me. People gave so generously, and every disaster always prompted them to give even more. They also loved a bargain and found a real treasure trove in my shop. I was happy there, with a deep joy that money could never buy.

Vee had written to tell me about the chaos the new decimal coinage had created when it had been introduced in Australia. It was not received in England either with any degree of enthusiasm, not amongst ordinary people anyway. For one pound sterling, which had been so powerful, to suddenly be reduced from two hundred and forty pence to a paltry one hundred was nothing less than a devaluation of our currency, no matter how much the politicians tried to pull the wool over our eyes. 'Decimalisation – my backside!' was the general consensus. 'Now just watch everything go up!'

This opinion held more than a ring of truth because there would be no more cheap food for Britain and butchers predicted that housewives would be paying a staggering one pound a pound for steak. The Royal Mail caused alarm bells with the news that the five-penny stamp was on its way. Inflation was beginning to bite hard. Under-the-counter tactics brought rich pickings for some, but the spending power of my little £500 nest-egg was slashed overnight.

I was thinking of this rather resentfully one day late in the summer as I wandered through the city centre, making my way towards MacFisheries at the end of Baldwin Street. I thought I would buy some fish and then hop on a bus home from the stop right outside the shop. I was walking past Bethel Gwyn's, the shipping agent, when a huge cardboard replica of a cruising ship caught my attention. I stopped to gaze in wonder. She was a Russian ship called the *Mikhail*

Lermontoff, recently completely refurbished and cruising to the Caribbean from November through to March on five twenty-eight-day cruises from just £240 per person, per cruise.

I sighed heavily, forgot about the fish, and the time, and just stood there dreaming of sailing away to the Caribbean, sunbathing by day and leaning on the ship's rail at night, looking at a shimmering path of silver moonlight over a warm blue tropic sea.

Rebellion made my thoughts race. What had I ever done? Where had I ever been? All my life I'd worked, brought up my family, and for what? My marriage was a mockery and there was no companionship between John and me. And here I was in middle age, with nothing to show for my entire life.

Inflation might have bitten hard into my five hundred quid, but that holiday was something that nobody would ever be able to take away from me. On the spur of the moment I walked into the shipping agent's and bought a ticket for the first November sailing.

My head swirled when I thought of the enormity of blowing all that hard-earned cash on a cruise and going off on my own. I closed my eyes and felt quite faint when I thought of how I would tell John that I would be absent without leave for a whole month. Added to that, the fish shop was closed when I got there and I missed my bus. All the way home I kept looking at my cruise booking receipt with a mixture of excitement, trepidation and great rushes of fear. Though as a matter of fact John said very little when I finally gathered enough courage to tell him about the coming event.

In the ensuing weeks I took advantage of the end-of-the-summer sales to buy my pretty clothes for the holiday. I bought summer dresses and beachwear and, very extravagantly, a deep-pink satin evening dress for those special occasions. I had heard that some rich women voyagers took trunkloads of designer clothes on cruises and that 'Captain's Night' was an evening to remember. Because I'd never owned one, I splashed out on a brand new suitcase big enough for all my purchases and easy to carry. And that left just one last thing I had to do. I was determined to change my personality by having my hair peroxide-bleached and dyed blonde. I paid a visit to the hairdresser, who hesitated as she ran her hands through my mop of dark brown curls, now liberally sprinkled with grey.

'Well, I rather think you would be better suited with a chestnut rinse,' she said helpfully. But I had made up my mind. Blond or nothing. 'You'll need at least two applications to achieve the effect you want,' she said stiffly, indicating her disapproval.

'Whatever it takes,' I said with gay abandon. I was determined that a new look and a new personality were coming with me on this trip of a lifetime – gentlemen might prefer blondes! (Although my mission was not to attract a man, but to get right away from one.) The hallmark of my independence was to be my new blond topknot.

Unsurprisingly, John refused point-blank to drive me to the station. So I phoned for a taxi and when my case had been safely stored away I waved goodbye to him – but the door was already closing behind me. It was a cold November morning and patches of fog made visibility difficult, but at last I was on the train bound for Southampton. I lugged my new case onto the seat beside me and gave a sigh of relief. I was on my way.

Cruising to the Tropics

The fog had thickened by the time I stepped off the train at Southampton and I mingled with my fellow voyagers. We shivered in the cold, damp air. The usual noise, the hustle and bustle of a busy dockside area, was strangely missing. The fact was, we had arrived in the middle of an unofficial dock strike, which had a pretty depressing effect on all of us. I pulled up the hood of my brand-new zipper jacket and followed the crowd down the short covered subway steps that led down to the quayside. There was little conversation and we seemed to unconsciously huddle together for warmth.

When we reached the quayside we had our first glimpse of our luxury cruiser, the *Mikhail Lermontoff*. She was moored alongside with her main deck ablaze with fairy lights. A band suddenly struck up with the tune 'Seventy-six Trombones' and, the weird silence having been broken, we all laughed with relief. Under an awning that led directly to the gangway, gold-braided ship's personnel stood ready to welcome us aboard. I lugged my case up to the warm, elegant reception area for more hand-pumping and smiles, and was rather relieved when a young, attractive steward came forward to take it from me, indicating that I follow him. I noticed, as we descended downwards from main deck to boat deck, that the thick-pile carpet ended abruptly as we reached lower C Deck.

The steward knocked on the door of cabin 426. Two voices trilled out in unison for him to come in. He opened the door and slipped my case inside, waited politely for his tip and quickly disappeared. I took stock of my surroundings. Two women were lying full-length on each of the lower berths of the double bunk beds that ran the length of one wall. A wooden ladder by the side of each of the bunks gave access to the vacant top berths. It was obvious that my cabin mates had arrived first and staked their claim. The older woman spoke first, in a strong Cockney accent.

'I'm Flo,' she said. 'And this 'ere is Veronica. We've bin waitin' fer you. Our other messmate's gorn off in a huff to see if she can git a cabin all to 'erself. Me poor ol' legs won't let me do gymnastics, especially in the middle of the night, and besides,' she lowered her voice conspiratorially, 'I 'ave to be near the loo. You any good at climbin' ladders?'

I laughingly introduced myself and assured them that the ladder would present no problem for me. They both looked relieved, and instantly got off the beds. We spent the next hour or so having a friendly wrangle about drawer and wardrobe space. There was really not a great deal of room and we all agreed that a fourth cabin mate could be a bit of an overspill. 'P'raps she won't come back.' Flo uttered what we all hoped.

There were several hours yet before sailing time and we decided to make a tour of the ship. In the lounge we joined a lively crowd of friends and relatives all sipping tea before the warning bell sounded to usher all non-passengers ashore. We were all excited now, gripped by the holiday mood that had evaded us for so long.

It wasn't long before we were all exchanging confidences, although my admission that I was on a cruise as a break for independence, and Veronica's holiday treat was being paid for by her parents, both faded into insignificance against Flo's startling saga: left a widow at forty, she did a bit of cleaning for a lady she thought was down on her luck and in need of a bit of company. Flo looked after her for fifteen years and then the lady died, leaving Flo all her considerable fortune.

'Well, dear, you could've knocked me dahn with a feather!' was Flo's comment.

With the money banked, Flo decided to take a cruise. She liked that so much that she tried several more, mostly the take-a-chance standby cruises and often on the *Loret La Mar*, which Flo said was far nicer than the *Mikhail Lermontoff*.

The lounge began to empty when the ship's bell eventually sounded. My two companions thought I was mad when I told them I wanted to go on deck and watch the ship actually cast off. I ran down to the cabin to put on my outdoor things. Passengers were shouting and waving their last farewells to well-wishers standing far below on the dock-side. In the half-light of that foggy and dismal November dusk, at least the cheering and interchange of friendly banter was heart-warming. The band struck up again and an impromptu quayside dance followed. Moving limbs to encourage circulation added amusement to the situation. Up on deck, watching the antics of those below, my teeth chattered in the cold and misty damp air. Above the sounds of the band I heard the gangway being removed, and seconds later the throb-throb of an engine sent a reverberation along the deck.

A loud cheer went up and suddenly there was a strange cacophony of sounds: instructions shouted through loud-speakers, ship's bells and whistles, sirens and foghorns. This was the moment then. I watched the distance between the ship and quayside become wider and wider, figures franti-cally dancing and waving, becoming smaller and smaller, their voices becoming fainter, until in that grey, choking mist they disappeared altogether.

I was bemused, for there had hardly been any movement on the ship at all. We seemed to have glided away from the dockside so effortlessly. Now the activity seemed concen-trated on the hooting of the siren and the shrill ringing of bells. Between these sounds and the curt instructions on loudspeaker and megaphone, a conversation seemed to be going on. I spoke to a fellow passenger standing near to me, watching as intently as I all that happened. His face was barely visible because of a warm woollen scarf he had tied around his neck and mouth. He lowered the scarf from his mouth to answer my enquiry and explained that the tugs in front making all the racket were pulling the ship, stern first, up Southampton Water to the mouth of the Solent. There the ship would slowly turn her bows to point in the right direction for our trip to the tropics.

We couldn't fail to recognise our departure point. All the tugs blew whistles, foghorns and sirens. Once again *Mikhail Lermontoff* responded with bells and whistles. Then we passed the Isle of Wight and the Needles and I thought to myself, Caribbean Islands, here we come!'

Excitedly, I hurried back to the cabin to give a running commentary on what I had seen and learned. I also wanted to have a shower to warm myself because it had been so bitterly cold up there on the deck. I sang as I turned on the shower and began to undress. Vanity impelled me to look into the mirror, for I could not resist the new sexy blonde nymph I had become.

The face that stared back at me was a stranger. The sea air had taken every bit of golden tint out of my hair and left it a mop of brassy peroxided straw. I gave a little shriek and dived into the shower. Completely and utterly devastated, I thought I might be able to wash it out somehow. After three washes I realised the futility of this procedure. In fact, every wash seemed to make it worse and worse. It just accentuated the brass and it now resembled the colour – and was frankly almost the texture – of the inside of a very rusty tin. Furthermore, I thought it looked as common as muck.

I trailed miserably back to the cabin and sat and howled.

Veronica remembered that the hairdresser was still open, taking bookings for Captain's Night in a few evenings' time. She would come with me for moral support. When we arrived at the salon I felt hot with humiliation because of the stares and the suppressed giggles as I passed. The assistant looked up from writing in the appointments book and said in a very loud voice so that everyone could hear, 'I can't do anything with that!'

With head bowed, my face red with embarrassment and unable to cover my brassy locks, I slouched and cowered out. I went for my first meal on the luxury liner in a trouser suit and turban. Flo said that from a distance my rusty mop looked just like a flower – 'like a bronze chrysanthemum!', she explained helpfully.

It was all so different from the glamorous new identity I'd planned for myself.

The *Mikhail Lermontoff* ploughed her way through murky weather, leaving behind a trail of white foam. We sailed out of the fog and into pale sunshine. On the second day we strolled along the deck, still muffled in winter woollies, and in sheltered places we stopped to exchange greetings with our fellow passengers. The biggest thrill of all came on the day when over the Tannoy system came the message 'We are now entering the tropics.'

There was also a warning of possible windburn. The warm zephyr-like breezes now blowing could inflict as much damage on sensitive skin as could the sun. However, we were all too feverishly excited to worry about the possible danger that might be done to our lily-white skins. And we pushed our winter clothing to the back of the wardrobe and donned shorts and cotton tops.

Stewards, now attired in white tropical uniforms, arrived on deck looking tanned, handsome and efficient. They began unloading the stacked deck chairs, placing them along the side of the deck. They unrolled the big tarpaulin cover of the swimming pool. Minutes later, sounds of splashing and laughter came from the upper deck. Games were organised; even a Russian-language class was introduced for those with an academic desire to learn the basics. A buffet lunch was served every day. Trestle tables were erected and piled high with the most exotic and mouth-watering meats, seafood and salads. No shortage of food on this ship, and we could come back and back again for more. This was life on the ocean wave in a huge, extended family setting – and it was great fun.

I had toyed with the idea of giving Captain's Night a miss. Despite reassurances from my two shipmates I was still feeling very delicate about the disaster that had befallen my hair and my short-lived new personality. Flo made last-minute remonstration with me in the cabin that evening:

'You can't hide yerself away from everything. Why not accept wot you can't change and enjoy yerself? It'll all grow out eventually.'

This philosophy sounded so much like my own mother, I was convinced. With my brassy hair I could literally brazen it out. I also thought the deep-pink satin evening dress I had purchased might have been a bit of a mistake; it did nothing to tone down the patchy, deeper orangey hues of my hair, which the sun and warmer trade winds seemed to have encouraged and made even more pronounced.

We tripped our way to the ballroom, where the captain was resplendent in gold braid and white uniform and stood just inside the doors shaking hands with all the assembled guests. To give me moral support, one on either side, my two companions elbowed me towards him. He was not very tall and his eyes seemed immediately to make contact with the top of my crowning glory. I distinctly saw a flicker of pain cross his face. He very limply touched the tips of my fingers with his white-gloved hand and instantly lowered his gaze to the ground.

Then I felt myself being steered towards the long drinks table, where a very dishy-looking steward was pouring wine. He lifted his head a second to ask us what we'd like. I was just about to explain what I'd like to drink when I noticed he appeared almost transfixed, staring at my hair, with the wine already filling the glass and overflowing onto the tray. All three of us escaped with our drinks to a secluded corner of the room, leaving behind a very harassed young man now intent on mopping-up operations.

We spent most of the evening admiring the expensive evening wear that some of the ladies were wearing, and making fun of the affected and outrageous way some of them played for the attention of the officers and captain. Nobody asked us for a dance, and Flo was the first to give a big yawn. We slipped out onto the deck and stood for a while leaning on the ship's rail, watching the wide white wake behind us as we ploughed through the tropical night. Then we made our way down the carpeted companion-ways to where the lino started on C Deck and to cabin 426.

In those relaxed, idle, sunny days, the three of us were inseparable. In the evenings we were entertained with Russian songs and Cossack dancing. There was a games room where we could play cards. This was where Veronica first introduced me to a game called Scrabble, and I quickly became an addict. Veronica was a good coach and I was soon competing with her. Scrabble set my nerves a-tingle and I became quite adept at the game. I spent many an exciting hour playing Scrabble in the years that followed the cruise and it is with a warm sense of gratitude that I remember Veronica.

We anchored a little way off shore at our first Caribbean island. Clustered around the ship's rail, we gazed spellbound as the native boys dived into the clear blue waters of the bay for coins that we threw down to them. We watched as they twisted and turned to retrieve the coins on the sandy bottom of the bay. When they again broke the surface of the water, their impish faces were wreathed in smiles.

Meanwhile, the boats were being lowered to take us ashore, where young taxi drivers haggled with us over the price of taking us on sightseeing tours of the island. Our driver took us to a beach where a steel band was playing. We sat under a big coloured umbrella and ordered long cool drinks. And so the happy carefree days slipped unwarily by. All too soon the precious days ticked themselves off, like falling leaves in autumn, and we had to say farewell to this Caribbean paradise. The whole of the population seemed to swim out to wave their goodbyes.

Three days out from Southampton, we again thrust our now golden bodies into winter coats and scarves. The swimming pool was covered and the deck chairs stacked and battened down. The last evening at dinner the captain came over to our table and handed Flo an envelope. The whole restaurant/dining room seemed to go quiet, the clatter of silverware and chatter suddenly cut off. All eyes were on our table as an officer appeared to pour us drinks with the captain's compliments. I felt the unconcealed curiosity of the stares. In his perfect English, our captain explained to the assembled passengers that the coveted tickets for a free cruise on the *Mikhail Lermontoff* had been awarded to Mrs Florence Woods, because she was the only person on the ship who reminded him of the Russian peasant women of his beloved homeland. After his speech, it was several seconds before a single, rather hesitant hand-clap was followed by a few more, and finally, to great applause, Flo was acclaimed the worthy prize winner.

The next day, the same noisy little tugs which had nosed us out of the Solent four weeks before now escorted us safely to the dockside, where we arrived on a cold December morning amidst the hustle and bustle of a busy port. The teeming activity demonstrated that the strike of a month ago was now forgotten and normality once more restored. I went to sit in the lounge. There is always something sad and nostalgic about the last days of a holiday.

This floating palace had been my home for the last twenty-eight rather wonderful days. The lounge was filled with noisy knots of people exchanging addresses with new-found friends, fervently promising they would keep in touch.

I gave a big sigh and turned my attention to lugging my case back down the gangway and up the steps to the train and home. If only I possessed another £240 I could have gone back to the cabin and staked my claim, and this time for a lower berth bed.

At the top of the gangway was a familiar figure and I gave a quick intake of breath as I instantly recognised John. After his flat refusal to drive me to the station or to wish me *bon voyage*, I hadn't expected him to actually drive to Southampton to welcome me home. However, I gave a wide grin and went forward to meet him. I dropped my heavy case so that I might receive the welcome hug. Instead, he held me at arm's length and right there in the middle of the gangway, amidst the amused stares of my fellow passengers squeezing by, he exclaimed in loud, shocked tones, 'My God, Joyce, whatever's gone wrong with your hair? You don't half look common!'

Why had he greeted me like that? And why did I always react with anger? I'd not seen him for a month. In my own way I had missed him, as I'm sure he'd missed me, and I had so wanted to show him over the ship and to describe to him the thrill of that wonderful holiday. All my good intentions blown to the four winds, as usual. Guilt, remorse, resentment – I stood there feeling all these things. I knew I would never be what he wanted me to be no matter how hard I tried. But I had taken that great leap towards a kind of independence by going off on my own. Things really never would be quite the same again now.

Bereavement

Just like the lush warm days of an Indian summer, those idle carefree days at sea faded into the storeroom of my memory. That cruise was a kind of turning point for me. Even the bleak November fog and sailing into warm sunshine symbolised a pointer along the way. My new personality, not dependent upon the colouring of a new hairstyle, was gradually asserting itself.

John was not a bad man, he was merely the product of the social conditioning of the time. He'd been deprived of a proper father and was terribly insecure and untrusting. I understood how his childhood had made him like that. My own childhood had been similarly deprived. Because I'd spent nearly two years at Painswick, away from my mother at a very impressionable age, I had never regained the closeness to her that gives a child real security. Both John and I sought in each other the love and security we'd never had as children. And we let each other down badly.

He thought the only way he could assert himself was by keeping me at arm's length. He was afraid that I would come to dominate him in everything if I was given a say in anything. He was close and secretive. I never knew how much he earned each week, nor how much we paid out in bills, because he kept all the household accounts, together with his chequebook and savings and personal effects, in a bureau that was always kept locked. He handled all the money, wrote all the cheques, made all the important decisions that affected us, and referred to me in front of strangers throughout our forty years together as 'the wife'.

But by the 1970s there was a massive swing of the pendulum, away from the repressive Victorian values of our youth and the dominant male role. It was not enough any more for women to remain passive, to endure what had always been and think things could not be changed. Women were beginning to change things for themselves. A lack of warmth, a lack of communication, and a lack of generosity were all black marks I stacked against John. He resisted all the changes that were happening and he sometimes made me feel pretty lonely and worthless.

I bought myself a new motor scooter and a black-leather motorcycle jacket. All I wanted now, I joked, was my name in big silver studs on the back. When I set out for work on my brand-new two-stroke motorcycle, the morning was filled with the scent of midsummer fragrance and almost every garden bore witness to the popularity and splendour of the rose.

All seemed well with my world. During the five years Vee

had been away, we had kept in constant touch. She bought herself an old typewriter and bashed out her long, chatty letters with two fingers. It seemed only natural that I too should sally forth and buy myself a second-hand portable – just to keep up with her. So our letters to each other passed to and fro, with their wobbly margins and typing errors and often a complete lack of capital letters. Although we both agreed that neither of us would ever get a job in a typing pool, the joy and pleasure those letters gave us more than compensated for the dreadful typing mistakes. She wrote to me to say how much my letters meant to her, and how they were passed around from hand to hand, and read and re-read.

Vee had worked extremely hard to help her son get established in Australia and had taken a variety of jobs – at one time she worked in a foundry, then in a local hospital, and had even spent time packing chickens on a 'chook farm'. She wrote with a kind of dreamy nostalgia of her homesickness, and her longing for the green fields of England. Then one day in a supermarket the customer behind her in the queue heard her voice and said, 'That sounds like a West Country accent to me – I come from Bridgwater myself!' Vee just went to pieces and wrote to me that the woman's West Country accent sounded just like her own mother. 'I just bent my head over my trolley and howled, Joy, and then we all broke down and had a good cry. There and then I decided I'd had enough – I've started saving to come home.'

I received the news of her homecoming with inexpressible joy. She chose to come home by sea on one of the last cruise journeys – and how agonisingly long those weeks of waiting for her seemed! Then came the day when her family collected me and we all went to Southampton to welcome her home. The policeman on the dock gates smiled and nodded and thumbed a direction when we enquired if the *Southern Cross* had already docked. At last we were reunited. I stood aside to allow her family to hug her and shed their tears, and I noticed with a start how ill and tired she looked. Those six weeks at sea had not erased the deep lines in her forehead, or restored the ravages to her yellowed and tired-looking skin. The five years under the fierce Australian sun had really aged her. When she held out her arms to me I just ran to her and for several minutes the two of us remained locked together, our tears falling fast and making damp patches on each other's shoulders. Vee was home. It was all that mattered. Five years ago it had been tears of sorrow. Reunited at last, now it was tears of joy.

In due course Kingswood Council allocated Vee a top-storey flat. She boasted about the view her lounge window commanded, which was of Kelston and Lansdown. And she claimed, 'I have my lovely flat, my family and my precious friend – what more could I ever ask for?'

There were times, though, when she and I came back from a shopping trip, when the three flights of stairs to her top flat brought on a fit of breathless coughing in her, and I would make her sit still on the stairs until it passed. She would sit there until she regained her breath, then lighting yet another fag she would joke, 'It's not the coughing that carries you off, but the coffin they carries you off in!' And I wondered if perhaps the only thing missing from her life just might be good health.

I heard through the grapevine just after Vee's return that War on Want were intending to open another shop at Staple Hill – just a mile or two down the road from my own shop – and I urged her to apply for the job of manageress. My joy was complete when I heard that she had netted the job. In time, she came to have the same sense of satisfaction as I did, and it also meant I had my dear companion on what had been lonely trips to London for our training courses.

I was thinking of all this as I rode to work one June morning, feeling the warm air on my face as I pulled the twist-grip of my bike to reduce speed around the corner into the main stream of traffic on the Fishponds Road and the last lap of my journey. I thought I might pop over to see my father when I'd finished at the shop that night and take him some of his favourite sweets. He loved mint humbugs – the huge, sticky brown-and-cream striped triangular shaped mints. There was a special little corner shop halfway along Chalks Road where they sold them, but I would have to leave a bit early to catch them open.

About six months before, Dad had gone into hospital to have a kidney removed, but when he came home again as a semi-invalid he was not a good patient and grumbled about his inactivity. His blue eyes would always light up when he heard the rustle of the white-paper bag containing the giant humbugs. As I neared my War on Want shop I noticed a council road-sweeper rifling through a box of clothing that had been left in the doorway. Over the man's yellow nylon dustcoat he was wearing a smart Harris tweed jacket. On such a warm June morning the jacket looked slightly out of place, but it had obviously proved to be such a find that he was now wearing it with pride, while scattering the contents of the carton in all directions in order to discover if there were other treasures of like value.

When I came up behind him, intending to rebuke him for the mess he had made in the doorway and for taking stuff without permission, he moved guiltily into the gutter, where he once more picked up his long-handled broom, and began pushing it quickly up the road. I opened up the shop feeling slightly irritated because now I would have to pick up and move the heavy carton into the shop before I could even put my bike away – otherwise the mess would attract other would-be bargain hunters.

By ten o'clock my two helpers arrived and I stopped to make coffee and to chat. I told them the story of the road-sweeper and the Harris tweed jacket. We were still laughing at his audacity when the phone rang. My mother's voice sounded cold and distant. Her one curt sentence seemed clipped short. I stood stock-still with the receiver frozen in my hand, listening to the buzz of a disengaged line and wondering if I'd heard the message right: 'If you want to see your father alive, you had better get over here as quickly as you can.'

My mother answered the door but brushed aside all physical contact and mention of condolence. My no-tears, no-nonsense mum, with all her feelings bottled up tight as usual. I followed her along the narrow passageway and into the back room. Dad was lying with his face pressed close to the skirting board, where he had died. It looked as though he had been sitting on the side of the bed and fallen forward onto his face. He looked so small and helpless. My first instinct was to rush forward and cradle him in my arms. I made a move towards him, at least to cover him with a blanket – to be so exposed was undignified, not right at all.

My mother's voice, like a command, halted me in my tracks. 'He must not be touched or moved until the doctor comes,' she said. 'They said so.'

I sat, with my chin resting on my hands on the back of a chair, just looking at that small, crumpled heap. 'Oh Dad,' was all I could say.

Mum came to stand beside me. She bent her head so that she was level with my face. 'You thought your father loved you, didn't you?' Her voice was matter-of-fact, with never a tremor to betray the turmoil she must have been suffering. It was as though she was musing on events long past but clearly memorised and recorded. For a moment, I thought she was reaching out to repeat something kind to ease the pain that the pair of us were now sharing. 'Your father never loved you. He couldn't stand you. You or your kids.'

The gurgle of disbelief that half rose in my throat turned into a wail of anguish and grief. A great pain seemed to weigh me down. There were stones in my chest.

The doctor came and pronounced my father dead. He took my mother out into the hall where they spoke in low tones for several minutes. The man at the chapel of rest was very kind to me when I went to pay my last respects to Dad, and asked if I would like him to stand with me. I shook my head; those last few moments could not be shared. My father had never hurt me when he was alive and it was inconceivable that he would want to hurt me when he was dead. He looked so peaceful lying there, and strangely young. Just like a photograph of him with my mother when they were in their twenties, just starting out on their life together. They had been such beautiful people then. I felt a lump come into my throat. Those blue eyes would never shine and dance at me again. There never would be an answer now to that vexing doubt my mother's dreadful words had raised in me.

I gently pressed the backs of my fingers to that cold waxen face.

'Goodbye, Dad,' I whispered softly.

Then I turned and walked quickly out into the noise and bustle of the living world and the warm June sunshine.

After Dad's funeral I experienced a strange kind of apathy. The fragile emotional bridge I had tried to construct to get close to my mother for so many years suffered irreparable damage, and a strange inertness prevented me from any desire to rebuild it. I no longer felt like visiting her. It wasn't that I didn't care – perhaps I cared too much, or perhaps I had always tried too hard to be close to her. There was certainly a kind of emotional relief in trying to shut off painful memories of that awful day, and all the other times she had hurt me in my life.

I did a lot of soul-searching in the months that followed, and would like to believe that it was just lack of communication that made her say what she did in the way that she did. Perhaps she was just trying to be honest and convey to me that her love for Dad died because of a lack of generosity and communication that he could not express, and she was just trying, in her own way, to get close to me by telling me that.

Mum was remarried within a year. She married George, a widower who lived in the same road, and they decided to join forces for companionship and to share their expenses. It was a big wedding and the *Evening Post* gave it middle-page coverage, with a picture of a pink and white bride cutting the cake. I like to think that in her last years my mother was happy with George.

Ireland

At seventeen Julie, who had always been a most attractive and appealing child, was quite simply beautiful. If she had been taller, she could have been a fashion model, and she already had a clutch of male admirers. So it should have come as no great surprise to me when she announced she wanted to get married, although I had grave reservations about both her choice of partner and the dim chances of a marriage working out well that was entered into so young.

At seventeen, of course, she was still under-age and had to have our consent. She had always been close to John and it was to him that she and Bob turned for permission to wed under-age. I was not consulted at all. I did feel very hurt, but consoled myself by thinking that everyone must be free to choose for themselves and to make their own mistakes.

So for some years Darrell was the only one still at home – my baby. It even occurred to me that he might well be the

408

solitary quiet one, so unlike his noisy extrovert sisters, who stayed at home with his old mum and dad. And then one morning at breakfast he began to tell us about a young girl who exercised her horse on the common every morning and passed the garage where he worked. 'How can I get to know her, Dad?' he asked.

John said, 'I should get to know the horse first, son. Get to know the nag.'

It was some months later that we were made aware that things were developing in that direction. Darrell was a transformed young man now, with aftershave and body lotion and wearing a freshly laundered shirt. He was off to meet a young lady called Ruth, and asked could she come to tea on Sunday.

'We can cater for the young lady, but not for the horse!' John laughed, throwing down his paper and slapping his son on the back, beaming. And I knew it would not be long before my last little bird left the nest.

Patty and Dave bought a motor caravan and invited us to join them and my grandsons on a tour of Ireland. There was great excitement as we all pored over maps to determine the route we should take and places we would visit. Sixteen wonderful days were planned, taking in the Ring of Kerry and Connemara. John had read about a place called Glendalough that he was particularly interested to see, and Dave promised that we would endeavour to get there if possible.

We set off driving through the wet lanes of Wales to Fishguard and the ferry to Rosslare. The slower pace of life in Ireland was immediately apparent – hardly any traffic on the roads, people in the fields making hay in the traditional way who waved to us as we passed by, and all the time in the world to stop and chat whenever we got out of the van to go shopping or sightseeing. It combined in perfect serenity to add to our holiday mood and the feeling of being at complete peace with the world.

There was just one fly in the ointment – John kept complaining of a pain in his back. At times he claimed it was so severe he could only get relief by lying flat on his back on the floor for several hours. I freely admit I was not entirely sympathetic. For one thing, John had a long history of playing the old soldier, and just like the little boy who called 'Wolf!', over the years we had come to take his dramatic claims of being at death's door with a big pinch of salt. We all made fun of him while he protested, 'I tell you I'm ill, I'm really ill.'

These claims got even less credence when an incident occurred that proved just how fast he could move when highly motivated. We were parked up in a delightful setting in the countryside one day, enjoying a picnic in the warm sunshine. The boys paddled in a nearby stream and I could hear their excited laughter as I sipped my welcome cuppa and listened to the carolling of a lark. Just then a baker's van came roaring down the winding road and as it passed us we noticed that its back doors were unsecured. They were opening and closing, banging to and fro. All of us were riveted by this sight.

'Just look at that!' John said, starting to his feet.

As the van took the corner with a squeal of brakes, the back doors flew open once more and out rolled a large freshly baked loaf. John was off down the road as if his life depended on it, claiming as his rightful prize that precious free loaf of bread, while the rest of us were helpless with laughter.

'How's your back, Daddy?' Patty called out wickedly, but no one could dent his enthusiasm for that loaf of bread, which he cradled in his arms, beaming with pleasure.

One of my customers in the War on Want shop, hearing that I was going on holiday to Ireland, had begged me to stop at Blackwater Bridge on our way to Killarney and take a present to her brother and sister who farmed there. She pressed a carefully wrapped box into my hands and said with a tear in her eye, ''Tis only a bottle of Paddy's, but tell them I send my love and miss them dearly, that's for sure.'

'Oh I will, I will that,' I said in friendly imitation of her lovely soft voice.

So we found ourselves at Blackwater Bridge, which lay tranquil and still in the hot August sun. We drew up by the old post office and went inside to ask directions to the O'Connell farm. At first the postmaster eyed us with suspicion, but when Dave held the bottle of whiskey aloft and explained that we had to deliver it as a present, he smiled, came round the corner and began talking to us like long-lost friends.

'You'll not miss the farm nor the gate,' he said, 'and the dog will spot you before you spot him, so he will.'

The dog spotted us all right, and he came bounding down the field towards us as soon as we stepped through the five-barred gate. He made circling movements behind us, crouching down on his belly and growling whenever any of us turned towards him. In this way, he literally rounded us up like a small herd of sheep, and drove us towards the farm cottage at the top of the field.

The barking meanwhile had alerted the woman in the house and she stood waiting for us to come up to her – looking slightly puzzled and rather on the defensive as she watched us six strangers coming up her field. She wore faded cords with braces, a man's flannel shirt with the sleeves rolled above the elbows of her brawny arms, and a man's trilby tipped on the back of her head. When the dog continued to bark, she picked up a handful of gravel and threw it at him, saying in a harsh voice, 'Be quiet, Rex, or I'll split ya!'

The dog sat down obediently with his tongue lolling, panting, and with his round brown eyes watching us intently to make sure none of us would stray. When I thought it safe to speak, I held out the whiskey and explained it was a present from Nora in Bristol. After the first initial shock of surprise and delight, she took the whiskey and cradled it in her arms and then let out a wail of despair.

'Holy Mother of God, and here's me keeping you all standing on me doorstep. Away inside with you all. Come along now, come along in.' Then, in that harsh voice of hers, she called out into the interior of the cottage, 'John! John! Stir yourself now – we've got visitors come.'

The inside of the cottage was flagstoned and there was an ancient black range in the kitchen, but we were swiftly ushered through into the parlour, where a new cloth was laid and very beautiful Victorian china brought out especially for us. Then the table was laden with cake, scones, jam, sandwiches and a big pot of tea while Mary pressed us for news of her sister, and all the details of our trip and where we would go next, and what we would see. All the while she pressed food upon us and said to the two boys, who had remembered their manners and refused a second piece of fruit cake, 'Sure and there's no law that says you can't have another!'

Mary and John were a brother and sister who had lived on the farm all their lives, struggling to make a living. It was only when Ireland joined the Common Market that things got a lot more comfortable for them, with all the subsidies they were able to claim. But John was getting old now, and suffered from something he called 'the heaviness' which made him fall down sometimes. The farming work was beginning to get too much for him, she thought.

By this time it was early evening and we said we'd have to find a campsite for the night. Mary was going off up the mountain to join her brother, who had gone to bring the cows down to the lower pasture for the night, and she said we should bring the van to a little field at the start of the lane where we would be welcome to stay. We were overjoyed with her suggestion, for it was an idyllic spot in the mauve and misty mountains, with the green of the pastures running up towards the rocky outcrops against the deep blue of the sky, and there was a babbling stream nearby.

So we got the van parked up ready for the night. It had been an eventful day and we were looking forward to the journey tomorrow to Killarney, where we planned to walk through the Gap of Dunloe. As darkness was falling there came a scratching and a whining at the door. 'Rex!' we all said in unison. The dog crouched and barked and ran a little way and then came back and repeated the exercise.

Dave got the big torch from the van in case we should need it, and we all set off to follow Rex as he ran to and fro, not towards the cottage but up the mountain. There were sharp dips and slopes to manoeuvre around and more than once we cursed and hoped it wasn't some kind of wild goose chase – though both the boys thought it a great adventure. At last we came to a little tumbledown cowshed in front of which was a great pile of cow dung. Mary was there, distraught, wringing her hands and standing over the prostrate form of her brother, who had fallen on his back in the cow dung.

'Oh, the heaviness has come upon me, so it has!' said the poor man from time to time as he lay there.

Mary caught sight of our rescue party and again wrung her hands and called out in thankfulness, 'Oh, me prayers have been answered, God bless ya! God bless ya!'

Well, it was obvious that we should have to help John up from where he lay in the cow dung, though needless to say it was not a job we looked forward to with relish. In the end we managed to get him to his feet and made our way back down the mountain. He was still shaking and staggering and the smell of course was indescribable. I think now that the poor man must have suffered a slight stroke. The farming really was too much for the both of them.

When we finally got back to the cottage we laid John out on the cold flagstones and proceeded to help Mary divest him of his smelly coat and trousers, thinking perhaps we could wash him and make him comfortable. Propped up against the table leg, he glared at us all and protested when Dave pulled at his coat and then slipped the clip from his braces. His arms flayed from side to side in an attempt to shoo us off.

'Away with you. Bugger off. I'll not be parted from me wherewithals in front of women, so I won't!'

Mary pushed us through the door and assured us she could cope. We were glad to make our escape and to walk back to the motor caravan, where we left our boots outside. The following morning we called on Mary and John O'Connell. John's smelly trousers were hanging on a rose bush outside – they had not been washed and more than a faint aroma of the countryside still came from them. There was no sign of John. Mary stood at the door waving to us as we left.

'God bless all of ya. Me poor heart breaks to say goodbye to new-found friends.' Then she called harshly to Rex, and once again, just as on our arrival the day before, he rounded us all up neatly and herded us to the gate.

Compared to the warmth and the scenic beauty of the south, with the lakes and lush greenery of mountain and meadow, travelling northwards brought a contrast in both the landscape and the people. We spent a week in the Gaeltacht in Connemara on the white rocky island of Lettermore. We were privileged during our stay to witness one of their local festivals when the men brought open-backed lorries and old farm carts and the young girls danced to Irish music played on violin and flute, and the men and women sang their sad traditional songs. We didn't hear a word of English spoken all day.

That week in the bungalow on the beach was a weird and wonderful experience. Every morning after the tide had washed the tiny strip of sand on the rocky beach we would dig for big fat cockles and clams in the soft wet sand. At night we went to sleep listening to the sea snaking up the beach and dragging back its swishing load of sand and small gravel. A lovely old shepherd dog made friends with us and followed us back to the bungalow each day. We made the big mistake of feeding it and thereafter it slept outside on the verandah and guarded us. When we packed up to leave it put its head on one side and whined as though it knew that this time we'd be leaving for good. Much to our dismay, it ran behind us for several miles before at last giving up the attempt as a lost cause.

The day before the end of our wonderful holiday we went to Glendalough, which John had so much wanted to see. We arrived there in the late afternoon with the sun slanting across the valley and touching everything with a slight haze of gold. The whole area held an aura of complete peace and tranquillity. This was where the monks had kept alive knowledge, culture and civilisation during the Dark Ages. When God and his angels slept across the rest of Europe, this was an international centre of learning and devotion. I stood in the ruins of a small church. Outside was a tiny churchyard with the ancient Celtic crosses still standing amidst the tall grasses and yellow buttercups and the busy droning of insects.

Nearby I could see a tall, narrow, tower-like structure where the monks had fled in times of trouble, when the invading Danes came to pillage, kill and rob the monastery of its riches. Once inside the tower they would be safe from harm.

The warm afternoon sun shone through a Celtic cross and bathed me in its rays. I sat on a seat and closed my eyes. It was so warm and peaceful. It seemed that as I dozed the sun shone through the Celtic cross onto my face and poured a kind of pure knowledge through to my brain. It was in no sense a religious revelation, and yet I felt that the Celtic cross meant that there was no beginning and no end, just a complete cycle of birth and life and death. I felt I had stood on this spot before, and would do so again.

As I progressed slowly through this shade of sleep I dreamed I saw John being followed by three men in white. When I tried to intercept him to lead him to the tower, where I knew he would be safe from them, they sadly shook their heads and very gently but firmly held him. We were now standing by a signpost but I could not read the words. The three men in white pointed for me to take a direction on my own and then all four of them waved farewell.

I awoke to see my family laughingly coming up the path towards me. 'She's dozed off again,' they joked, and pulled me to my feet.

I noticed that John looked very strained and tired, so I took his arm. 'Come on,' I said gently. 'Let's get back to the van, I could murder a cup of tea.'

417

Illness

Darrell and Ruth were married just after Christmas 1978 at Chipping Sodbury Register Office. Afterwards, a small group of parents and friends went for a meal in the local steakhouse, where we could watch the chefs cooking our orders on a giant grill.

We shared their enthusiasm and delight when they found a small cottage at Pucklechurch. They made plans to improve the property themselves and set about knocking down walls to make one big lounge-cum-dining room from the two rather dark rooms. The cottage was one of five miners' cottages situated at the bottom of a small valley called The Vale and was surrounded by woods and fields. Each cottage had a substantial plot of land front and back, and both of them had ambitious plans to become self-supporting.

Ruth was an outdoor girl, never happier than when mucking out her horse and her face shone with radiant health. It wasn't long before she bought a goat and ducks. Then they bought an acre of woodland and built a stable for Roderick the horse just in front of the wooded area at the bottom of the garden. Several trees were felled and used for fuel to heat the rooms and hot-water system. *The Good Life* was a title that fitted them perfectly, and the happiness reflected in everything they set out to do. John and I often spent weekends visiting them, and one day we heard that the cottage at the end of the rank with an extra side garden and the field beyond had become vacant and was put up for sale.

John dropped the bombshell a few mornings later at the breakfast table: 'I'm putting this house on the market.'

I continued grilling the bacon and dishing it onto the plates, trying to control my irritation. It might be a tease, just something to get me going. After a while he could stand my lack of reaction no longer and repeated, 'Did you hear what I said?'

I placed the plate of egg and bacon in front of him and looked around for the sauce bottle. John was partial to tomato sauce. 'I'm buying the end cottage at Pucklechurch,' he said.

He grinned and stuffed his mouth with bread soaked with egg yolk and tomato sauce. There was bravado in his voice. Just for a second my heart sank, but I went on eating my meal and still hoped he was joking. After a while he looked up and demanded, 'So what d'you think of that?'

I didn't think anything of that, and said so.

'Well, there's nothing you can do about it,' he said belligerently. 'The house is in my name and if you want a roof over your head you'll have to go wherever I say you'll go.' He began drinking his tea noisily and then spluttered, 'What's your objection anyway?'

'Well, I'm surprised you give me the chance to object,' I retorted sarcastically. 'But, since you ask, I can put forward quite a few. For a start, since a garden has always been too much for you, how come an end cottage with at least an acre of land suddenly holds such attractions?'

'Darrell would work the garden.'

'Objection number two: how could I get to work from there? I have no car and I don't fancy twelve miles a day on my scooter.'

'You'd have to give the shop up then, wouldn't you?'

I detected a slight contempt in his tone that made me angry and I burst out, 'And just look at the cottage. A two-up, two-down with narrow winding stairs and low, beamed ceilings and the electric light on all day might seem quaint to you, but it's not my idea of comfort or bliss in my old age.'

Thwarted and angry, he got up from the table and made for the door. 'I don't care what you say,' he shouted. 'I'm selling the house and there's nothing you can do about it.'

'We'll see about that,' I said, and meant it.

During the next few days I made an appointment to seek legal advice about the house and to find out just where I stood. I explained my position to the young lawyer: if the house was in his name, could he really sell up and force me to go wherever he chose? He sat opposite me and surveyed me quizzically, all the while tapping his fingers together in a kind of tattoo. He confirmed that the Marriage Act, which had recently come into force, entitled me to half the matrimonial home. Since the house was not in joint names John did have the right to put it on the market, but I would then be the beneficiary of any new dwelling. I could, however, put an 'F order' on the house, which would prevent him selling my half. All I had to do was pay a pound and the address would be forwarded to the Land Registry.

'Do it,' I said without hesitation, and fumbled in my purse for the money. I was feeling elated. Confidently I gave him our address.

He looked at me searchingly and then said, 'Think very carefully please, Mrs Storey. Your husband may divorce you if you do this.'

As the days slipped by and nothing happened, I began to feel safe and less sick at what I had done. I scanned the papers and the property pages just to make sure that our house was not hidden between the adverts. I began to think that perhaps after all John had been winding me up again and hadn't meant at all that he really wanted to buy the cottage at Pucklechurch.

One of the reasons I was always so angry was because he made decisions without consulting me. Then, after he'd made me angry, he would buy me some little treat and expect that it would put everything right. What he completely refused to do was to consult me. Never having a choice in the matter was the thing that made me want to explode; it wasn't really the cottage – after all, I'd dreamed of nothing else for years myself.

Over the years, John's casual walking away, whistling, always made me frustrated and angry almost to boiling point. Selling our house just to be near his son, and allowing Darrell to work the garden, was something that should have been discussed with me. Like with so many other things that happened in our marriage, I was beginning to think there had been no real relationship at all. There was this dark rage inside me all the time, like some evil entity ready to leap out and explode.

I knew by the look on his face and by the way that he threw off his jacket viciously over a chair that John had found out about the F order I had put on the house. He faced me coldly and calmly, but with his mouth quivering he levelled the words at me: 'If you were a man, I'd kill you.'

I looked into those icy, cornflower-blue eyes, returning his intense stare until he lowered his gaze and turned away from me. The laugh I gave was cynical. 'No! You would not have killed me. If I had been a man, we would have been buddies sharing everything. What this is about is the eternal power game that we have always played and that you as a man must always win. So go ahead, divorce me if you like. I want this house split right down the middle and I want what is due to me!'

He slumped heavily into a chair. Lines of tiredness and utter defeat made him look suddenly crumpled and aged. He threw up his hands as if to ward off further conversation: 'Don't talk to me, woman, can't you see I'm ill?'

In John I had once seen the Peter Pan little boy, the eternal child, whose dreams, like bubbles in the air, faded and came to nothing. Now I saw a selfishness that reduced him to nothing. It was me who had changed and left him far behind. And I saw that I fell far short of what he had always wanted me to be, and I was tired of following his illusive dreams and schemes.

Besides, buried deep down inside me, waiting to break the surface, I had dreams of my own.

The divorce papers that John served on me a few weeks later I pinned to the middle of the kitchen door, as a last act of defiance, for public scrutiny. John had put down incompatibility as the grounds for the break-up, and since this put the blame on neither partner we could both retire to our corners undefeated champions. We spoke little but glared at each other a lot. I left for work as usual every morning, and took no notice of John, still sitting at the table looking moody and sipping tea.

So he looked a bit tired and more than a bit worried. Well, that was more than likely because he couldn't bear to have the house sold and half the proceeds go to me. Hard cheese! Sour grapes! He could chew on those and serve him right!

One Friday night when he returned from the doctor's with yet another sick-note, John gloomily confided that he had been weighed at the health clinic and for the third week in a row had lost weight. I was tackling the dirty dishes that had been left around all day and I was not in a good mood. Expecting sympathy and not getting any, he loped to the settee and lay there. 'I have to go to hospital for tests,' he said quietly.

Impossible ever to forget that warm April day with the green tubs of yellow daffodils outside the big white hospital building, and the vibrant colour and movement everywhere. I was on my way to visit John and I felt happy as I walked along the corridor to the little side ward where he had been for a week now, having X-rays and tests. A woman doctor intercepted me, and together we walked back to the small records office close to the entrance. In that cheerless little room, lined with metal filing cabinets, she told me with impersonal and clinical correctness that my husband had cancer and was a terminal case. Six months, in her professional judgement, was all the time we would have to discuss the situation and come to terms with it.

A pneumatic drill was tearing up the road outside and I could hear the sound of cars changing gear on the busy main road. Everything else outside this room was shockingly normal. Inside, looking at her, I wanted to shout, 'Talk to John – about death? Why, we have never talked about anything deep in the whole of our lives together!'

They had given him ample opportunity to ask questions about his treatment and his health. He had not done so. And in the circumstances they thought it best to leave me to tell him. Scared and frightened at the enormity of what I had just been told, I shivered in my fear.

I felt inadequate, convinced I would never be able to face it, never be able to cope with his illness and the care he would need. Never be able to do it alone. More than anything else, there was the awful finality of death so close to me amidst all the glory of the spring outside that made me rebel. It just wasn't fair.

John came home and we made up a bed for him on the settee. For the first time in his life he was dependent on me. Now that he had to trust me at last, things changed between us. One evening as I gave him his medicine he looked at me levelly, his blue eyes staring into mine. 'Square with me, Joyce,' he said. 'I've got cancer, haven't I?'

I held his gaze steadily. 'Yes,' I answered him truthfully. 'But we'll fight it. Both of us together.'

He closed his eyes, but said calmly and very quietly, 'I wasn't going to ask them in there how long I'd got.'

I held his hands tightly. 'Are you asking me now?'

'No!' he said emphatically.

It was out. It was over – and he had known all along. I admired him for that – it showed a real strength in him that I had never suspected, and a weakness in me. I felt a bit ashamed.

Throughout the whole of his illness, despite the fact that he came to rely on me more and more and our relationship gradually developed into a gentle, caring one, he never quite relaxed his hold on the financial side of the household. His bureau with all its secrets remained locked.

But I did learn how to nurse him and care for him and he was grateful for the concern I showed him. 'No man could be cared for better,' he would often comment. I never ever heard him cry out in pain or complain. I often saw him hobble to the medicine chest to take his medication, which now contained stronger and more effective painkillers. I had a great compassion for his attitude towards this wicked wasting illness, and he brought out all my instinctive maternal and nurturing side. It seemed so painfully ironic that this was the same man who for years had behaved like such a hypochondriac that any little ache would give him an excuse to get a note for time off work. This was the man who today was meeting a life-threatening illness with such fortitude and courage.

He did have a simple conviction that he could fight the disease, and in the early warm June days he used to sit in the garden and confidently predict that he would soon be well enough to return to work. Friends and neighbours came to sit with him and he was pleased when they told him how well he was looking.

On the morning of my birthday I was surprised to find him up and dressed and saying he was going to take me out for a drive to Clevedon. There was a brand-new, bright-canary-yellow Opel Cadet standing out in the garage that he'd only ever driven twice. That was his excuse for taking it out now, that it was doing no good to the car to have it standing idle. Filled with misgivings, but happy to see him so much more like his old self, I sat with him and felt good being driven through the countryside in the warm July weather. As a precaution, I had not forgotten to slip his medicine into my handbag. When we arrived in Clevedon we parked in the High Street and walked the short distance to a quaint little bow-fronted shop that held a collection of china cats.

'Choose any one you want,' John said. 'I don't care how much it costs.'

I had always envisaged a cat lying amongst the lavender bushes, along with the cherished dreams of a cottage with roses round the door. And not just any old moggy, either. For me it had to be a short-haired Burmese Blue – a cat that was not only exclusive but wickedly expensive as well. The trouble was, John hated cats. Not even a stray, a homeless little waif, was ever welcome in his domain.

'Oh Joyce, no – not a cat,' he would plead. 'You know how I hate them.'

Now, today, I was supposed to choose a china one. Just like the cold china dolls that I could never get warm, no matter how I kissed and cuddled them as a child. The confusion and the emotion I experienced at that moment almost choked me. I wondered if his sudden decision to buy me a cat was some last-minute contrition, a desperate plea to make amends, a way of giving me the cat I'd always wanted. Except that I wanted a real, warm, living creature.

I saw the beads of pain contort his face and knew I could never stand there and argue with him. I had to go along with this last wish and get him home again as quickly as possible. And so I chose a marmalade pussycat in a relaxed, curled up pose which I thought would look well on top of the telly. John hobbled back to the car with the aid of a walking stick, and the grip of his hand on my shoulder was hard, and it was difficult to walk along what with that and the awkward parcel I was carrying that held my curled-up cat. It seemed an age getting back to the car and another

427

age waiting for the medicine to take effect and ease the pain.

John never dressed, or took the car out, again. The St Peter's Hospice carers came each day to give him his injection and to help wash and shave him. John died just as summer merged into autumn and the first strong breezes blew all the leaves from the trees. I like to think that in those last few months we both reached out and found something to give each other at last.

John found it impossible to let go of the dominant role and Victorian values in a rapidly changing world. We grow and move forward only when we can change. 'Adapt or die' is the primitive law of survival. If only fate had dealt John a fairer hand. My dream always was about the freedom to choose, the freedom to make your own mistakes and the chance to start again. In the end, freedom itself is the basic right of all people and the only thing worth fighting for.

Mum died that same year, just a couple of months later and just as the Christmas celebrations were under way. She died from a massive heart attack, which gave none of her children time to say goodbye to her. And then I was made redundant. So I became an orphan, a widow and unemployed all at the same time. It was a triple blow. Grief and bereavement took their toll on me and it was a year or more before I had the courage to face the world on my own.

It took me a long time to realise that it was not the ending of my life, but a new beginning.

As a senior citizen I enjoyed a pension that far exceeded

any housekeeping money John had ever allowed me. I found I could meet the financial commitments of running a house and paying the bills quite adequately. With my redundancy money and the small amount of capital my mother had left me, I set about making a few alterations to the house to make it comfortable and secure now that I was sixty-three. I bought a new suite. I put in patio doors. The girls bought me a black pussycat, who I called Natasha. I bought my red-velvet curtains at long, long last.

And I joined a writers' group. I realised at the first session that I had come home and all my searching was over. This, then, all along, was all I had ever really wanted to do. And the thrill of seeing my name in print! Even now I can't really believe it. At school, an author was someone you looked up to in awe and wonder. It wasn't for the likes of me from the solid working class. 'Don't get ideas above your station,' my mother would have said.

But I thought, 'If only I'd started sooner . . .'

Then, just as life seemed comfortable, and the feeling of sweet contentment filled me as I learned how to write, fate dealt me a bitter, bitter blow. I suffered a slight stroke, which damaged my eyesight and left me only partially sighted. Never to read a book or write again. Never to properly see my grandchildren. Never to see a bluebell wood in spring. I wept bitter tears of frustration and grief. 'If I can't read any more and I can't write my books then I don't want to live. I just want to die.'

Sometimes in my sleep I dreamed I could see perfectly once more and I woke excitedly, only to relive the awful experience of being nearly blind. This was one mountain I felt I could never climb. But my children supported and encouraged me. I went to the Blind School and learned to touch-type properly at last. And they gave me a small magnifier, which allows me to read one word at a time. And my daughter comes and reads back to me the work I've done. It's a long and painful process, though, trying to write when you can't see your words, and having to wait until someone comes in to read it back to you.

There is the saddest blow of all, though, that I have never come to terms with and now I think I never shall. That is the death of my lifelong and dearest friend Vee. Our friendship spanned a lifetime – through school years to the workroom, marriage and widowhood. Vee was the nurturer and carer, the mother I never had. She was the one who looked after me. She enjoyed cooking for me and watching with satisfaction as I polished my plate clean. She listened to all my tales of woe, tempering my anger and frustration with her playful banter so that she dispelled my bitterness. And if we had a difference of opinion she was never antagonistic. She could dissipate my angry moods with her level-headedness, and I always came away from a visit to her feeling loved and cherished. Hers was the voice on the other end of the phone and we spoke every day. She was the one I really loved. Now my life will never be the same again. This pain I feel is grief for part of myself that is lost; it is like a wound in my side.

Vee and I often laughed to think that if there had been a

strong feminist movement when we were growing up, we would have been at the forefront of the struggle, carrying the banner even on wet and windy days.

But perhaps my dream of equality for all women will become a reality now that the torch has truly been lit and there are so many of us working towards that end. That's all I ever wanted, all I ever fought for. The most important things in life are equality and freedom.

Postscript

*J*oyce died on 14 November 2001 in Southmead Hospital, surrounded by the people who loved her. She simply and quietly curled up with her hands under her chin as she'd so often done at home, and fell asleep for the last time.

No one who knew her only in the last few years of her life would recognise the fiery tiger of her younger days. At eighty-four she really was a very sweet, delightful and often surprisingly youthful person – full of good humour and wise advice. She could also express herself, as she had done all her life, in shockingly salty language and, just as easily on another occasion, roundly condemn us for using it. I can see her now, in her rocking chair, with needles clicking, listening to one of her talking books or sitting with quiet enjoyment at one of our big family reunions.

But that rather sweet old lady with the white stick is not the figure that strode through my childhood, nor indeed the person who decided to write the story of her life in these pages.

So what was she *really* like, my mother? Well, she was often outrageous and sometimes stupid, and she could be boring and amusing and caring, and she was unkind and unfair to my father and perhaps far more forgiving than he deserved. She said terrible, searing, destructive things that she never, ever meant. Echoing through the whole of my early life there come her words. Words of frustration from a woman we kids never really acknowledged as gifted: 'What did I ever do with my life except have four bloody kids I never wanted?'

She could go on and on and on for hours about the unfairness of her lot and how life had dealt her such a bitter blow. Words flowed out of her: funny, descriptive words that had us helpless with laughter, or harsh, angry words from a woman who was secretly loving and soft. They were her currency, and she was a spendthrift with them. They tumbled and rushed as she sought for expression, and long, long before she started writing them down they filled our days and dominated our thoughts and shaped our lives.

There was nothing, *nothing* in the world that she cared about that she did not do with passion. And that passion drove her. Often it was searing anger, occasionally Rabelaisian wit, sometimes a terrible sadness, longing and a sense of loss. But always it was a deep, Technicolor feeling. There was nothing neutral or pastel-tinted about Joyce or her relationship with anything or anyone. All her life she resented the description of her as a strong person, yet she was almost indestructibly strong, I'd say. And people were drawn to her and the strength they recognised in her; so she collected waifs and strays like a Pied Piper.

I can't pretend we had a happy childhood. She often said she and Daddy should never have married, and perhaps that was true. Desperately they sought in each other what they thought they most needed – she wanted nurturing, John wanted stability. Neither of them was able to give what the other most needed. It was sad for them, and the resulting earthquake was truly awful for us four children. Perhaps my mother should never have married at all. My father, on the other hand, could have been happy, so very, very happy, with a wife who could bake and sew and bottle and who loved children and was simply a contented homemaker.

None of these attributes was anywhere near the top of Joyce's priorities. It was not that she despised them, or that she was not good at them (although, actually, she wasn't), she just knew there was something beyond them – a magic landscape where everything was possible for her, where the liberty and creativity she craved were only limited by her own imagination. But what she lacked in practical skills as a mother she more than made up for by giving us children something of her sense of magic, her deep love of the countryside, and her fighting determination for equality and freedom.

I can remember when she took us all back to Painswick, where she had been in hospital as a baby. She showed us the fields and the lanes where she had danced and wandered, and made us lie down by a tumbling stream and close our eyes and listen to the music of the water as it played amongst the stones. At Blaise Castle when I was eight she thrust my face deep into the seductive satin darkness at the heart of a rose and told me to breathe and smell and remember it all my life. Only too obviously, she could have been a poet or an acclaimed writer of short stories, but she was fettered by the constraints of childbearing and the demands of domesticity, played out against a background of grinding poverty and ignorance, and it took her all her life to break free. At last, when John was dead and we'd all left home and she was sixty-five, she began to write. And then she went blind.

So she learned to touch-type, and waited until one of us called in and read back to her what she'd written so she could correct and rewrite. All the words written in this book were done by someone who could only read one word at a time with a magnifying glass. It has often been said that there is a story inside all of us. But not all of us can tell it. Joyce's story is riveting not just because of her strange background, nor because it records part of an age gone by, but because she tells it with such brutal honesty and self-deprecating humour. And because, above all, she was a born story-teller, with an instinctive feeling for the power of words and their dramatic effect. All these stories really happened, but not necessarily in the order she gives them. So what? That doesn't make her a liar, it just makes her a good story-teller. The world needs story-tellers. They weave their magic spells for us and transport us into another, infinitely more varied and colourful world than our humdrum everyday existence. Joyce was poor all her life and longed to live in luxury. But she has left us something truly priceless – the legacy of her own extraordinary story.

Joyce, you were funny and brave and strong all your life. We four children thought you were truly wonderful, and all of us who knew and loved you miss you so very, very much.